Global Perspectives on

Industrial Transformation

in the American South

New Currents in the
History of Southern
Economy and Society

This series, New Currents in the History of Southern Economy and Society, puts the history of the American South in an important new light. It demonstrates the complexity of the southern economy across time and place and its profound impact on the varieties of people who have inhabited the region. It conveys southern economic development as consistently diverse and dynamic. The series stresses the importance of comparative and transatlantic perspectives and strives to reintegrate southern history in relation to the rest of the nation and the globe. The series is purposefully organized around central themes rather than chronology to highlight new ways to conceptualize economic change and industrial growth.

The series grew out of the work of the Southern Industrialization Project (SIP), a professional organization that seeks to foster a greater understanding of the history and culture of industrialization in the American South. Each year SIP meets to discuss scholarly papers organized around key themes. This series represents SIP's commitment to developing these conference themes into substantive scholarly volumes that further promote research in southern economic and social history. In addition, SIP maintains a discussion list on H-Net of more than one hundred academic and public historians with research interests that encompass many industries, eras, and geographic locations.

Global Perspectives on

Industrial Transformation

in the American South

Edited by Susanna Delfino

Michele Gillespie

University of Missouri Press
Columbia and London

Copyright © 2005 by
The Curators of the University of Missouri
University of Missouri Press, Columbia, Missouri 65201
Printed and bound in the United States of America
5 4 3 2 1   09 08 07 06 05

Library of Congress Cataloging-in-Publication Data

Global perspectives on industrial transformation in the American South /
edited by Susanna Delfino and Michele Gillespie.
        p.   cm. — (New currents in the history of Southern economy and
society)
    Summary : "Essays analyzing the economic evolution of the American
South from the late colonial period to World War I and beyond. Examines
the South in respect to long-held assumptions about industrialization and
productivity and draws comparisons to the larger Atlantic and world economy"—Provided by publisher.
    Includes index.
    ISBN 0-8262-1583-1 (alk. paper)
  1.   Industrialization—Southern States. 2.   Industrialization.
3.   Comparative economics.   I. Delfino, Susanna, 1949–   II. Gillespie,
Michele. III. Series.
    HC107.A13G535 2005
    330.975—dc22
                                                              2005008095

∞™This paper meets the requirements of the
American National Standard for Permanence of Paper
for Printed Library Materials, Z39.48, 1984.

Designer: Jennifer Cropp
Typesetter: Crane Composition, Inc.
Printer and binder: The Maple-Vail Book Manufacturing Group
Typefaces: Minion and Brighton

For Stanley L. Engerman

Contents

Preface

Since the 1960s, revisionism in many areas of American history has increasingly brought the South to the center of historians' attention. After several decades of innovative historiographic contributions, the once-staple interpretation of a backward, wholly agricultural, antebellum South peopled only by wealthy planters, poor whites, and more or less contented slaves has at last given way to one of economic and social dynamism as well as regional prosperity. Both southern society and economy now look more complex, articulated, and diverse than their classic representations would once have had us believe. The notion of southern cultural difference compared with the North has changed accordingly, acquiring new, less negative underpinnings.

Within such a fast-growing field of investigation as the South is today, the particular is often likely to prevail over the general, for it is only by detailing previously ignored or neglected facts that the historian can develop the larger picture of a society's history. To this day, no synthesis fully represents this revisionist approach, which endeavors to place southern economic and social development in a dynamic and expanding context. Aware of the need to begin synthesizing the vast body of data and facts patiently collected and documented by dozens of scholars, we intend New Currents in the History of Southern Economy and Society to address what we perceive as the most urgent task toward the rewriting of southern history: a reassessment of the South's economy from the antebellum days to the present. This approach is deemed crucial for a more correct understanding of southern society and culture.

With hindsight, the course of southern economic history in the nine-teenth and twentieth centuries can be seen as emblematic of larger issues, first within the United States, then in the hemisphere, and per-haps, as comparative perspectives will show, in the world. To signify the importance and desirability to this end of interdisciplinary collabora-tion between historians and economists, the volumes in the series will feature contributions by both sets of scholars as much as possible. Because a comprehensive synthesis remains unfinished, we have chosen to organize each volume thematically, rather than chronologically, to help the reader become better oriented to the developments in different areas related to industrial growth (technology, labor, entrepreneurship, the transformation of southern society, etc.) across time and space, rather than in a single historical period. Indicating the ways in which new directions and developments in this field can be adopted and inte-grated with one another constitutes a primary purpose of this series of volumes; it elects the comparative approach and the broad Atlantic per-spective as indispensable organizational principles. Ultimately, the aim of this series is—to borrow William Freehling's phrase—the "reintegra-tion" of southern history on its own terms, in its relation to the rest of the nation, and in its global dimension.

Global Perspectives on

Industrial Transformation

in the American South

Introduction

Susanna Delfino and Michele Gillespie

During the past half century, the traditional understanding and interpretation of the history of the American South, and especially of the Old South, have undergone major—one might say spectacular—revisions. This season of reappraisals and revisitations owed much to the economic historians of the cliometrics school, to whom all historians of the South should be indebted for stimulating social and cultural studies. In the act of adding "thickness" to their findings in the economic realm, historians began in fact to describe southern society and its changes in all their diversity and articulation.

This research encouraged the complete revision of the classic representation of the white South, which began with the U. B. Phillips model at the turn of the last century. As a result, by the last decade of the twentieth century, large planters began to be described more as businessmen and entrepreneurs than as agrarian patriarchs. This new research also wrested from historical obscurity a vast world of small producers, both slaveholders and nonslaveholders, as well as tenants and farm laborers, highlighting in important new ways how and why the agricultural setting was interdependent with the nascent industrial order. Large planters who were investors in southern manufacturing ventures, and even became manufacturers themselves, for example, sent their sons to work in the factories, either as full-time or part-time employees. Moreover, contrary to popular myth, many sons of farmers made careers in industry,

1

becoming factory agents and superintendents.[1] Historians have also documented the seasonal nature of the shift between agricultural and industrial labor, as well as its largely migratory character within the South, which further united these two kinds of economies.[2] Other scholars have brought evidence of the wide involvement of slaves in artisanal and industrial pursuits, alongside white artisans, whose very existence in the Old South historians once denied. Women, free and slave, white and black, constituted a large share of the antebellum industrial labor force of the South, both in traditional areas, such as textile manufacturing, and nontraditional ones, such as iron-making and mining. While much study has focused on manufacturing concerns, which were principally rural during antebellum times, the urban South has also elicited attention, revealing the existence of class formations pretty similar to those of northern towns.[3]

Yet, for all the advances made, by the early 1980s the debate on economic development and social change in the antebellum South seemed to be in a quandary. Many scholars contended that by 1860 the economic performance of the region was far inferior to that of the North. Consequently, there seemed to be little use in studying industrial transformation in a region that ostensibly lagged behind in this branch of the economy and that, during the second half of the 1850s, with rising cotton prices and the movement to reopen the slave trade, seemed to renew its commitment to slave-based plantation agriculture. Despite the brilliant foray into the international/comparative realm made by Robert W.

1. Susanna Delfino, "Invisible Woman: Female Labor in the Upper South's Iron and Mining Industries," in *Neither Lady nor Slave: Working Women of the Old South,* ed. Susanna Delfino and Michele Gillespie (Chapel Hill: University of North Carolina Press, 2002), 285–307 and 293–94 in particular.

2. See for instance Bill Cecil-Fronsman, *Common Whites: Class and Culture in Antebellum North Carolina* (Lexington: University Press of Kentucky, 1992).

3. On slave industrial labor in the antebellum South, besides the classic Robert S. Starobin, *Industrial Slavery in the Old South* (New York: Oxford University Press, 1970), see Ronald Lewis, *Coal, Iron, and Slaves: Industrial Slavery in Maryland and Virginia, 1715–1865* (Westport, CT: Greenwood Press, 1979). On white labor, either male or female, see Michele Gillespie, *Free Labor in an Unfree World: White Artisans in Slaveholding Georgia, 1789–1860* (Athens: University of Georgia Press, 2000); id., Michele Gillespie, "'To Harden a Lady's Hand: Gender, Politics, Racial Realities, and Women Millworkers in Antebellum Georgia," and Bess Beatty, "I Can't Get My Bred on Them Old Lomes: Female Textile Workers in the Antebellum South," both in *Neither Lady nor Slave,* ed. Delfino and Gillespie, 261–84 and 249–60, respectively.

Fogel and Stanley L. Engerman in *Time on the Cross* (1974), the general—and generalizing—North/South comparison was still predominant in most historians' frame of mind, and it remained so for a very long time.[4]

From the second half of the 1970s, historians made several important steps toward a less-conventional approach to the study of the southern economy, away from the generalized comparison between North and South. By the end of the decade, Gavin Wright portrayed planters as economically rational beings (who embraced cotton planting on the basis of its "comparative advantage") and the agricultural South as an economically thriving region.[5] In a series of articles appearing between the early 1980s and the early 1990s, Thomas Bateman, Jeremy Atack, James Foust, Kenneth Sokoloff, Vicken Tchakerian, and others established fruitful comparisons between the South and the West in terms of agricultural productivity and industrial performance of the South and that of the West, respectively. These works showed that between 1840 and 1860, the South generally compared well, and sometimes favorably, with the West.[6] By the mid-1980s, Susanna Delfino had observed that the breaking down of regional aggregate values for capital investment and manufacturing output clearly indicated lack of uniformity in industrial development within each of the three main geographical subdivisions of the United States. Adopting Alan Pred's model in the delineation of economically integrated areas in the antebellum United States, she identified four of them in the South and argued in favor of

---

4. Robert W. Fogel and Stanley L. Engerman, *Time on the Cross: The Economics of American Negro Slavery* (Boston: Little, Brown, 1974).

5. Gavin Wright, *The Political Economy of the Cotton South: Households, Markets and Wealth in the Nineteenth Century* (New York: W. W. Norton, 1979). Wright has long insisted on the low population density of the South as an important factor limiting the size of markets. His argument ties in very well with that made by Majewski and Tchakerian in this volume.

6. See, for instance, Fred Bateman and Thomas Weiss, "Manufacturing in the Antebellum South," in *Research in Economic History* 1 (1976), ed. Paul Uselding; id., "The Participation of Planters in Manufacturing in the Antebellum South," *Agricultural History* 48, 2 (1974): 277–97; Viken Tchakerian, "Productivity, Extent of Markets, and Manufacturing in the Late Antebellum South and Midwest," *Journal of Economic History* 54, 3 (1994): 497–525; Kenneth L. Sokoloff and Viken Tchakerian, "Manufacturing Where Agriculture Predominates: Evidence from the South and the Midwest in 1860," *Explorations in Economic History* 34, 3 (1997): 243–64.

a subregional approach to the study of antebellum industrialization in key American regions.[7]

In the 1980s, yet another important approach came to maturity. The study of the Atlantic economy from the European expansion toward the Americas to the age of revolutions and, ultimately, to the abolition of slavery helped broaden the intellectual horizon of American scholars and prompted them to recast the experience of the American South in a new light. Linking capitalism to slavery as integral components in the expansion and development of the Atlantic economies and in the fostering of British industrialization, this approach strongly suggested the need to reassess the South's economic course, from colonial times on, in an international perspective. In recent years, Atlantic history has definitively established itself as an important field of investigation and is already yielding its first fruits in the delineation of the origins of globalization. The essays in this collection address this issue.

Certainly, the contrast between the idea of a South permanently sealed into the role of a backward and dependent region within the United States, which informed the older studies (a view that also influenced the post–Civil War era), and a vision of the same as continuously evolving over time as part of the international economy was too vast not to solicit attention on the part of historians. Following Fogel and Engerman's suggestion, the comparative-international approach thus appeared as the only meaningful way to place the evolutions of the southern economy in a more realistic context, divested of the "exceptionalist" bias that had for a long time confined discourse on the American—and southern—economy to the domestic scene, on the grounds of a supposed "uniqueness" of the American experience within world history.

Stanley Engerman led the way again, committing himself to the exploration of the connections between slavery, capitalism, and industrialization in the southern United States in a broadly comparative perspective, and produced many important works on this subject.[8] The fact that the present volume hosts an introductory essay by him has spe-

---

7. Susanna Delfino, *Yankees del Sud. Sviluppo economico e trasformazioni sociali nel Sud degli Stati Uniti, 1790–1860* (Milano: Franco Angeli, 1987), 46–49, 102–9.

8. See, for instance, Stanley L. Engerman, ed., *Trade and the Industrial Revolution, 1700–1850,* 2 vols (Celtenham, UK: An Elgar Reference Collection, 1996); Barbara L. Solow and Stanley L. Engerman, eds., *British Capitalism and Caribbean Slavery: The Legacy of Eric Williams* (New York: Cambridge University Press, 1987); Robert W.

cial significance not only because of Engerman's role as a major trail-blazer in establishing new directions in the study of southern history, but also because of his pioneering achievements in the field of comparative studies.

This quick sketch of the main historiographic developments that have occurred over the past fifty years in the fields of southern society and economy, although well known to many, is a necessary starting point for this volume. It is our intention to illustrate for readers the circumstances that prompted us to initiate a series of volumes devoted to the exploration of New Currents in the History of the Southern Economy and Society.

The word *globalization* is in common usage nowadays, but when applied to the emergence of a "global South," it is generally associated with post–World War II developments. Furthermore, the term conjures up in many ways the crystallization of distinctions of colonial origin between centers and peripheries in the development of the world economy, by which the latter become structurally dependent on the former. Consequently, theories of colonial or quasi-colonial dependence of the southern economy on the northern one have always received wide consensus.[9] Despite the still widespread view that long stretches of the South's history were marked by marginalization and isolation, this volume, the first in the series, establishes instead that the American South was an expanding economy. Its growing strength enabled it to gain high-ranking positions within the Western world. As a major exporter of valuable cash crops, the South had in some ways to adapt itself constantly to the general conditions and changing circumstances of the international economy, but its vast wealth, sheltered within a strong, independent nation, allowed it to stand as a respectable counterpart to the most developed countries of western Europe.

The fact that the South was able to free itself from the sort of post-colonial dependency that affected the countries of Central and South America has not been fully appreciated in all its implications. However,

---

Fogel, *Without Consent or Contract: The Rise and Fall of American Slavery,* 2 vols. (New York: W. W. Norton, 1986); Joseph E. Inkori and Stanley L. Engerman, eds., *The Atlantic Slave Trade: Effects on Economies, Societies, and Peoples in Africa, the Americas, and Europe* (Durham: Duke University Press, 1992).

9. See Gavin Wright, *Old South, New South: Revolutions in the Southern Economy since the Civil War* (New York: Basic Books, 1986).

if the U.S. South did enjoy a more independent status internationally, its regional economic concerns often clashed with larger national ones, making the implementation of economic policies suitable to its needs increasingly difficult to obtain after 1820. During the last few decades of the antebellum period, the region's economic dependence on the north-eastern United States became increasingly apparent to many white south-erners. On the basis of the prominent role the South played within national politics, southerners cherished economic independence as well. Herein lay, however, the southern dilemma. While industrialization ap-peared to be a good way to free the South from northern dependence, economic emancipation could not occur without the region's reinforc-ing its commitment to plantation agriculture, the main source of its wealth, thus making the South more dependent on Great Britain.

The comparative approach with other Western countries thus ap-pears to be an indispensable step toward the rethinking of the entire course of southern history. It allows historians, for instance, to account for the development of a distinctive political economy, and thus helps shed light on and give more depth to the political stands that the South took during the antebellum decades, until the momentous decision to secede from the Union. Ultimately, this volume can be understood as the *manifesto* of a revisionist scholarship on southern history that aims at bringing together the vast knowledge accumulated by historians of the southern economy and the fresh perspectives of Atlantic history.

Generally speaking, comparisons are not necessarily established to demonstrate similarities; rather, by teasing out explanations for both similarities and differences, they serve the larger purpose of sharpening historical interpretation. For instance, comparing the slave-based econo-mies of the Americas may help us understand how and why the North American case differed from the others; how and why the southern United States was able to achieve a level of industrialization under slav-ery that was unknown to Latin American countries, and in which ways the plantation system of the South differed from those of the latter, and so on.

The adoption of a global approach to a study of the southern econ-omy from its very inception serves the important purpose of helping to identify themes of continuity that have largely been obscured by the general belief that the Civil War constituted a watershed. Consistent with this proposition, the nine essays in this collection cover the period from late colonial times to the post–World War II era. Pushing the argument beyond the Civil War and into the twentieth century, a number of these essays explore how the South tried to answer the new challenges posed by changes in the national and international economies between the 1870s and the 1910s. At the core of these changes were the growth and affirmation of corporate capitalism, both industrial and financial, the monopolistic or oligopolistic concentration of industry by sector, and the internationalization of labor markets, signaled by massive migration movements.

While the post–Civil War southern economy has generally been dismissed as a colonial economy incapable of catching up with the North, insufficient attention has often been paid to the larger, uncontrollable forces that shaped it. On closer analysis, the respectable performance of the South's economy during the first decade or so following the Confederate surrender indicates that the region had already developed a sufficient industrial basis to weather the early phases of the new, globalizing trends of the economy.[10] Simultaneously, however, the agricultural sector that had provided immense wealth under the plantation system started to show the drawbacks connected with the transition from slave labor to free labor and new types of organization of production. What had once been the South's strength became its weakness. Occupational segregation between whites and blacks, and the general confinement of the latter to unremunerative agricultural jobs, contributed decisively to the onset of a dual economy.[11]

Stanley Engerman opens the volume with an important essay that goes to the very heart of the debate on the performance of the southern economy in the antebellum decades, by delving into the myths on the South's failure to industrialize because of slavery. After summarizing the several positions expressed on this subject over time, Engerman uses the comparative approach to show that the antebellum South, if considered as a separate nation, although lagging behind the North and Great Britain, would have ranked among the wealthiest and the most industrialized countries of the Western world. Agriculture was indeed the basis of its economy, which did not make the South unique among pre-1860

10. Ibid., 43.
11. According to Gavin Wright, the creation of a labor market which was separate from the national one was largely responsible for the recurrent difficulties of the southern economy.

world economies. While some European regions concentrating on agricultural production to meet the growing demand of highly industrializing areas consequently experienced a process of deindustrialization, the American South did not. The comparative approach also shows a slave society dissimilar to others in Central and South America. In the U.S. South, sustained industrialization was in fact carried on simultaneously with the fostering of a thriving agricultural export sector. The destruction of old myths about the South has taken much effort and time on the part of scholars. Now, in light of twentieth-century, especially post–World War II developments, the creation of new myths is likely to occur, and it is probably already under way. It will be the task of future generations to grapple with them. The breadth and scope of Engerman's essay provides the backdrop against which to set all other contributions in this collection.

Taking heed of the latest revisionist work on British industrialization, Emma Hart examines the role of Charleston, South Carolina, as a town located at the periphery of the empire between 1750 and 1790. Through a perusal of its productive sectors, she classifies Charleston as a town devoted to the "leisure industry"—pretty much like other towns were in contemporary England—but nonetheless closely connected with the general process of industrial development. Cabinetmaking emerged as a major sector of enterprise. The way in which this industry was organized in the town of Charleston strongly suggests patterns of rationality in organizing the production chain, involving highly sophisticated division of labor, which were typical of early industrialization. Hart's overview of the highly articulated urban economy of Charleston, including white and black workers, raises questions about the traditional view of this colonial town as a mirror of a drowsy plantation society largely aloof from industrial developments occurring in the "center economy." Quite to the contrary, Hart shows Charleston as fully participating in them.

Southern concerns about economic dependence and the development of a system of global interdependence are the subjects of Brian Schoen's essay. Analyzing the economic philosophy of cotton producers during the antebellum period, Schoen explains how the adherence of southerners to free trade was consistent with the pursuit of their own interests, in that "it reflected the realities of an interdependent nineteenth-century global economy dominated by Britain's commercial and manufacturing empire." From the 1830s on, southerners endeavored to lessen what they perceived as increasing economic dependence on the North by developing a railroad network and fostering industrialization. To achieve this end, they were initially able to obtain financial assistance from the British, whose capital had long been operating in the region, especially through merchant houses. In the face of a domestic climate inhospitable to their economic interests, in the late antebellum period, southerners tried to achieve independence from the North through pursuit of new international opportunities and increased interdependence with Europe. These prospects were at the basis of the secessionist impulse, but, as history would prove, expectations of unconditional British support for southern political independence rested on false assumptions.

Reinforcing Engerman's arguments, Shearer D. Bowman invites the reader to rethink the traditional image of a backward South in an international and intercontinental comparative perspective. In this way, "the South's relative 'backwardness' appears in a very different light." In view of recent scholarship that has shown the economy of the antebellum South and its industrial sector in particular as definitely successful in comparison with those of most contemporary Western countries, not to mention the Latin American ones, Bowman reminds us that the bottom-line question nowadays is why the South did not industrialize more. He concludes, based on a number of important studies, that the answer to this question seems to point to a broad idea of fragmentation, or lack of integration, which, as John Majewski and Viken Tchakerian's essay also indicates, probably stemmed from the region's geographic and environmental features. These, in turn, produced separateness and rivalry among the people living in different areas. The failure of the South to achieve internal homogeneity and coordination emerged dramatically during the Civil War and constituted the Confederacy's greatest weakness. Bowman's conclusive comparison between the U.S. South and six Prussian provinces over time, based on the many similarities existing between the two as "peripheral" regions in a developing world-system, illuminates the strong connection between the political power of the agrarian elites and regional economic success. Because of the differences existing between them in this regard, the economic paths of the two regions began to diverge toward the end of the nineteenth century.

Bowman's concern for the interconnections existing between the state, politics, and power as important factors in shaping the course of an economy is shared by Susanna Delfino, whose essay builds on this very assumption to explore the cultural implications of such interconnections in shaping assessments on the economic performance of a region. Exploiting the similarity between the United States and Italy in terms of a growing North/South contraposition in public discourse between the 1830s and 1860, she shows how the idea of southern backwardness, which was not in fact supported by absolute economic failure by these two southern regions, stemmed from the processes connected with the rise and affirmation of the liberal state in the Western world. Under the banner of "modernization" and free labor, it aimed at mustering wide political and economic consensus to an expanded role of the state in public life and to a massive program of industrialization. In both countries, a northern elite needed to exploit the wealth of the South to launch its program, yet feared the political influence of a southern ruling class, which would forward the interests of a staple-producing, export-oriented economy, which was antithetical to its schemes. Under the pretence of their supposedly archaic social institutions and structures, the two Souths were declared incapable of modernizing and, no matter what their degree of economic well-being and industrial development, were thus indicted for backwardness.

Yet, the fact remains that while the Italian South before 1860 was not dramatically lagging behind the North of the Peninsula (if nothing else because the Italian North itself was among the least industrialized parts of Europe), some substantial disparity existed, by that time, between North and South in the United States. Rejecting the traditional, generalized North/South comparison, John Majewski and Viken Tchakerian address this issue by establishing a comparison between the South and the Midwest. In particular, following the soundest Adam Smithian tradition, they approach the subject from the point of view of the extent of the market. While they confirm the long-standing view that "slavery and mountainous topography did indeed help limit the growth of southern markets," they point to agricultural land-use patterns as a further, important variable to explain the limitations of southern markets. According to them, southern farms included a much higher number of unimproved acres than farms in the Midwest. As the authors explain, the "far more dispersed settlement pattern" was responsible for major difficulties in creating a suitable transportation network. Crop selection determined the location of manufacturing and, in this regard, some areas of the South managed to keep pace with the Midwest, but, generally speaking, the far lower rural population densities of many southern areas exerted an obvious effect on the extent of markets. Majewski and Tchakerian argue, however, that this pattern of land use and settlement made economic sense to white southerners. The problem with southern agriculture, they conclude, "was a combination of geography and climate." Southern planters were economically rational in deciding to keep a large portion of their lands unimproved. Slavery may have played a partial role in shaping their decisions, but southern landholding patterns deeply influenced the potentials for the development of manufacturing.

Majewski and Tchakerian's essay raises important questions about the objective factors that influenced the pattern and extent of southern industrial development in the antebellum era, suggesting new understandings of the distinctiveness of southern culture as one primarily shaped not by slavery, but by a combination of factors among which geography and topography played major roles. Their essay establishes some interesting premises for the analysis of the southern textile industry in a global context as explored by David Carlton and Peter Coclanis. In their wide-ranging overview of the development of the textile industry in the southern U.S. from antebellum days to the present time, they observe from the very beginning that, although the story of industrialization has mostly been written as one separate from the phenomena simultaneously taking place outside of America, "globalization has been a presence in southern textiles since the modern industry arose out of the ashes of the plantation regime." In this way, historians have failed to appreciate not only the impact exerted on the southern textile industry by the important changes engendered by the transition from the "First" to the "Second" Industrial Revolution, but also "the deep historical roots of its current crisis."

From the 1870s on, textile production, and especially that of cotton, experienced in fact a steady shift from the northern regions of Europe and the United States toward more southerly areas of the world. Within the United States, this process led to the definitive transferal of the industry to the South. This migratory pattern of the industry, however, created new problems for the southern-based textile manufactories. Whereas they had previously relied on the domestic market, from the 1920s on, they were increasingly confronted with competition for that market from Brazil, India, and other East Asian countries. The South had long enjoyed the advantages of a "peripheral" position within the American economy, but it was now projected into its very core. Indeed, the American South was unique among competitors in that it was American. After a period of indecision following World War II, from the 1960s on, the new challenges posed by the low production costs of foreign competition prompted the devising of new strategies on the part of southern textile manufacturers that presently anticipate a revitalization of the industry.

Beth English's essay exemplifies the first phases of the globalization of the textile industry, that is, its southward migration. She focuses on the example of the Dwight Manufacturing Company, a concern originally based in Chicopee, Massachusetts, to illustrate the factors that prompted northern firms to open branches in and eventually relocate to the South (unfavorable labor legislation, union activism, and high state taxes, above all). The whole process took some forty-odd years to complete, but by the 1930s, the American South had become the "core" of the American textile industry. In 1894 the Dwight Manufacturing Company had opened a branch in Alabama City. In 1927 it shut down its Massachusetts premises and definitively relocated to Alabama. Early on, however, the industry was bound to face all the problems arising from global competition that impinged upon the long-held low-wage, antiunion policy previously adopted by southern states to attract businesses. This was especially true for the oldest textile manufacturing southern states, like the Carolinas, which faced competition from other southern firms first. When the threat posed by labor organizations began to wither toward the end of the century, the southern states, including Alabama, renewed their efforts to make themselves attractive for business, including repealing labor legislation. The globalizing tendencies of the economy, however, were shifting labor markets from the local, to the regional, to the national, and finally to the international dimension, dramatically altering the issues the southern American textile industry would have to face in the following decades.

The problem of labor was a constant concern with southern industry from the very beginning and, after emancipation, it became closely intertwined with racial considerations. In her essay, Erin Elizabeth Clune illustrates the debates taking place in the South during the first few decades of the twentieth century about how to supply the region with a suitable labor force, especially in the agricultural sector, without relying much on blacks, in order to limit their ascendancy as freeholders. White immigrants, mostly Italians and other southeastern Europeans, seemed to provide the needed workers. As Clune explains, "White ideologues cast black economic activity as incompatible with modern civilization" and therefore advocated measures to control them. In effect, black progress might destabilize the South's class and racial hierarchies. The encouraging of emigration from southern and eastern Europe raised objections from some quarters of the southern political establishment, however, and many began to support emigration from the British Isles. Between 1906 and 1907, British businessmen visited the South intent on supporting an immigration campaign. Although mass emigration from the British Isles never materialized, the campaign exposes the uneasiness of Americans toward the shift of blacks up higher on the socioeconomic ladder and underlines the limits imposed on southern economic development by the pursuance of a racist labor policy. In what marks an important development, Clune casts her argument within the broader context of the Atlantic world, where many colonial societies, not just the American South, deliberately sought out mass white immigration to limit black freedom and shore up racial segregation after emancipation.

The innovative essays included with this volume illustrate the most important directions that future studies might take to achieve a new synthesis of southern history. Despite their diverse disciplinary approaches, they collectively provide a multifaceted picture of the transformations that the South's economy and society underwent, one that transcends the traditional framework of historical discourse.

We thank all the contributors for their enthusiastic commitment to this project, and we hope that the volume may constitute a good starting point for many more reassessments of the course of southern economic and social history. Gordon A. Melson, Dean of the Graduate School, and the Research Funds Committee of Wake Forest University receive our sincere gratitude for granting us financial support that enabled us to complete this volume. We offer special thanks to our good friends at the University of Missouri Press, especially Beverly Jarrett, editor-in-chief, and Sara Davis, our editor. As always, we thank Catherine Clinton for all her friendship and support. Finally, we wish to express our deepest gratitude to everyone else who, in many ways, has encouraged and supported us in the realization of this first volume of the series.

Southern Industrialization

Myths and Realities

Stanley L. Engerman

Historical myths may be considered inaccurate observations that people prefer to believe.[1] Often, they are not all wrong, which enhances their believability, but they are not accurate or detailed enough to serve as useful bases for historical understanding.

Often people of otherwise quite different views find it convenient to accept a similar belief about structures or events. Thus the power of a common belief gains strength from its rather different political and cultural starting and concluding points. For this reason, it often takes a great deal of scholarly work to revise a historical myth and reorient scholarship in a more useful manner. This apparently common belief may, however, reflect rather different questions being asked of the historical record, and a confusion about what is at the time, and what might be in the future.

---

1. In writing this introductory essay I have been concerned mainly with the broad issues regarding the debate concerning southern industrialization in the antebellum period. I have, therefore, greatly limited the number of footnote references. The standard works on southern industry, both those pointing to its limited nature and those arguing for a more positive depiction, contain numerous citations to the basic works, as do the essays included in this volume. Susanna Delfino has been most helpful in the preparation of this essay.

The study of slavery has provided some of the South's most important myths, myths based on what people thought to be accurate depictions of reality. Although believers in these myths may have had different underlying beliefs, the policy implications of those beliefs were not, at first, dramatically different. For example, many abolitionists and many slaveholders claimed that slaves were basically damaged and incompetent individuals, without culture or any family attachments. Among the many problems of the effect of slavery on slave personality was the inability of slaves to work successfully in agricultural and industrial pursuits. The southern pattern of inefficient agriculture and the lack of industry were, therefore, seemingly easily explained by the characteristics of the enslaved. Of course, abolitionists and slaveholders explained this incapacity differently: to abolitionists it was created by the slave system and was therefore reversible (but how long after the end of slavery was not always clearly presented); to slave owners, it was inherent in the slave's African background and racial characteristics, although, even in U. B. Phillips's argument, there was some hope (limited, however), for slaves' schooling, education, and improvement.[2]

Clearly, scholarship over the last several decades has completely revised this myth of slave destruction, and we continue to learn more about slaves as agents and independent (within constraint) actors, in both the plantation and the urban setting. While the past misinterpretation is generally attributed to planters and southerners, we should not ignore the role played with the best intentions by abolitionists, and subsequent historical critics of the slave societies, in shaping these views of the enslaved as a central aspect of their description of the evils of slavery.

Although the initial myths and their need for correction in the case of southern industrialization are not as striking as in the case of the patterns of behavior of southern slaves, similarities persist. The relative shortfall in southern industry has been the basis of the many contemporary and subsequent writers' arguments that the slave economy of the

2. In his *Life and Labor in the Old South* (Boston: Little Brown, 1929), Ulrich B. Phillips describes the plantation as not only a factory, but also a school in which training in crafts and other aspects of labor were undertaken. To Phillips the ultimate weakness of the plantation school was "the fact that even its aptest pupils had no diploma in prospect which would send them forth to fend for themselves." Despite its role in educating and "civilizing" slaves, this was a school without graduates.

South suffered severe economic difficulties and would not have survived prolonged competition with that of the North. This argument on
southern economic backwardness and lack of industry contrasted the
modernization of industrial societies, such as those in the North and
England, with the backwardness of societies elsewhere lacking in industry, whether slave or nonslave. Societies based on slavery and with a
labor force predominantly in agriculture were seen as less efficient and
productive than industrializing societies, and the contrast of modern
free labor and nonmodern slave labor became a central part of the abolitionist antislavery arguments. This contrast was not unique to the regions of the United States but, as Susanna Delfino points out, was also
central to debates on the unification of Italy at the same time. Similar issues were raised about European serfdom and other nonindustrialized
parts of the world. The American South was not the only part of the
world with limited industry, and many areas without slavery had similarly low levels of industrialization.

This contrast has persisted despite the development of critiques of
modernization and some renewed attention to the social costs of modernization and industrialization. While the arguments concerning the
possibilities of different routes to economic growth and development
have attracted current adherents, the concern with antebellum southern
industrialization seems often to reflect the opinions of an earlier era.

To the abolitionists and their subsequent supporters, the failures of
the slave system generated incapable labor and incapable businessmen,
an inefficient, unproductive economy, low rates of innovation, limited
capital availability, a limited share of the market, and a lack of entrepreneurial mentality. In contrast with the North and with England, critics
argued, the South lacked a modern business structure. This lag behind
northern industry became particularly apparent after the 1820s, when
cotton textiles and related industries expanded in New England and the
middle Atlantic states.

To the planters and their subsequent supporters, the failure to industrialize reflected, in part, the South's choice of a higher way of life than
would be provided by embracing the crassness and evils of a modern
industrial economy. To industrialize, and be like the North and western
Europe, would have meant the introduction of many of the social, economic, and political problems then confronting industrialized areas.
The South was willing to sacrifice industrial growth in order to main-

tain a higher way of life, for whites at least. Limiting industrialization was explained, also, as the cost of the South's bearing, for the nation, the burden of maintaining and controlling the black population. This burden arose, in part, because of the historic role northerners had played in the transatlantic slave trade, in which they had profited by bringing slaves to the South. Thus, it was not rooted solely in the behavior of southerners.

Here, again, agreement on the persistence of the limited degree of southern industrialization in antebellum years had some similar implications. Limited southern industrialization was attributed to the failure to achieve a productive slave economy, in agriculture as well as in industry, and to the limited market demand due to a maldistribution of income. This failure was abetted either by the incompetence of slave labor or else by the South's unwillingness or inability of southern planters and farmers to pursue income-maximizing economic goals, aims that would have meant a change in southern patterns of living. Both of these propositions pointed to a belief in a stagnant southern economy, with poorly prepared businessmen, entrepreneurs, and workers. The failures of both laborers and owners, and the costs of controlling the slave population, explained the absence of southern industry, and these failures were taken as indications of southern economic backwardness. There is an alternative set of explanations for limited southern industrialization and agricultural development based on the characteristics of southern climate, soils, and geography. This is the emphasis of John Majewski and Viken Tchakerian, who argue that what some regard as an inefficient southern pattern of production reflects a rational response to the constraints imposed by natural forces. Presumably the human failure here was the decision made as to where to settle and produce. The focus on climate and resources points to differences in comparative advantages and the role of different growth paths, rather than to dramatic differences in levels of efficiency at particular points of time.

There have been, in recent decades, some reinterpretations of the nature of the southern economy and of southern industrialization. This does not deny, obviously, the relatively small size of the southern industrial sector compared with that of the North, particularly the states of the Northeast, at least after 1840. Nevertheless, these new reinterpretations help to place southern industrialization in a somewhat different perspective.

Recognition of the slave-based sugar plantation as a "factory in the fields," and of slave-based agriculture as among the first businesses to be concerned with problems of coordination, labor productivity, and incentives and with a need to deal with issues of production and distribution, and, more generally, the role of the plantation in sugar, cotton, rice, and coffee production, as among the largest business activities of the time, has given more attention to the operations of slave-based economies. Sugar production was based on advanced technology and mechanization, and in the United States, sugar plantations were among the major users of steam power before the Civil War. Slave-based production might not, as some argue, have survived much longer in the nineteenth century, but it should be noted that slavery had survived for over two centuries as a profitable institution.

There have also been some new comparisons of the South with the rest of the world and with the Midwest, which place the debate about the southern economy in some perspective.[3] While the South (if it were treated as a separate nation) had less industry than the northeastern United States and Britain, it had a relatively high industrial and economic ranking relative to the rest of the world. It was about fourth in per capita income, ahead of all of Europe except Britain, ranked high in canal and railroad construction, was sixth in the world in cotton textile production (despite the absence of air cooling to keep threads separate), and was eighth in pig iron production. It had an extensive education system for whites, and even the degree of literacy for the total population exceeded that in most of Europe. It had a well-developed banking system, and state and local governments were active in economic development.[4] As Brian Schoen notes, also, the South was able to attract foreign capital and advocated policies to decrease imports from the North

3. The following section draws upon Robert William Fogel, *Without Consent or Contract: The Rise and Fall of American Slavery* (New York: W. W. Norton, 1986), 60–113; and Robert William Fogel and Stanley L. Engerman, *Time on the Cross: The Economics of American Negro Slavery* (Boston: Little Brown, 1974), 191–257.

4. See, on banking, Larry Schweikart, *Banking in the American South from the Age of Jackson to Reconstruction* (Baton Rouge: Louisiana State University Press, 1987); on the role of state governments, see Milton S. Health, *Constructive Liberalism: The Role of the State in the Economic Development of Georgia to 1860* (Cambridge: Harvard University Press, 1954); and John Majewski, *A House Dividing: Economic Development in Pennsylvania and Virginia before the Civil War* (Cambridge: Cambridge University Press, 2000).

and increase industrial production in the South. The impact of the 1857 Panic, more severe on the North than the South, provided an important argument for the wisdom of southern economic structure. And an examination of the effects of King Oil in the 1970s suggests that the earlier belief in King Cotton may have been wrong but was not completely irrational.

Moreover, the comparison of industrial structure within the United States raises questions concerning the definitions of manufacturing output and classifications used by the census. In some measure the shortfall in manufacturing output in the South relative to that in the North reflects the census classification scheme. At the time much of manufacturing was involved with the processing of agricultural products. In the North, with small farms and independent factories, most agricultural processing took place in separate firms listed in the manufacturing sector. In the South this was more often part of the plantation sector listed in agricultural output. Thus sugar production of large plantations, generally on units larger than northern textile firms, was agricultural, not manufacturing output. Similar allocations occurred for rice cleaning (larger than flour mills) and cotton ginning, as well as the more general output from coopering and blacksmithing. Thus the South lacked a large modern industrial sector as in the North, but its manufacturing output was larger than was indicated by the census, and the basic economic structure, in both North and South, was still predominantly agricultural.

Businesslike attitudes and actions of planters and other southerners have been seen in a wide variety of behaviors, all of which suggest that there were multiple responses to changing economic conditions, with prices and outputs responding to these changes, and these permitted profits from slaves, from land ownership, and from industry, to persist. These commercial, trading networks, with societies based on wealthy consumers, artisans, and exports, were not confined to the late antebellum era. Emma Hart's survey of late-eighteenth-century Charleston indicates the many ways that the city was an integral part of the British Atlantic world and how its development was influenced by this linking. It raises the rather difficult question of whether the South's economy was too open or too closed for the region's long-term interests.

Prices of slaves reflected the changing prices and productivity of commodities produced by slave labor and purchased for them. This was found not only in the United States, but also in the British West Indies, Cuba, Brazil, and Saint Domingue. Indeed rising prices for prolonged periods characterized all societies where slave prices can be analyzed.[5] The changing mix of crops and the choice of urban-versus-rural location reflected the relative returns to planters. Despite many claims of the inflexibility of slave economies, a rather different pattern is apparent in the historical record. From early settlement until about 1800, U.S. slavery was quite different in terms of geographic location, major crops produced, and size of plantation units from the patterns that developed in the more frequently studied "Cotton Economy" of the nineteenth century. There was rapid movement westward and southward so that about half of the southern population in 1860 inhabited areas that had not been in the southern part of the thirteen colonies; cotton replaced rice and tobacco as the major export crop; and the size of plantations increased.

Similar flexibility in crops and location was found in other slave societies, particularly Cuba and Brazil, in the mid-nineteenth century. Slaves performed many different functions in rural and urban areas, and even when sugar and cotton were the major crops, these generally accounted for less than half of the slave's labor time on the plantation. In short, the view of a static, stagnant plantation sector, based on a monoculture, is not accurate as a portrayal of the southern (or any other slave) economy.

More attention has also recently been given by historians to the trappings of the business sector in the South—financial newspapers, market newsletters of slave traders, a complex legal system essential for commercial and other purposes, a generally effective and efficient banking system, extensive state and local aids to transport and financial developments, the availability of schools for white education, and many other aspects of what would be considered necessary in modern business societies. The agricultural journals of the South had frequent discussions

5. For comparisons of slave prices in the United States, Cuba, and Brazil, see Manual Moreno Fraginals, Herbert S. Klein, and Stanley L. Engerman, "The Level and Structure of Slave Prices on Cuban Plantations in the Mid-Nineteenth Century: Some Comparative Perspectives," *American Historical Review* 88 (Dec. 1983): 1201–18; and Laird W. Bergad, "American Slave Markets during the 1850s: Slave Price Rises in the U.S., Cuba, and Brazil in Comparative Perspective," in *Slavery in the Development of the Americas,* ed. David Eltis et al. (Cambridge: Cambridge University Press, 2004), 219–35.

of optimum ways to organize and control labor.[6] These discussions should not be interpreted as a sign of weakness; rather they were a sharing of information that was one of the explanations for sustained growth. Many plantations kept detailed, standardized account books, listing daily outputs, numbers, and values of slaves and other assets owned and providing related information on commercial matters. Whether capitalist, pre-capitalist, or acapitalist, the planters were clearly commercially oriented in much of their behavior, both within agriculture and in other sectors, including industry.

What this data on the southern economy has done is shift the interpretation of southern industrialization. Whereas earlier it was argued that economic backwardness retarded industrialization of the South, it is now argued that the strength of the agricultural sector held back industrial change. While the same findings regarding the limited size of the southern industrial sector are present, the interpretation of why it happened, and how these findings fit in with our knowledge of the South, has now changed. The antebellum South now is seen as another of the regions in which high levels of agricultural or mineral productivity slowed the pace of industrialization—a rather different and more fruitful way to approach the issue than that provided by earlier slaveowners, abolitionists, Marxists, and those others who argued that it was due to the failures of the southern economy. It was the great antebellum profitability of cotton production, with rising prices throughout the period, that served to limit the size of other sectors of the economy, a phenomenon now called by economists the "Dutch Disease."[7] The production of crops and other commodities was not based on unthinking decisions, but rather the changes were responses to price differentials and their shifts, with a movement into other sectors based on relative demand conditions.

There is another question raised about the costs to the South of its limited industrialization: the effects upon the outcome of the Civil War. In some ways the response in the Civil War, with expanding imports of

6. See, for example, James O. Breeden, *Advice among Masters: The Idea of Slave Management in the Old South* (Westport: Greenwood Press, 1980).

7. The "Dutch Disease" is an explanation given for the consequences experienced by the Dutch after the 1960s due to the presence of material gas. So high was the demand for natural gas, and so profitable its production, that difficulties were experienced by other potential export sectors.

manufactured items and the internal development of war-related industries provides some indication of the possible flexibility of the South in response to a decline in demand for cotton, which gave rise to the southern ability to sustain a longer-than-anticipated war effort.[8]

Recently, there has been a reversal in the argument about the impact of differing degrees of labor skills and labor mobility in the North and in the South. The flexibility of the southern economy has now come to be considered a source of its failure and particularly of its failure to industrialize.[9] Moreover, the ability of female and child labor to produce more cotton than it could wheat meant that a labor pool of women and children who would otherwise be underemployed developed in the North and was used in industry. In New England, it is argued, labor was less mobile than in the South, thus increasing the industrial labor force in the region, with, in particular, the importance of women and children in the developing textile factories. Northern industrialization, therefore, is now seen as the outcome of economic and social weakness, not strength, while southern economic flexibility and strength in agriculture had short-term benefits, but some scholars believe they may have meant long-term costs to the South, depending on future changes in world demands and the possibilities for flexibility of supply adjustment in the southern economy.

These comments do not deal with all of the questions asked about southern industry before and after the Civil War, but they do provide an essentially different and important starting point from which to study southern economic issues. It is useful to remember that the South was not the only part of the world with limited industrialization and extensive agricultural production. Indeed the South was probably among the most productive economies in the world at the time. Its great agricultural production aside, the South was also ranked among the world's

8. See, for example, Raimondo Luraghi, *The Rise and Fall of the Plantation South* (New York: New Viewpoint, 1978); and Mary A. DeCredico, *Patriotism for Profit: Georgia's Urban Entrepreneurs and the War Effort* (Chapel Hill: University of North Carolina Press, 1990).

9. See Claudia Dale Goldin, *Urban Slavery in the American South, 1820–1860* (Chicago: University of Chicago Press, 1976); Claudia Goldin and Kenneth Sokoloff, "The Relative Productivity Hypothesis of Industrialization: The American Case, 1820 to 1850," *Quarterly Journal of Economics* 49 (1984): 461–87; and Gavin Wright, *The Political Economy of the Cotton South* (New York: W. W. Norton, 1978), 107–20.

leading industrial producers. In some nations in the nineteenth century, there may have been deindustrialization, with a shift back into agricultural and mineral production to meet the expanded demands for those commodities by the few nations of Europe and North America that had recently begun to experience industrialization, but such an example of deindustrialization was not a southern pattern. Explaining the South may be a problem, but the idea that the region's economic problems were unique is a falsehood. When the downturn of 1857 hit northern industry but not southern agriculture, commentators stressed the advantages of the southern economy in confronting international economic problems.

I regard the discussion of southern industrialization thus far as mainly presenting a factual record for the antebellum South. I would argue, further, that many of those scholars suggesting that the South would ultimately pay for its limited industrialization were really basing their contentions on counterfactual propositions, statements about what would or could happen at some future unspecified date, not what had actually happened. Those forecasts, since that is what they were, were based on claims concerning particular specified conditions; most important among them was the presumption that the southern slave economy was capable of only limited flexibility. It is seldom specified what time in the future the southern industrialization rate should shift upward in order for the South to maximize its rate of economic growth, and how much time might be allowed for any necessary transition to occur. It is not that the idea of counterfactuals is inappropriate; they are a central tool for most historical analysis. Their usefulness, however, is set by the reasonableness of the underlying assumptions going into them. It might have been expected that the findings of past decades on southern economic development and the flexibility of the economy would raise some questions about the continued use of the earlier assumptions of a backward and inflexible economy in the counterfactual analysis. But, here as elsewhere, it often seems as if old myths about southern economic behavior and structure remain dominant in influencing historical interpretations.

As we have learned from the analysis of the plantation sector after the Civil War, it is not easy to use the postemancipation southern economy to explain what might have happened if the antebellum regime had continued in the absence of the political changes due to the Civil War.

Clearly there were gains in welfare to the ex-slaves with emancipation, but the changes in the system of social organization, triggered by the end of the plantation system, led to some significant negative changes in the economy, with a weakened financial system, a movement to smaller, less efficient farms to produce cotton, and a limited effort to repair a damaged transportation system. Much of the initial reduction in per capita incomes reflected the social and economic changes introduced by the loss of the extensive labor control under slavery due to the outcome of the war, not generally to actual wartime damages.[10] Manufacturing did recover more rapidly than did agriculture after the war, and its growth continued throughout the following years.

The rather sharp legal change in the status of slaves in the United States after the Civil War is somewhat different than the more prolonged procedure of the ending of all aspects of serfdom in the area of Prussia studied by Shearer D. Bowman, so that the ending of serfdom does not seem to have had the dramatic effects that the ending of slavery had in the South and elsewhere in the Americas. Yet the nature of the endings of European serfdom and of southern slavery did have some important relations. The ending of serfdom in Europe was followed, if not immediately, within a few decades, by renewed migration from Europe to the American North. In the South, after 1865, there was little out-migration interregionally. In the aftermath of World War I, there was legislation reducing immigration into the United States, and this along with World War I led to the beginnings of a wide-scale migration of ex-slaves to the North, starting in the second decade of the twentieth century.

Based on the estimates of regional incomes in the nineteenth-century U.S, there is yet another puzzle regarding the southern economy. The regional income data had indicated that in the antebellum era the South's per capita income grew at about the same rate as the North's. Similarly, after the once-and-for-all adjustment to the legal ending of slavery and the end of the plantation system, over the next several decades of the nineteenth century and into the early twentieth century, the same pattern of equal growth rates between regions occurred.

10. See Stanley L. Engerman, "Comparative Approaches to the Ending of Slavery," in *After Slavery: Emancipation and Its Discontents,* ed. Howard Temperley (London: Frank Cass, 2000), 281–300.

The South had many problems, but these did not seem to impede the relatively high growth rate of income and the South's maintaining of its relative per capita income position during a large growth spurt in the North. Manufacturing expansion was part of the growth, with growth in non-natural-resource–based industries as well as in industries based on natural resources. Dramatic was the movement of the cotton textile industry from New England to the South, accelerating in the 1880s. As David L. Carlton and Peter Coclanis point out, by 1910 the South had the third largest installed spindlage capacity in the world, behind only Britain and the North, not only taking markets throughout the United States from northern producers, but also selling in Asian markets. As Beth English points out, the southward movement of textiles was facilitated by cheaper labor in the South, as well as state government policies. In the South the states provided subsidies and other benefits to manufacturers and investors, while the northern concern with improving working conditions and labor standards served to raise the cost of labor there. Erin Elizabeth Clune describes another important aspect of southern industrial development, the attempt to attract white immigrants for southern labor, with a particular interest in laborers from England. The choice of locale reflects, as much else in the South, ethnic preferences about what would seem desirable for southern society.

New technologies aided southern growth, with innovations such as air-cooling, which permitted the humid South to expand its cotton textile industry. This was a precursor of later innovations, such as air-conditioning, which led to southern demographic and economic growth, with considerable migration from the North. This expansion meant that the South, at the end of the twentieth century, had a per capita income almost equal to the national average and a substantial southern manufacturing sector. Thus, given time enough, and with enough changes in the economy, the early problems of the southern economy apparently could be overcome, even if belatedly. The explanations given for the growth of southern industrialization have now provided us with a new set of myths, intended to explain this achievement, with different presentations of the relative importance of the public and the private sectors. There is, for some, the myth of the central role of the government and, for others, that of the key role of private individuals. It seems too early in the scholarship, however, to determine which, if either, myth will seem more plausible to future generations.

Charleston and the British

Industrial Revolution, 1750-1790

Emma Hart

In their efforts to understand the character of early American settlement, historians have invariably approached their task region by region.[1] By doing so, they have discovered that each of the component
parts of colonial British America often achieved its greatest coherence
through its specific economic traits. In the case of the Lower South "rice
branded a distinct. e mark on the social structure and economic organization of the region."[2] South Carolina and Georgia were, therefore,
distinguished from Britain's northerly colonies by their slave majority,

1. Perhaps the best regionally focused survey is Jack P. Greene, *Pursuits of Happiness: The Social Development of Early Modern British Colonies and the Formation
of American Culture* (Chapel Hill: University of North Carolina Press, 1988). For a
survey of economic regional difference see John J. McCusker and Russell R. Menard, *The Economy of British America, 1607–1789* (Chapel Hill: University of North
Carolina Press, 1991). On New England, Daniel Vickers, *Farmers and Fishermen:
Two Centuries of Work in Essex County, Massachusetts, 1680–1830* (Chapel Hill:
University of North Carolina Press, 1994); Margaret Ellen Newell, *From Dependency to Independence: Economic Revolution in Colonial New England* (Ithaca:
Cornell University Press, 1998). On the Chesapeake, Rhys Isaac, *The Transforma-
tion of Virginia, 1740–1790* (Chapel Hill: University of North Carolina Press, 1982);
Lois Green Carr, Russell R. Menard, and Lorena S. Walsh, *Robert Cole's World:
Agriculture and Society in Early Maryland* (Chapel Hill: University of North Carolina Press, 1991).
2. McCusker and Menard, *Economy of British America,* 175.

their lack of towns, and the emergence of the plantation as the building block of society.[3]

This ongoing concern with rice production has allowed scholars to show how the Lower South became an important and distinctive region in the history of early America. Today, South Carolina and Massachusetts are accepted as equal partners in the creation of a New World society. However, concern for plantation agriculture has also encouraged historians to place the Low Country outside of the twin processes of industrialization and urbanization that were shaping many other areas of the British Atlantic world from the 1740s on. So, while Charleston became the fourth largest town in British America in the course of the eighteenth century, its success is wholly attributed to the rise of the rice economy. In the Lower South, features that are interpreted elsewhere in early America as indicators of hastening industrial development are instead used to illustrate the region's exclusion from this process. For instance, whereas the growth of New York, Philadelphia, and Boston by the mid-eighteenth century is often read as a sign of the beginnings of a process leading to northern industrialization, the expansion of Charleston during the same period is seen as an indication of the increasing wealth of South Carolina's rice planters and merchants.[4]

3. Standard works on the early South Carolina Low Country include Converse D. Clowse, *Economic Beginnings in Colonial South Carolina, 1670–1730* (Columbia: University of South Carolina Press, 1971); Peter H. Wood, *Black Majority: Negroes in Colonial South Carolina from 1670 through the Stono Rebellion* (New York: W. W. Norton, 1996); Clarence Ver Steeg, *Origins of a Southern Mosaic: Studies of Early Carolina and Georgia* (Athens: University of Georgia Press, 1975); Daniel Littlefield, *Rice and Slaves: Ethnicity and the Slave Trade in Colonial South Carolina* (Urbana-Champaign: University of Illinois Press, 1977); Peter Coclanis, *The Shadow of a Dream: Economic Life and Death in the South Carolina Low Country, 1670–1920* (New York: Oxford University Press, 1989); Richard Waterhouse, *A New World Gentry: The Making of a Merchant and Planter Class in South Carolina, 1670–1770* (New York: Garland Press, 1989); Joyce Chaplin, *An Anxious Pursuit: Agricultural Innovation and Modernity in the Lower South, 1730–1815* (Chapel Hill: University of North Carolina Press, 1993); Robert Olwell, *Masters, Slaves and Subjects: The Culture of Power in the South Carolina Low Country* (Ithaca: Cornell University Press, 1998); Jack P. Greene, Randy J. Sparks, and Rosemary Brana-Shute, eds., *Money, Trade, and Power: The Evolution of Colonial South Carolina's Plantation Society* (Columbia: University of South Carolina Press, 2001).

4. On southern towns see Richard Walsh, *Charleston's Sons of Liberty: A Study of the Artisans, 1763–1789* (Columbia: University of South Carolina Press, 1959); Joseph A. Ernst and H. Roy Merrens, "'Camden's turret's pierce the skies!' The

There is little doubt that Charleston fulfilled an important function as a trading entrepôt in the plantation Lower South. However, this does not preclude us from investigating the town from an alternative perspective, especially as new work on early British America has shown that the regional paradigm can sometimes be a constricting, as well as a constructive, framework for analysis. David Armitage, for example, has advocated the usefulness of a "cis-Atlantic" approach—namely "the history of a particular place . . . in relation to the wider Atlantic world"—in order to overcome the artificial divisions that regional studies can create between places and societies. In particular, Armitage argues for the utility of this cis-Atlantic framework for the study of the port towns and cities that so embodied the connections between colony and metropole.[5]

This essay seeks to apply this British Atlantic approach to the study of Charleston, in particular focusing on groups within the urban population who have been overlooked because they operated outside of the rice economy. For although Charleston was brought to life by rice and indigo money, it soon began to develop functions not directly connected to the region's staple crops. In the 1790 census, only 28 percent of Charleston heads of household were either planters or merchants, and their households were home to only 30 percent of the city's black and white population; artisans headed up 27 percent of the town's households; professionals and service workers headed 14 percent.[6] This

---

Urban Process in the Southern Colonies during the Eighteenth Century," *William and Mary Quarterly* 3rd ser., vol. 30, no. 4 (Oct. 1973): 549–74; Carville Earle, "The Evolution of a Tidewater Settlement System: All Hallow's Parish, Maryland, 1650–1783" (Ph.D. diss., University of Chicago, 1973). For Charleston in a wider early American urban context see Carl Bridenbaugh, *Cities in the Wilderness: Urban Life in America, 1625–1742* (New York: Oxford University Press, 1938); and *Cities in Revolt: Urban Life in America, 1743–1776* (New York: Oxford University Press, 1955); Jacob Price, "Economic Function and the Growth of American Port Towns in the Eighteenth Century," *Perspectives in American History* 8 (1974): 123–88; Gary Nash, "The Social Evolution of Pre-Industrial American Cities, 1700–1820: Reflections and New Directions," *Journal of Urban History* 13 (Feb. 1987): 115–45; Richard L. Bushman, *The Refinement of America: Persons, Houses, Cities* (New York: Vintage Books, 1993).

5. David Armitage, "Three Concepts of Atlantic History," in *The British Atlantic World, 1500–1800,* ed. David Armitage and Michael J. Braddick (Basingstoke: Palgrave, 2002), 21–23.

6. Figures calculated by cross-referencing the 1790 city directory and the 1790 federal census data.

essay investigates this diverse urban domestic economy as one of many similar urban economies throughout the contemporary English-speaking world in order to show how the Lower South was involved in a British Atlantic industrial revolution. Furthermore, I will argue that viewing Charleston from this additional, global perspective, can help us better to understand its economic character and its importance to early America.

To illustrate the ways in which Charleston's economic development was connected to wider processes of urban industrial change, I have chosen to analyze its working community from two perspectives. First, I survey the overall contours of the town's economy and show how its profile made it part of an industrializing urban system. I then explore the structure of some individual businesses to uncover how their evolution was representative of broader industrial trends.

Here, it is important to note that while this essay finds commonalities between Charleston and its British urban counterparts, it does not set out to deny the very major particularities of the region's economy, and most especially the influence of slavery. A majority of the artisans and service providers discussed in the following pages owned slaves whom they employed extensively in their businesses. Although this caused social tensions and altered class structures, it is my contention that it did not fundamentally reshape the urban economy. As Robert Olwell has shown, while African Americans may have been able to test the law of the market in the Low Country, they could not overturn it completely.[7] Slave men and women were essential to the growth of Charleston's economy, as they traded in the marketplace, labored in workshops, and served as domestics in homes. However, since they did so mostly within roles prescribed by their white masters and mistresses, their work often facilitated the construction of a complex British Atlantic urban economy.

Understanding Charleston's place in British Atlantic industrial development requires that first we understand the nature of that development. After decades of research and writing, the debate about the character of Britain's industrial revolution remains as vital, and almost as unresolved, as ever. Recent scholarship, however, has been especially marked by an increased diversity in the approaches taken to the study of industrial change. Whereas earlier historians tended to be concerned with

7. Olwell, *Masters, Slaves and Subjects,* 141–80.

macroeconomic analysis, later studies have turned away from this "numbers" approach, looking instead toward more qualitative accounts of change. Suggesting that patchy national data had been pushed to their limits, these scholars focused on the experience of workers and entrepreneurs throughout different regions and industries with the goal of understanding the pace and nature of change on a micro level.[8]

Unsurprisingly, opinions about what constituted industrial revolution have changed as a result of these new approaches. In the first instance, the revolution has become more evolutionary as scholars have posited a more stately pace of development that started as early as 1750 and ended over a century later. Moreover, this measured change, although visible on the broadest scale with growth in national income and domestic expenditure, made for an uneven advance across industries and regions. So, where iron and cloth were manufactured in large-scale enterprises quite early on in the eighteenth century, the shift from workshop to factory was later and less clear-cut in the majority of trades, with "pre-industrial" work patterns persisting well into the 1800s.[9] And, although certain areas and cities (Lancashire, Birmingham, and Manchester, for example) were rapidly swept forward by change, others deindustrialized or took on new roles. Industry in the Welsh border county of Shropshire, for example, was initially lively but tailed off as overall development forged ahead.[10] In sum, we are now as familiar with the place of the West Riding's woolen industry in the industrial revolution as we are with that of Sheffield cutlers, London cabinetmakers,

8. David Cannadine, "The Present and the Past in the English Industrial Revolution, 1880–1980," *Past and Present* 103 (1984); Joel Mokyr, ed., *The Economics of the Industrial Revolution* (London: Rowman & Littlefield, 1985); N. F. R. Crafts, *British Economic Growth during the Industrial Revolution* (Oxford: Oxford University Press, 1985); Maxine Berg, *The Age of Manufactures* (London: Fontana Press, 1985); E. A. Wrigley, *Continuity, Chance, and Change: The Character of the Industrial Revolution in England* (Cambridge: Cambridge University Press, 1988); Pat Hudson, *The Industrial Revolution* (London: Arnold, 1992); Patrick O'Brien and Roland Quinault, eds., *The Industrial Revolution and British Society* (Cambridge: Cambridge University Press, 1993); R. C. Floud and D. McCloskey, eds., *The Economic History of Britain since 1700* (Cambridge: Cambridge University Press, 2000).

9. For an excellent summary of these discussions see Hudson, *The Industrial Revolution*.

10. Eric Richards, "Margins of the Industrial Revolution," in *Industrial Revolution and British Society*, ed. O'Brien and Quinault, 209.

women workers, Wedgwood's advertising innovations, and Watt's steam engine. Together, entrepreneurs and artisans, rural dwellers and towns-folk, and northerners and southerners all represented the diversity that characterized eighteenth-century British industrial change.[11]

This new and wider-ranging approach to Britain's industrial revolution has also recognized that events other than the building of factories, or the implementation of innovation, were key to economic development. Perhaps the most important of these associated processes was the emergence of what Peter Clark has labeled a "diffuse and polycentric" urban system.[12] This was a system where London retained its central importance but was increasingly unable to fulfill an economic role without the many other types of towns that dotted Britain's provinces. Together, port towns, leisure and spa towns, and manufacturing towns increasingly interacted to provide metropolitan Britons with all of their material and cultural requirements.[13] This system witnessed all urban entities working together to produce and distribute goods. For example, before a Bath socialite obtained a fashionable silk gown, raw silk arrived in a port town from the Far East; it was then woven and dyed at Spital-fields in London, and the material was finally stitched together by the mantuamaker at Bath. If our socialite was to accessorize her new outfit, she would then need to buy Manchester-made ribbons from the haber-dasher and Birmingham-wrought jewelry from the goldsmith.

11. N. McKendrick, "Josiah Wedgwood: An Eighteenth-Century Entrepreneur in Salesmanship and Marketing Techniques," *Economic History Review* 12 (1959–1960); Pat Hudson, *The Genesis of Industrial Capital: A Study of the West Riding Wool Textile Industry c 1750–1850* (Cambridge: Cambridge University Press, 1986); Maxine Berg, "Women's Work, Mechanization and the Early Phases of the Industrialization in England," in *The Historical Meanings of Work,* ed. Patrick Joyce (Cambridge: Cambridge University Press, 1987); "Small Producer Capitalism in Eighteenth-Century Britain," *Business History* 35, 1 (1993).

12. Peter Clark, ed., *The Cambridge Urban History of Britain: Volume 2 1540–1850* (Cambridge: Cambridge University Press, 2000), 10.

13. Examples include Peter Earle, *The Making of the English Middle Class: Business, Society and Family Life in London, 1660–1730* (London: Methuen Publishing, 1989); Paul Langford, *A Polite and Commercial People: England 1727–1783* (Oxford: Oxford University Press, 1989); Rosemary Sweet, *The English Town, 1680–1840: Government, Society and Culture* (London: Longman, 1999); Peter Clark, ed., *The Cambridge History of Urban Britain: Vol. 2, 1540–1850* (Cambridge: Cambridge University Press, 2000); Joyce M. Ellis, *The Georgian Town, 1680–1840* (Basingstoke: Palgrave, 2001); Peter Clark, *British Clubs and Societies, 1580–1800: The Origins of an Associational World* (Oxford: Oxford University Press, 2000).

As well as recognizing the complexity of economic change, the broadly defined industrial revolution opens up a new space for cities like Charleston. By increasing the ways in which people and places might be part of economic change, this urban-based "industrial evolution" encourages a reassessment of the relationship between the Low Country and the metropole.[14] We already know that as a hub for the import of British goods, slaves, and rice, Charleston was fully enmeshed in one transatlantic system—the triangular trade between Africa, America, and Britain. But, was the town also party to other systems based around manufacturing and industry?

One way of working out Charleston's position within a transatlantic urban system is to draw up an occupational profile and place it alongside that of its contemporary towns in Britain and America. Admittedly, establishing such a profile accurately, over time, is made extremely difficult by a lack of sources. For while scholars working on the Anglo-American town have customarily turned to tax records and freeman's admissions for a guide to townsmen's business activities, no such records exist for Charleston. Clearly, we will never have access to more reliable sources of such data, but enough records do survive to ascertain the general shape of the urban economy. By using newspapers, city directories, census data, and court, church, and government records, along with probate information, it is possible to piece together enough about the Charleston business community to unearth useful details of its character.

The data reveal that Charleston's economy did indeed have a distinct profile. In particular, figures demonstrate an economy that, as well as being shaped by the merchant and seafaring activity commonly found in port towns, was oriented toward the luxury and service trades. Charleston's numerous tradesmen and women were devoted to providing for the consuming needs of the Low Country population. This particular profile is best supported by the 1790 federal census, which shows that 40 percent of Charleston heads of household could be described as being part of a "leisure" industry—that is to say, they were gentlemen planters at leisure, artisans working in luxury trades such as cabinetmaking and silversmithing, or professionals and service workers like lawyers, teachers, or dancing and music masters.

14. As Eric Richards has suggested, the most "distant margins of a widening economic world" could easily get dragged into an "increasingly articulated British market system" ("Margins of the Industrial Revolution" in *Industrial Revolution and British Society,* ed. O'Brien and Quinault, 203).

By eighteenth-century standards, Charleston's occupational profile was not unusual. Studies of eighteenth-century Shrewsbury, a provincial town in the county of Shropshire with a comparable number of inhabitants to the Low Country metropolis, have revealed that by 1775 a similar proportion of freemen (36 percent) were occupied in such a "leisure" sector. The character of Shrewsbury's economy had undergone a marked transformation from the late seventeenth century, when leather and textile processing had dominated the urban economy. However, with the advent of industrial change, and the rise of towns such as Leicester and Manchester, these sectors had withered away, and the town had been reborn as a place where provincial gentry could purchase new consumer goods and pursue new leisure activities. That Charleston's occupational profile was akin to Shrewsbury's would therefore suggest that it had come to serve a similar function in the Low Country and occupied a similar place in a British Atlantic urban system.[15]

With its leisured disposition, Charleston's economic character was the opposite of Britain's growing regional manufacturing centers, where an even spread of trades was overlaid with certain industrial specializations. Among these regional centers was Birmingham, which, by the late 1770s, was home to an unusually large number of buttonmakers and toymakers, and Manchester, a town that played host to almost two hundred fustian and check manufacturers.[16] What is more, as table 1.1 shows, Charleston's economy contrasted in a similar fashion with its more northerly New World counterparts. Where Boston's large community of shipwrights signaled the emergence of a maritime economy, and a nascent leather processing industry in Philadelphia was indicated by a high concentration of master tanners and shoemakers, Charleston had a disproportionately large number of retailers, cabinetmakers, doctors, and attorneys. Overall, although the Low Country town had almost as many heads of household in nonagricultural pursuits as other cities of the period, the profile of the business community was nevertheless distinct.[17]

15. Angus McInnes, "The Emergence of a Leisure Town: Shrewsbury, 1660–1760" *Past and Present* 120 (1988): table 1, 56.

16. Ellis, *The Georgian Town,* appendix 2: "Trades and Professions in Five Major Towns."

17. Jacob Price, "American Port Towns." Although Price classifies the urban economy under different categories, reclassifying his figures according to categories

Table 1.1

Occupational Profile of Three American Cities

Sector	Boston (1790) %	Philadelphia (1780–83) %	Charleston (1790) %
Government	3	3	9
Professional	4.5	3	10
Retailers	10.7	14	24
Retail Crafts	8.9	14	9.3
Building Crafts	11.1	8.4	8.4
Travel & Transport	8.3	12.3	5.2
Textile Industry	2.4	1.6	0
Leather Industry	6.1	11	4.2
Food	2.6	1	1.2
Shipbuilding	9.5	5	2.1
Metalworking	3.5	3.8	3
Furniture	1.6	1.1	3
Maritime	10.2	7.4	4.5
Merchants	17.7	14.4	16.1
	100	100	100

Source: Jacob Price, "American Port Towns" Appendix C,
Charleston City Directory 1790. Correlation of the city directory
with the census reveals that the directory is comprehensive in its
coverage of urban households.

---

used in this study shows that artisans in Philadelphia made up (according to
whether the 1775 or 1780–1783 source is consulted) either 51 percent or 58 percent
of male household heads identified with an occupation. In Boston, the proportion
in 1790 was 51 percent and in Charleston in 1790 it was 40 percent.

Certainly, it could be argued that the trends evident in table 1.1 emerge as a result of the free black and enslaved peoples who constituted a substantial proportion of Charleston's working population throughout this period. Indeed, scholars have suggested that the training of slaves as tradesmen noticeably reduced the numbers of white artisans in the town. This practice could well distort a head of household occupational profile by emphasizing highly skilled luxury trades, such as silversmithing, where slaves were much less likely to replace white masters.[18] However, a number of features of this data suggest that such distortion is unlikely. First, the vast majority of slave artisans worked as carpenters, blacksmiths, or tailors, meaning that it is in the building and retail craft sectors that we would expect to see much lower numbers of white master artisans.[19] Significantly, though, the figures show that these sectors occupied a proportion of Charleston's heads of household similar to those in Boston and in Philadelphia, suggesting that slaves probably had a minimal impact on the number of established white master craftsmen. And although shipbuilding occupied an especially low number of white heads of household in Charleston, this tallies with the much lower tonnage of shipping built in the city during the eighteenth century.[20] It would, therefore, seem more likely that Charleston's slaves worked in positions that were usually taken by white journeymen and laborers in Boston or in Philadelphia, and since such men would invariably be listed as part of other people's households in a census, the occupational structure of the town suggested here is probably reliable.

The profile of the town in the 1790 census indicates the result of sustained development of its economy. The early years of Charleston's growth were characterized by the emergence of a construction sector, with shipwrights, carpenters, bricklayers, and blacksmiths all arriving to build the basic infrastructure of the town. The growth in this sphere continued as, characteristically for a growing provincial town, carpenters and

18. Carl Bridenbaugh, *The Colonial Craftsman* (New York: New York University Press, 1950); S. Max Edelson, "Affiliation without Affinity: Skilled Slaves in Eighteenth-Century South Carolina," in *Money, Trade, and Power,* ed. Greene, Brana-Shute, and Sparks.

19. See Philip Morgan, *Slave Counterpoint: Black Culture in the Eighteenth-Century Chesapeake and Low Country* (Chapel Hill: University of North Carolina Press, 1998), 204–44.

20. Joseph A. Goldenberg, *Shipbuilding in Colonial America* (Charlottesville: University of Virginia Press, 1976).

bricklayers were required to build the public and private edifices that constituted the new urban landscape.[21] However, from the 1720s until 1790 (apart from an interruption around the time of the Revolution), artisans in the luxury and clothing trades flooded into the town. By the time of the first federal census, those working in trades such as cabinet-making, tailoring, millinery, silversmithing, and coachmaking were ubiquitous among the town's artisans. A lack of workers in heavier manufacturing sectors such as cloth and leather processing, shipbuilding, or iron-founding, meant that despite the size of the construction industry, luxury and service trades remained the most populous. Structurally, rather than being oriented to either heavy manufacturing or to the industries traditionally associated with port towns, Charleston was devoted to servicing the needs of the region's wealthy consumers.

Even though Charleston was a port town, its seaboard location does not seem to have been the primary influence on either its regional or its colonial role. As its occupational structure shows, the town had developed in significant ways beyond its mercantile and agricultural functions. In particular, the profile of the business community bore a strong similarity to the British provincial leisure town: a type of urban place that was increasingly being pushed to the fore by new consumption patterns among local elites, and by new manufacturing trends in Britain's regions. Hence, as well as developing into a port town that would serve a regional plantation economy, Charleston was also growing in such a way as to allow it to fit into an urban system that was an essential part of industrial revolution.

The nature of the town's economy permeated the physical character of Charleston, and the geography of its streets also bore the hallmarks of a service and leisure town. As table 1.2 shows, by 1790 the town's thoroughfares had become clearly demarcated by their commercial functions. According to the 1790 city directory, the nine major downtown streets were home to five hundred eighty-three different businesses. Merchants, shopkeepers, and artisans could be found on all the major roads, but they were distributed according to an identifiable pattern. The waterfront was characterized by a large number of retailers and importers and a scattering of artisan shops that provided services to

21. Jon Stobart, "Shopping Streets as Social Space: Leisure, Consumerism and Improvement in an Eighteenth-Century Town," *Urban History* 1998, 25(1), 10.

ships and sailors. Broad Street, on the other hand, was devoted to merchants and artisans in the luxury and clothing trades. Overall, Broad, Church, and Elliott streets presented the best opportunities for luxury shopping, while King and Meeting streets were home to more basic services such as bakers, saddlers, and carpenters. This pattern meant that the oldest areas of the town, closest to the waterfront and nearest to the grandeur of the State House, the Exchange, and St. Michael's Church, were clearly a cut above the more newly developed areas to the south. Charleston's streets were lined with evidence of its role as a town that catered to the needs of a wealthy consuming population.

These shops not only constituted the commercial complexion of the town's center, but also increased in sophistication as the eighteenth century progressed. Indeed, by 1790 Charleston's retail spaces had achieved a complexity equivalent to those in many British provincial towns. That many Charleston buildings became designated as artisan workshops rather than residential properties marked the first step in this process. Charleston property owner Barnard Elliott advertised that he had edifices specifically described as a barber's shop and a gunsmith's premises for sale. Other buildings remained multipurpose but were classified as being "suitable for trade." Elliott was also in possession of a house occupied by a vintner and a printer, but he implied when selling it that other tradesmen would find it equally capacious.[22]

By the 1760s, the records of local painters and glaziers show that these craftsmen were often receiving commissions to fit out shop interiors to make them more recognizable as "shopping" spaces. In 1767, perukemaker James Duthie employed painters Hawes and Flagg to fit up his barber's shop with a pole, "wigg signs," new glazed windows, and a new coat of paint.[23] During the 1780s, Crawford and Wallace, also painters and glaziers, fitted out a retail space for Charleston grocers McCawley and Company, putting in large shop windows and a full range of drawers, canisters, and bowls, all inscribed with the name of their contents. Other contracts saw Crawford glazing "show cabinets" in a jeweler's shop, a "shoe case" in a merchant's store, painting numerous sign boards, and painting and glazing bow windows for a

22. Advertisement of Barnard Elliott, *South Carolina Gazette and Country Journal,* May 24, 1774.
23. Hawes and Flagg vs. James Duthie, Charleston County Judgment Rolls, vol. 83A, no. 110A, South Carolina Department of Archives and History (hereinafter SCDAH).

Table 1.2

*Distribution of Commercial Premises in
Charleston's Major Thoroughfares, 1790*

	East Bay	Broad St.	Church St.	Elliott St.	King St.	Meeting St.	Qeeen St.
Merchants	33	30	12	12	8	10	5
Shopkeepers	22	3	12	3	72	11	18
Artisans:							
Luxury/Clothing	7	16	20	10	23	20	14
Food/Service	8	5	2	7	23	16	3
Construction	15	4	6	1	30	20	16
TOTAL	85	58	52	33	156	67	56

Source: 1790 City Directory and 1790 Federal Census for
St. Michaels and St. Philips Parishes, Charleston.

watchmaker.[24] After browsing carefully displayed wares and deciding on a purchase, a customer was increasingly likely to receive a printed receipt that bore the name and logo of the shop owner.[25] Overall, there is much to suggest that by 1790, downtown Charleston was defined by spaces devoted to shopping, making it visually similar to areas that had sprung up in British towns like Chester, Bath, and Shrewsbury.[26]

For Low Country residents, Charleston was not simply a shipping point, but a place where they could obtain a wide range of goods and services. Between 1750 and 1790 the town came to represent a regional node in a larger British Atlantic urban system and customers' purchases reflected this role. As table 1.3 shows, residents fostered a leisure and service economy by turning to Charleston's craftsmen and service

24. Account book of Alexander Crawford, MSS, South Carolina Historical Society.
25. Baker-Grimke Papers, Richard Bohun Baker Receipts, MSS, South Carolina Historical Society. This collection of receipts includes pre-printed examples from silversmith Philip Tidyman and merchants Mansell, Corbett & Robinson.
26. Stobart, "Shopping Streets as Social Space."

Table 1.3

Found Instances of Patronage of Charleston Tradesmen, 1710–1800

Service Purchased	Instances	As a Percentage
Luxury and Household Goods (Furniture, silver, upholstery, coaches, etc.)	174	32%
Personal Needs (Clothing, shoes)	138	26%
Infrastructure and Construction (Ships, carpentry, building)	147	27%
Food and Services (Carting, bakery, gardening, soap and candlemaking)	81	15%
TOTAL	540	100%

Source: Charleston County Judgment Rolls, SCDAH; James Laurens papers, MFM, MSE Library, Johns Hopkins University; Baker-Grimke Receipts, MSS, SCHS; James Waties Papers, SCL; Lowndes Family Papers, SCHS; Vanderhorst Papers, SCHS; William Ancrum papers, SCL; Henry Laurens account book, Robert Scott Small Library, College of Charleston.

workers for luxury items, clothing needs, foodstuffs, and on-site construction work. Low Country settlers had their suits and gowns made up, their hair dressed, their children given an elementary education and dancing or music lessons, their town houses built and repaired, their ships restocked, their horses saddled, and their coaches refurbished, all in Charleston. Coming from across the coastal Low Country, these customers also created a hinterland for Charleston that matched equivalent spheres of influence found around the British provincial town.[27] However, by choosing to buy manufactured goods such as tools, fabric, nails,

27. Jon Stobart, "County, Town, and Country: Three Histories of Urban Development in Eighteenth-Century Chester," in *Provincial Towns in Early Modern England and Ireland: Change, Convergence, Divergence,* ed. Peter Borsay (Oxford: Oxford University Press, 2002), 180.

ceramics, and glass from import merchants or shopkeepers, South Carolinians encouraged the development of service industries over heavy industries. As was the case in other British provincial towns, material needs were met by a combination of imported and locally produced goods.

Describing the kinds of businesses that lined Charleston's streets and uncovering the ways in which they served their customers reveals a new facet to the town's role within its region. And by setting this role in a wider British Atlantic context, we can see how it drew Charleston into an industrializing, polycentric urban system. As a leisure and service center, the colonial South's largest town did not stand alone but worked to include the Lower South in the economic processes that have come to define the eighteenth-century English-speaking world.

As much as developments in the overall shape of urban economies can now define industrial revolution, transformations within individual workplaces still remain crucial in interpreting economic change. However, scholars no longer see the rise of large-scale factory production as the sine qua non of industrialization. Indeed, many have shown that factories became a characteristic mode of production in only a very few British industries, and in only a few select towns, before the mid-nineteenth century. For the most part, manufacturing, especially in luxury and service trades, continued to be undertaken in workshops. This situation translated into a continuing need for artisans in every sizeable town in Britain. However, structural changes were still visible within these workshops, as they were sensitive to general advances taking place in British manufacturing. Such changes manifested themselves as master artisans in the same town came together to form production networks, masters took on a more managerial role, larger number of employees performed more specialized tasks, and individual firms achieved greater vertical integration.[28] It is essential to understand how these developments influenced the working practices of the tradesmen who made up Charleston's diverse business community.

Without doubt, tradesmen in the urban Low Country kept pace with their contemporaries across the Atlantic. Turning once again to the first

---

28. The strongest supporter of this model is Maxine Berg; see *Age of Manufactures*, "Small Producer Capitalism" and "Factories, Workshops and Industrial Organization," in *The Economic History of Britain*, ed. Floud and McCloskey, 123–50.

Table 1.4

Size of Artisan Workshops in Charleston, 1790

No. of Employees (Adult White Males + Slaves)	Number of Households	Total Number of Potential Employees (Black and White) N-2610	As a Percentage
1	99	99	3.8%
2-4	207	566	21.7%
5-9	111	738	28.3%
10+	74	1207	46.2%

Source: 1790 Federal Census for Charleston, 1790 Charleston City Directory

federal census, it is clear that by 1790, Charleston's white artisans had succeeded in establishing workshops that matched their British provincial counterparts in size. Mostly as a result of white masters' embrace of slaves as skilled workers, three-quarters of black and white artisans labored in an enterprise with five or more employees, and almost half were part of a workshop with more than ten workers. And, as table 1.4 shows, less than 4 percent of artisans were listed as living alone, without slaves or white men of apprenticeable, or journeyman, age. Although precise comparisons are difficult in the absence of similar data from other early American cities of the era, anecdotal evidence uncovered by Sharon Salinger would suggest that Charleston workshops were at least as big as their Philadelphia counterparts.[29]

Delving into the internal structure of the Charleston workshop reveals that there were many levels on which master artisans were part of transatlantic industrial development. Thomas Elfe, a cabinetmaker and

29. Sharon V. Salinger, "Artisans, Journeymen, and the Transformation of Labor in Late-Eighteenth-Century Philadelphia," *William and Mary Quarterly,* 3rd ser., vol. 40, no. 1 (Jan. 1983): 62–84.

one of Charleston's best-known master craftsmen of the eighteenth century, stood at the head of one of the most extensive and sizeable artisan enterprises in the prerevolutionary town.[30] Elfe's surviving ledger for the years 1768 to 1775 indicate that his business flourished; he took over one thousand orders for furniture, repairs, and renovations. The core of his enterprise comprised the master, Thomas Hutchinson (his business partner), and eight slaves. Since Elfe was a long-established mechanic, this nucleus could well have included one or two apprentices. Elfe's accounts show that both masters and employees specialized in a range of cabinetry tasks, namely the frame and panel construction of case and seating furniture, repairs, the assembly and disassembly of beds, the construction of tables, and the manufacture of small wooden objects such as tea trays and coffeepot handles.

However, the activity within this workshop unit was supplemented by the labor of some twenty-three other craftsmen whom the cabinetmaker employed to perform other jobs essential to the making of a complete piece of furniture. Of these men, three-fourths remained in the cabinetmaker's service throughout the seven years on record and were paid on an almost monthly basis. The stability of this wider workforce suggests that Elfe had created what amounted to a small factory, where as many as thirty-five workers were united in furniture production. What is more, the members of this extended enterprise were divided into five groups according to their role in the manufacturing process. The cabinetmaker had assembled a production line.

Production began with men like Jeremiah Sharp, a mahogany sawyer who cut the lengths of wood that Elfe purchased from local merchants. Carpenters, presumably including Elfe's slaves and apprentices, then prepared the timber that would be used for the frame of the furniture. The major part of the construction process would then take place in the shop itself, with all of the work for smaller items likely completed there. Elfe's workforce, however, obviously lacked carvers. These were the craftsmen that he employed most frequently to provide embellishment for items such as chair backs, bookcases, and table legs. The last stage of

30. Thomas Elfe account book, MSS, Charleston Library Society. For biography about Elfe see E. Milby Burton, *Charleston Furniture, 1700–1825* (Columbia: University of South Carolina Press, 1955); Richard Walsh, *Charleston's Sons of Liberty: A Study of the Artisans* (Columbia: University of South Carolina Press, 1959), ch. 1; Samuel A. Humphrey, *Thomas Elfe, Cabinetmaker* (London: Wyrick, 1996).

Figure 1.1

Thomas Elfe's Production Network

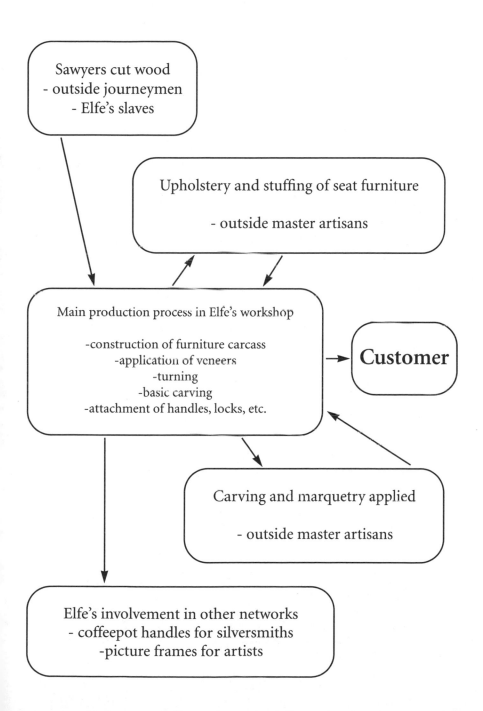

production was the completion of the upholstery, another task that was always done outside of the main shop. Significantly, by subcontracting work out, Elfe was recreating workshop network structures introduced by some of London's most prominent cabinetmakers of the same period. Famous furniture craftsmen such as Thomas Chippendale and Samuel Norman achieved higher output by forming alliances with neighboring carvers, gilders, and upholsterers to finish their product. By the third quarter of the eighteenth century, certain Charleston artisans were au fait with advances made within metropolitan workshops.[31]

As a single example, Thomas Elfe's workshop could simply have been an extraordinary anomaly. However, similar trends are detectable elsewhere in Charleston's manufacturing economy. Emergent among the town's master tailors and perukemakers was the custom of employing "foremen," a strikingly industrial position, in their workshops. The foreman was usually a white journeymanlike figure who, as the term suggests, generally organized and led the labor of apprentices, slaves, and other workers in the enterprise. As early as 1758, John Boomer advertised that "he has for sometime lived with Mr. Moses Audebert, perukemaker, . . . in the character of foreman." Setting up on their own, tailors Logan and Williams noted that they were "late foreman to Mr. Walter Mansell, and . . . have work'd with him several years."[32] The possibility that these tailor's workshops had reached a considerable size even before the Revolution is confirmed by the 1773 inventory of master tailor Alexander Cormack. In Cormack's "cutting room" were twelve adult slaves, and his estate executors noted that in addition to finalizing the extensive customer accounts, they still had to pay off a large number of white employees.[33]

In the immediate postrevolutionary period, Charleston's artisans consolidated their moves toward a more industrialized workshop structure. In addition to the census evidence already discussed, the case of the carpentry firm of Wyatt and Richardson illustrates the continuing shift toward capitalist working practices in the city. Between 1784 and 1797 the

31. For specific examples of this structure in operation circa 1755 see P. A. Kirkham, "Samuel Norman: A Study of an Eighteenth-Century Craftsman," *Burlington Magazine* 4 (1972): 501–13.

32. Advertisement of John Boomer, *South Carolina Gazette*, Aug. 18, 1758; advertisement of Logan & Williams, *South Carolina Gazette*, May 17, 1760.

33. Inventory of Alexander Cormack, Nov. 4, 1773, p. 624, WPA Transcripts, Charleston County Library.

company had forty-eight apprentices, journeymen, and free black carpenters in its employ. At any one time this workforce was made up of the three master artisan partners, eleven slaves owned by John Wyatt and often put to work for the firm, about seventeen carpenters, and an accounts clerk. The company's journeymen carpenters filled out timecards and were paid a weekly wage. What is more, Wyatt and Richardson seemed aware that by pooling their resources, and achieving vertical integration, they might be able to win out over their local competitors. To this end, John Wyatt planned to set up a sawmill to allow the firm to "get what lumber we wish and . . . have the advantage of others."[34] Following the successful establishment of this mill in suburban Charleston, the firm purchased additional lands at one of the city's wharves, where they enlarged their premises with a countinghouse, stores, a depot for their carting business, a brewery, and new workshops. To a greater extent than Thomas Elfe some thirty years before, Wyatt and Richardson had created a complex enterprise that illustrates how industrial change elsewhere in the British Atlantic world could influence the structure of Charleston's economy.[35]

Finally, from the Charleston building trades, we see an increase not only in the size and complexity of artisan enterprises, but also of professionalization among the ranks of mechanics. In Britain, rebuilding after the Great Fire of London in 1666 had accelerated changes already afoot in the construction industry. Guild regulations were relaxed as carpenters, bricklayers, and plasterers flooded into the city from the regions, and building contractors, master builders, and builder-architects became familiar managerial figures on construction sites. This professionalization of the building industry spread rapidly to British provincial towns, and more especially to those places experiencing significant development as regional service and leisure centers.[36] Within an American

34. Ibid., testimony of James Allison.

35. This section of the essay is especially in debt to the work of Sydney Pollard, whose charting of the impact of the first British industrial revolution on Europe serves as an excellent model. Sidney Pollard, *Peaceful Conquest: The Industrialization of Europe, 1760–1970* (Oxford: Oxford University Press, 1981).

36. C. W. Chalklin, *The Provincial Towns of Georgian England: A Study of the Building Process, 1740–1820* (Montreal: McGill-Queen's University Press, 1987); Peter Borsay, *The English Urban Renaissance: Culture and Society in the Provincial Town* (Oxford: Clarendon Press, 1989); Elizabeth McKellar, *The Birth of Modern London: The Development and Design of the City, 1660–1720* (Manchester: Manchester University Press, 1999).

context, Donna Rilling has charted the important contribution that a newly dynamic building industry made to the development of Philadelphia's economy from the 1790s onward.[37]

Yet from the 1750s onward, it is evident that similar figures were at work in the Charleston construction industry. Setting about the building of St. Michael's Church, the Exchange, and the State House, the provincial assembly employed artisan building contractors to coordinate the labor and design of each project.[38] As their role had been embraced across the private as well as the public sector, these general managers and architects were also employed by planters and merchants in the building of their Charleston houses. Carpenter-contractor Richard Moncrieff, in partnership with another builder, Kinsey Burden, directed the construction of the Miles Brewton house, and it is probable that both would have been involved in the organization of the considerable labor and materials that were required to undertake the substantial project. Peter Manigault's building activities during the 1760s showed a similar reliance on the contractor. In 1765, the merchant set about the construction of a substantial city house for the then-absent Ralph Izard. Manigault took the lead in the overall design of the house and kept Izard abreast of the work with letters and plans of his future residence. Having dabbled in the early phases of planning, however, Manigault handed over the project to house carpenter and contractor Daniel Cannon, who managed the necessary labor and materials and saw the house through to completion.[39]

That the general contractor was entrenched in the Charleston building industry is further reflected in the written agreements recorded by artisans and their clients. Accompanying the appearance of the professional builder in Britain was the custom of undertaking projects "by the great," which meant that a total price and a deadline were agreed for

37. Donna Rilling, *Making Houses, Crafting Capitalism: Builders in Philadelphia, 1790–1850* (Philadelphia: University of Pennsylvania Press, 2001).

38. Proceedings of the Lower House of Assembly, Feb. 26, 1767, microfilm, Milton S. Eisenhower Library, Johns Hopkins University; Records of St. Michael's Church, Charleston, MSS, South Carolina Historical Society.

39. Caroline Wyche Dixon, "The Miles Brewton House: Ezra Waite's Architectural Books and Other Possible Sources," *South Carolina Historical Magazine* 82, 2 (1981): 118–43; Peter Manigault to Ralph Izard Esq., not dated but estimated Sept. 1765, Peter Manigault to Ralph Izard Esq., Charleston, Oct. 9, 1765, transcript of the Peter Manigault Letterbook, Museum of Early Southern Decorative Arts, Winston-Salem, North Carolina.

work. These terms were then recorded in a contract. This new custom replaced previous, less formal building practices, where the client would pay off individual workmen, either at the end of the project, or according to a measurement of the wood or brickwork completed.[40] The emergence of the written contract suggests that master builders were not only increasingly likely to be literate and numerate, but also better aware that fixed costs would allow them to calculate their profit more easily.

A number of Charleston contracts strongly reflect these advances in building practice. One such document was drawn up in May 1770 between bricklayers and carpenters Axson and Gaborial and the planter William Clay Snipes. Axson and Gaborial agreed to build a Charleston residence for Snipes "with outhouses and other appurtenances agreeable to a plan given in and signed by the said John Gaborial." The house was "to be finished in a compleat perfect workmanlike manner on or before 6th November 1770," with Axson and Gaborial receiving half of their £3,500 fee when the house was "inclosed" and the other half when it was completed. For their money, the partners undertook to provide "all the materials and workmanship" and to pay a penal sum of £500 if the building was not completed on time.[41] The agreement was clearly couched in formulaic terms, implying that its writing was a familiar process for the builders. Furthermore, this is a language that recurs throughout contemporary documents. Contractor Thomas Robinson noted that he had built a shed "as per agreement" for Luke Stoutenburgh, while client Ann Middleton similarly recorded an "agreement with Andrew Gordon for building house."[42] Charleston's British, provincial townscape was being built using the evolved methods of building found in the British town itself.

Trends that are commonly seen as markers of industrial change in equivalent British towns were highly visible in many areas of the Charleston economy. Because this industrial change was still in its early stages, such developments were not necessarily momentous—the town was not home to any factories, and there was no mass production. Yet pro-

40. For a full explanation of this process, see McKellar, *Birth of Modern London,* esp. 81–89.

41. South Carolina Judgment Rolls, Jacob Axson Jr. vs. William Clay Snipes, 1771, vol. 99A, no. 255A, SCDAH.

42. South Carolina Judgment Rolls, Thomas Robinson vs. Luke Stoutenburgh Esq., 1768, vol. 88A no. 173A, SCDAH. Expense of Building Mrs. Ann Middleton's House and Kitchen 1799–1800, MSS 43/118, South Carolina Historical Society.

duction networks, professionalization, waged working weeks, and diversified firms with dozens of employees all lent a more industrialized tone to nonagricultural work in the urban Low Country. This level of industrial change placed Charleston, a provincial, service-oriented urban economy, alongside British towns of equivalent status. Ultimately, the city resembled a typical British Atlantic town of the period not just because its occupational structure gave it a clear position in an urban economic system, but also as a result of the internal dynamic within its workshops.

Thus we see how looking at Charleston's economy from a British Atlantic standpoint can add to our knowledge of the town's place within the immediate Low Country region, the colonies, and the empire. By delving into its businesses with an eye on similar urban structures within eighteenth-century Britain and America, we can see how Charleston's economy developed a distinct profile in the decades after 1750. This profile suggests that although the town grew as a hub for transatlantic trade, the demands of provincial settlers in an era of consumer and industrial revolution also influenced the town's role. In particular, settlers' need for certain goods and services made Charleston into a regional leisure and service center. Like other such towns throughout Britain, this meant that the Low Country metropolis had a modest, but nevertheless well-developed, manufacturing sector that embraced early indicators of an industrial revolution.

Charleston's comfortable integration into an industrializing urban system stretched across the turmoil of the American Revolution and into the early national period. The social and political unrest that characterized the twenty years leading up to 1783 could not, it appears, reverse the intricate economic ties forged in the course of the eighteenth century. In this regard, Charleston's situation highlights how, rather than forming their own discrete system, American cities remained deeply connected to their British counterparts even after political independence.

Running parallel to these ongoing transatlantic connections were the many ways in which Charleston had evolved into a southern city by 1790. Enslaved African Americans created a unique urban geography, and plantation agriculture provided the economic underpinnings of the region. As white wealthy excess collided with black enslavement and poverty, it created internal tensions and caused consternation among commentators like J. Hector St. John Crevecoeur, who dramatically portrayed Charleston as a place where "the chosen race eat, drink, and live happy, while the unfortunate one grubs up the ground, raises indigo, or husks the rice."[43] However, these regional tensions were played out against a backdrop of dynamic growth and change in cities throughout the British Atlantic world. It was the meeting of these two forces that gave eighteenth-century Charleston its Januslike quality. One of the city's faces looked to the plantation system, but the other was turned toward transatlantic industrial revolution and urban transformation.

43. J. Hector St. John Crevecoeur, *Letter from an American Farmer* (Oxford: Oxford University Press, 1997), 153. It should be noted that Crevecoeur probably never visited Charleston himself.

Alternatives to Dependence

The Lower South's Antebellum
Pursuit of Sectional Development
through Global Interdependence

Brian Schoen

In 1844 Senator Walter Colquitt of Georgia passionately appealed to
the United States Congress for a reduction of the 1842 protective tariff.[1]
He argued that international free trade and the "state of mutual dependence" it created was "a source of gratification rather than of regret,
since it gives to each nation an increased facility for the development of
its highest energies, enlarges the sum of its enjoyments, and affords the
surest guarantee for the peace and harmony of the world."[2] Though

1. The ideas guiding this essay are part of "The Fragile Fabric of Union: The
Cotton South, Federal Politics, and the Atlantic Economy" (Ph.D. diss., University
of Virginia, 2004). Some of the content was presented at annual meetings for the
Society for the Historians of the Early American Republic (Berkeley, July 2002) and
the Southern Historical Association (Baltimore, Nov. 2003). I would like to thank
Peter Coclanis, John Larson, John Majewski, and Michael O'Brien for their insightful comments in these forums. I would also like to thank Susanna Delfino, Stanley
Engerman, Michele Gillespie, Peter Onuf, and Kelli Coughlin Schoen for their sug-
gestions.
2. "Speech of Mr. Colquitt, of Georgia in reply to Mr. Berrien on the Tariff, delivered in the Senate of the United States," Apr. 10, 1844 (Washington, D.C., 1844), 16.
In Evans, *Early American Imprints: Pamphlets in American History,* 557T 1090.

Colquitt's words might resonate with early-twenty-first-century politicians and economists who praise the virtues of free trade, his optimism remains a difficult fit within a southern antebellum historiography tending to stress economic backwardness and hopeless colonial dependence. Rather than lamenting the retarding effects of merchant capital on southern economic modernization, Colquitt shared his southern contemporaries' faith that regional and global prosperity would emerge from the mutually beneficial possibilities of unfettered international trade. Such confidence in free-trade liberalism guided policymakers within the cotton-producing regions of the Lower South, providing the context for that region's efforts at industrial development during the antebellum period.

This essay examines how cotton producers' understanding of the economic and political challenges facing them guided their attempts to overcome those challenges. While recognizing the strong possibility that perceptions may have been mistaken, it evaluates them on their own terms and within the context of the broader world in which they were formed. The hindsight of Marxism, modernization theory, and developmental economics might make the Cotton South's surprisingly deep commitment to free trade seem retrograde. Historians have, at times appropriately, stressed dependency as the chief problem in southern economic development; some have argued that such a burden dominated regional economic thought. We must avoid, however, viewing such concerns as fundamental to southern views or as paralyzing for southern action. Within the context of European laissez-faire thought and an Enlightenment-derived faith in natural economic laws, southern free traders believed they were at the forefront of international economic thought. Nor did continued trust in free trade represent a fatalistic approach towards southern economic development. On the contrary, most advocates came to see international free trade as the best means to achieve regional economic diversification, development, and independence from northern capital and commerce. Free trade made rational sense to those who embraced it and, to some degree at least, genuinely reflected the realities of an interdependent nineteenth-century global economy dominated by Britain's commercial and manufacturing empire. Where historians and economists have stressed the obstacles presented by southern export agriculture, the groups from the Cotton South discussed here—mainly South Carolina, Georgia, Alabama, and

Mississippi—saw opportunity for continued prosperity and even true regional economic development.[3]

This is not to suggest that sentiments were static or uniformly held. Nor should it devalue the planters' fear or willingness to act when they perceived themselves in an unequal or exploitative economic relationship. Minority groups, composed primarily of artisans and hemp and sugar producers, sometimes questioned the alleged beneficence of free-trade practices and in some instances accepted the idea of legislative protection. The ideal of free trade, a concept emerging from the imperial crisis of the 1770s, also spawned measures that countervailed the principle itself. In the postrevolutionary period, continued commercial dependence on Britain, seen as a legacy of imperialism and mercantilism, led Jeffersonian Republicans to advocate neomercantilist policies. Later as the sectional crisis deepened and fears of "monopolist-minded" northern merchants, manufacturers, and capitalists heightened, many southerners proposed using similar tools against their northern brethren. As a general rule, Enlightenment-informed southern theorists like South Carolina College professor Thomas Cooper believed nature and natural development distinguished a healthy interdependence from an unhealthy dependence, seen as the byproduct of political oppression or artificial measures. Even as southern cotton interests considered erecting barriers to free trade within the union in the 1850s, however, they

3. Mark Smith provides a useful summary of the literature in *Debating Slavery: Economy and Society in the Antebellum American South* (New York: Cambridge University Press, 1998). See Eugene Genovese, *The Political Economy of Slavery* (New York: Vintage Books, 1967) and with Elizabeth Fox-Genovese, *The Fruits of Merchant Capital: Slavery and Bourgeois Property in the Rise and Expansion of Capital* (New York: Oxford University Press, 1983); Harold Woodman, *King Cotton and His Retainers: Financing and Marketing the Cotton Crop of the South, 1800–1925* (Columbia: University of South Carolina Press, 1990), 139–53; Fred Bateman and Thomas Weiss, *A Deplorable Scarcity: The Failure of Industrialization in the Slave Economy* (Chapel Hill: University of North Carolina Press, 1981). By contrast, Robert Fogel and Stanley Engerman, *Time on the Cross: The Economics of American Negro Slavery* (New York: Little Brown, 1974). Economist Gavin Wright has convincingly stressed the indirect ways that monoculture cotton production gradually retarded broader human and financial capital: *The Political Economy of the Cotton South* (New York: W. W. Norton, 1978). See also John Majewski, *A House Dividing: Economic Development in Pennsylvania and Virginia before the Civil War* (New York: Cambridge University Press, 2000), 1–7. Jacob J. Persky stresses fear of dependency in southern economic thought in *A Burden of Dependency: Colonial Themes in Southern Economic Thought* (Baltimore: Johns Hopkins University Press, 1992).

continued to stress their faith in the possibility for mutually beneficial dependence within an increasingly interconnected nineteenth-century world.

This essay provides further support for Harold Woodman's largely unanswered call for more intensive studies of antebellum southern commerce.[4] Specifically, it suggests the importance of taking a truly global perspective toward understanding southern economic development. The comparative approaches on which historians and economists have recently focused have provided considerable insight, but studies must move beyond comparisons of isolated organisms. Historians and economists must do more to show the economic ligaments that tied the South, especially the Cotton South, to other regions and to global processes. In addition to knowledge of the microeconomics of a plantation system, a proper understanding of thought and action must situate the region's decision-makers within the larger world in which they acted. At least as interesting, we must also seek to reconstruct how contemporaries themselves perceived the opportunities, as well as obstacles, available within that world. For a large and powerful segment of the southern United States the fate of "King Cotton" was critically tied to the global prosperity of international trade, much of which took place under the auspices of the British Empire.

While the imperial crisis and Revolution generated support for free-trade ideals, widespread southern consensus over free-trade policies did not emerge until the 1820s, when debates over a high protective duty consumed national politics. Early nationals balanced free-trade hopes with the realities of an Atlantic economy still guided by mercantilist policies and British naval dominance. For many in the Lower South, achieving long-term international free trade required first casting off the historical legacy and practical reality of British postcolonial commercial dependence. With the exception of a small Federalist minority, led by Congressmen William Loughton Smith, most Georgia and South Carolina planters and merchants embraced discriminatory duties against Britain, defending them as necessary to protect American interests and reroute trade to their "natural" markets on the European continent. Into the early nineteenth century, Anglophobia led agricultural Republicans like Georgia's George Troup and South Carolina's John C. Calhoun to

4. See introduction to 1990 edition: Woodman, *King Cotton,* xv.

support the Jefferson and Madison administrations' employment of an arsenal of retaliatory economic weapons and eventually war against their primary trading partner. Lower South ambivalence over the viability of free-trade policies continued after the War of 1812. Fearing a flood of British manufactures in 1816, Republicans in Congress, including Calhoun, supported retaining a peacetime tariff that would provide mild protection for the nascent manufacturers created during the war. Though continued labor shortages and recently secured lands in the Southwest prevented Lower South tariff supporters from expecting a significant manufacturing sector to emerge in Georgia or South Carolina, they believed a better American market could give commercial agrarians some leverage within a war-torn Atlantic economy.[5]

By the mid-1820s, however, economic and political realities had led earlier supporters of tariff protection to redefine their interest in favor of free-trade policies. Rapidly declining cotton prices in the 1820s suggested that protection hurt rather than helped southern agrarians. At the same time the rhetoric of Philadelphia publicist Mathew Carey and Kentucky Representative Henry Clay indicated that self-sufficiency had become an end in itself. Clamoring for even higher, many feared prohibitory, tariffs elevated concerns that northern manufacturers sought a monopoly on American commerce. In the meantime, relative international tranquility led many to conclude that Metternich's "concert of Europe" might have succeeded in bringing peace and prosperity to the

---

5. R. C. Nash and Peter Coclanis have shown that the colonial rice and tobacco trade ultimately targeted continental Europe, with Britain serving as a reexporter rather than a consumer. R. C. Nash, "South Carolina and the Atlantic Economy in the Late Seventeenth and Eighteenth Centuries," *Economic History Review* 45, 4 (Nov. 1992): 688; Peter Coclanis, *The Shadow of a Dream: Economic Life and Death in the South Carolina Low Country, 1670–1920* (New York: Oxford University Press, 1989), 134. For neomercantilist strands in southern thought, see William Appleman Williams, "The Age of Mercantilism: An Interpretation of the American Political Economy, 1763 to 1828," *William and Mary Quarterly* 15 (Oct. 1958): 419–37; John E. Crowley, *The Privileges of Independence: Neomercantilism and the American Revolution* (Baltimore: Johns Hopkins University Press, 1993), esp. 140, 144–45, 159. The emergence of southern free-trade thought in the antebellum period is explored in Brian Schoen, "Calculating the Price of Union: Republican Policy, Economic Nationalism, and the Origins of Southern Sectionalism, 1790–1828," *Journal of the Early Republic* (Summer 2003). Also Norris W. Preyer, "Southern Support of the Tariff of 1816: A Reappraisal," *Journal of Southern History* 25, 2 (Aug. 1959): 306–22.

Atlantic state system. Within this context political and economic leaders of an expanding Cotton Belt provided a nearly united front in favor of free trade and against an "American System" they believed would make the South economically subservient to the North.[6]

When opposing protective tariffs southern free traders drew on well-known arguments favoring free trade, beginning with a libertarian tradition opposing "artificial" measures that rerouted labor and capital away from so-called natural ends. Such arguments were, of course, incongruous with the region's commitment to slavery. At the time, however, few acknowledged the paradox, and those who did took refuge in the burgeoning language of scientific racism, arguing that Africans were "naturally" suited for servitude. Free traders also stressed that nature's blessings of cheap land and high wages meant America was simply not yet ready to become a manufacturing nation. The salutary results of global specialization and free international trade praised by Adam Smith, the French philosophes, and their successors provided further ideological support for the traditional assumption that America's "workshops remain in Europe."[7] The cotton business in particular seemed perfectly tailored to the international division of labor heralded in *Wealth of Nations*. As European textile manufactures became increasingly reliant on southern cotton, the interdependent and profitable trade would, many in the Lower South believed, guide the South toward never-ending prosperity. This helps explain Thomas Cooper's conviction that "the argument in favour of insulation and independence . . . is a bad feeling: it induces us to wish our gains dependent on the depression of our neighbours."[8] Widespread faith in "Say's Law," which assumed that demand would always keep up with supply, furthered their optimism. Southern

6. A close historical study of the tariff debates of the antebellum period is badly needed. With the exception of a narrowly focused study by Jonathan Pincus, one has to go back to useful but outdated and biased examinations from the early twentieth century. See Jonathan Pincus, *Pressure Groups and Politics in Antebellum Tariffs* (New York: Columbia University Press, 1977); F. W. Taussig, *The Tariff of the United States* (1892; reprint, New York: Putnam's Sons, 1923); Edward Stanwood, *American Tariff Controversies in the Nineteenth Century*, 2 vols. (Boston: Houghton, Mifflin, 1904).

7. Jefferson, "Notes on the State of Virginia," Query 19, in *Jefferson: Writings*, ed. Merrill D. Peterson (New York: Library of America, 1984), 291.

8. Thomas Cooper, *A tract on the proposed alteration of the tariff, submitted to the consideration of the members from South Carolina, in the ensuing Congress of 1823–4* (Philadelphia: Skerrett, 1824), 12.

politicians also argued, rather indignantly, that the War of 1812 had been fought in an effort to gain American access to international markets. They claimed that efforts to restrict overseas commerce betrayed the accomplishments of the previous decade, noting continued peace in the Atlantic and citing 1815 and 1818 commercial agreements with Britain that ended discriminatory duties on American ships and even granted limited access to the West Indian trade.[9]

Tariff opponents in the Cotton South now used the persistence of a lucrative Anglo-American cotton trade to argue that regional and national wealth necessitated open access to Atlantic markets. Propagandists used trade statistics to construct an image of a national United States economy similar to that later proposed by Douglass North in his classic study *The Economic Growth of the United States, 1790–1860*. Like North, advocates from the Cotton South suggested that cotton's international value had benefited not only growers but also northern merchants and capitalists responsible for financing and shipping the crop to its overseas destinations. Additionally, the comparative advantage of cotton growth increased cotton planters' reliance on western foodstuffs and supplies, thus providing a market for the nation's grain producers. Unlike protectionists, who used the Panic of 1819 to suggest structural problems with the U.S. economy, free traders from the Cotton South believed it to be just a temporary slump caused by overspeculation and bad banking policy.[10]

Though exaggerated these cotton-centered arguments were not irrational. Cotton had rapidly gone from obscurity in the 1790s to composing 40 percent of the total value of exports in 1825. By the mid-1830s that percentage had risen above 50 percent, where it remained for nearly a decade. If historian Robert Albion was correct, then New York's instrumental position within an emerging cotton triangle between north-

9. Early examples of this can be found in Georgia's representative Thomas Telfairs's arguments against the 1816 tariff in *Annals of Congress*, 14th Cong., 1st sess., 1316–1320 and John Taylor of Caroline, *Arator*, ed. M. E. Bradford (Indianapolis: Liberty Fund, 1977), no. 4–no. 7 and Taylor, *Tyranny Unmasked*, ed. M. E. Bradford (Indianapolis: Liberty Fund, 1992). Examples are scattered throughout the 1820 tariff debates; see, for example, James Hamilton, *Annals of Congress*, 18:1 vol. 2: 2180; George McDuffie, ibid., 18:1, vol. 1: 1677–1678. See also Schoen, "The Fragile Fabric of Union," ch. 4.

10. Douglass North, *The Economic Growth of the United States, 1790–1860* (New York: W. W. Norton, 1966), 67.

ern, southern, and European ports helped make it the leading United States port and financial center. The claims of southern dependence on western grains are harder to substantiate, particularly in the Southwest. Recent literature suggests that by the late antebellum period even the Southeast was more self-sufficient than previously thought. Regardless, attempts to stop importation of western foodstuffs in protest of western support for protection demonstrated that both supporters and opponents of the policy perceived a significant interregional trade to the Southeast. To the majority of elites in the expanding Cotton Belt free access to international markets would and should continue to provide, as in the past, national profitability based on healthy and natural regional and global interdependence.[11]

Higher tariffs in 1824, 1828, and 1832, however, demonstrated the South's inability to create a national coalition capable of preventing or significantly rolling back protective policies. The British Corn Laws hindered western grain producers' access to what was potentially their most lucrative market. This, along with hope for federally funded internal improvements, led farmers in the North and Northwest to embrace the idea of a stronger home market. Much of the northern merchant community had abandoned free trade and embraced a vigorous home market, leaving the South largely isolated in its advocacy of international free trade. Some believed the failure of the political effort confirmed that export-minded, slave-owning agrarians, particularly in cotton-growing

11. For cotton statistics, see Stuart Bruchey, *Cotton and the Growth of the American Economy: 1790–1860* (New York: Harcourt, Brace, 1967), table 3:K. Robert Greenhalgh Albion, *The Rise of New York Port, 1815–1860* (New York: Scribner's Sons, 1939), 95–121. The topic of interregional trade during the antebellum period remains a contested issue. See Albert Fishlow, "Antebellum Interregional Trade Reconsidered," *American Economic Review* 54, 3 (May 1964): 352–64; Diane Lindstrom, "Southern Dependence upon Interregional Grain Supplies," and Robert Gallman, "Self-Sufficiency in the Cotton Economy of the Antebellum South," both in *The Structure of the Cotton Economy of the Antebellum South,* ed. William N. Parker (Washington, D.C.: Agricultural History Society, 1970); Lawrence Herbst, "Interregional Commodity Trade from the North to the South and American Economic Development in the Antebellum Period," *Journal of Economic History* (Mar. 1985): 262–81; Paul Uselding, "A Note on the Inter-Regional Trade in Manufactures in 1840," *Journal of Economic History* 36, 2 (June 1976): 428–35. Nevertheless, contemporaries seemed to believe that a considerable trade in western grains and livestocks did find their way to the Lower South. See David Franklin Houston, *A Critical Study of Nullification in South Carolina* (Cambridge: Harvard University Press, 1896), 70–71.

regions, could no longer command a national political majority. Few embraced the extreme political remedies of secession or nullification, but all within the Lower South had been forced, as the secessionist-minded Thomas Cooper suggested, to "calculate the value of union."[12]

In calculating the economic price of a union guided by Henry Clay's American System, economic elites in the Lower South unsurprisingly imagined possible alternatives. The first was a global economy in which all nations accepted free-trade policies. But within the context of national debates, southerners also proposed that protection would force them into basic self-sufficiency that would hinder their opponents' vision of a home market. Lower cotton prices combined with higher prices for supplies, they argued, would make them unable to purchase high-priced northern finished goods or western supplies. Agricultural labor would be diverted to the production of corn, wheat, and livestock and possibly even manufacturing. While proposals for national economic autonomy had been heard during times of war, seldom had groups within the Lower South considered regional self-sufficiency, particularly in a time of international peace. It is within this context that planters, particularly in South Carolina and Georgia, joined artisans and shopkeepers to herald infrastructure development through steam railroads and tentative investment in textile factories and ironworks.[13]

Yet, agrarians' gestures toward southern industrialization were incomplete, in large part because the tariff controversy had highlighted the desirability for more rather than less international trade. The debates over protection led cotton-producing free traders to defend the importance of Anglo-southern free trade, leading to a shift in economic outlook that has been underappreciated by historians. The emergence of a lucrative and enduring Anglo-American cotton trade after 1815 challenged the Anglophobic perspectives that had previously domi-

12. Though few southerners embraced the extreme remedies, most lamented the unequal effects of the tariff and may have accepted the premise that tariffs for manufacturers were unconstitutional, in spirit if not in fact. See, for example, debates of an 1831 free-trade convention, *Journal of the Free Trade Convention* (Philadelphia: T. W. Ustick, 1831), esp. 19–20, and Mississippi, Alabama, and Georgia resolutions in *State Papers on Nullification* (Columbia, S.C.: M. Morris and Wilson, 1830), esp. 217–40, 238–43, 269–96.

13. For example, McDuffie, *Annals of Congress*, 18:1, 1677–1678. Ernest McPherson Landers, *The Textile Industry in Antebellum South Carolina* (Baton Rouge: Louisiana State University Press, 1969), 31–42.

nated southern Republican economic thought. British naval power opened new markets for textiles in South America, Africa, and Asia, making it a good reciprocal partner for cotton growers. All U.S. manufacturers could offer were consumers already clothed in textiles derived primarily from southern raw cotton. Consequently, to Mississippi Congressman Christopher Rankin, "the idea of a home market for either our produce or manufactures to any considerable extent, is most fallacious . . . calculated to delude and deceive the people."[14] In this calculus, national or even regional independence did not make economic or political sense. In the 1820s it seemed increasingly clear to cotton planters that only European, and perhaps only British, manufacturers could provide the technology and the markets to consume rapidly ballooning quantities of American raw cotton. In the Lower South, politicians were singing the praises of Anglo-American trade.

The perception that Europe was finally committing itself to the abandonment of trade regulation deepened southern frustration with the advance of a so-called mercantilist system at home. Even as slaveholders cautiously eyed Wilberforce's Parliamentary advances on behalf of abolition, southern theorists hailed the first stirring of a British free-trade movement, symbolically marked by Alexander Baring's presentation of an 1820 petition for repeal of the Corn Laws. Cooper and John C. Calhoun praised the "wise" Tory ministries, which under the leadership of George Canning, William Huskisson, and the Earl of Liverpool had, it seemed, finally embraced the sound theories of Adam Smith and his followers and would seek to turn them into free-trade policies.[15] As history would demonstrate, southern hopes for a British free-trade triumph went unfulfilled, at least until 1846. National interest rather than ideology guided British policy, and only after a severe Irish famine were the most powerful vestiges of British protection, the Corn Laws, finally removed. Still, most in the Cotton South remained convinced that a

14. Ranklin, *Annals of Congress,* 18:1, 2010. From a practical standpoint, it may be noted that refusing to collect duties would have made Charleston and other South Carolina towns free-trade ports, making them attractive destinations for foreign commerce. Some skeptical northerners believed this, rather than allegiance to spurious states' rights principles, motivated nullification.

15. Thomas Cooper, *Lectures on the Elements of Political Economy,* 2nd ed. (1830; reprint, New York: A.M. Kelley 1971), 30. Calhoun to L. W. Tazewell, Apr. 14, 1829, *Papers of John C. Calhoun,* 10, 23; and to recently appointed United States Minister to France, William Rives, June 21, 1829, ibid., 11, 55.

transatlantic free-trade movement would succeed and benefit their economy.[16]

The North's acceptance of protection and Britain's slow movement toward free trade redefined the perceived problem of dependence. It was not overdependence on Britain, but a northern monopoly created by a protective system that would make the South an economic dependency. Writing to the president of the Anti-Corn Law League in 1845, South Carolina politician, planter, and arch free-trade economist George McDuffie confessed his enthusiasm for British allies and abhorrence of northern protectionists,

> I habitually look[ed] upon the prosperity of Manchester with as much interest & gratification as I do upon that of Charleston or New York & much more than I do upon that of Boston, which I am constrained to regard as the fruits of an unjust & oppressive system of legalized plunder, which confiscates at least one fifth of the annual income of the cotton planters to sustain a mercenary monied aristocracy of pampered & bloated monopolists.

McDuffie conveyed his hope that "the time may speedily arrive when the banner of free trade shall wave in triumph over the whole world, & that beneath its ample folds the nations of the earth may pitch their tents in peace."[17] In the postnullification period, many sectional-minded southerners hoped that a natural reciprocal interdependence between the South and Europe would provide a way out of economic dependence on the North. It is difficult to imagine slave owners as economic liberals, but in regards to macroeconomic policy they believed themselves to be the true liberal progressives.

The rise of cotton prices in the mid-1830s, continued gestures toward

16. Bernard Semmel, *The Rise of Free Trade Imperialism* (Cambridge: Cambridge University Press, 1970), esp. ch. 6; Boyd Hilton, *Corn, Cash, Commerce: The Economic Policies of the Tory Governments, 1815–1830* (Oxford: Oxford University Press, 1977).

17. George McDuffie to George Wilson, Mar. 11, 1845, MSS, Papers of George Wilson, Manchester Central Library, M20/vol 8. For a reciprocal gesture, see F. C. Mathiesson to Edward Tootal, forwarded to Robert Peel by Tootal, MSS Peel Papers, British Library, 40588 ff 70–71. The myth of peace-loving southerners no doubt obscured their treatment of Native Americans and slaves and was tested by potential conflict with Britain over the Texas annexation. The first was rationalized as being for long-term peace between races; the second was settled diplomatically.

free trade in Britain, and the anticipation of continued reductions provided by the 1833 Compromise Tariff made the postnullification period a time of considerable optimism in the Cotton South. Given these expectations, and the continued comparative advantage that cotton offered, one might suppose that cotton producers remained complacent in their agrarian outlook. That may have been the case in the still largely unsettled states of Alabama and Mississippi, where high profits in cotton continued to point investment toward land and slaves. Yet even there, and more noticeably in the Southeast, economic and political elites pursued the challenge of economic diversification and commercial development. Specifically, cotton planters and merchants embarked on a campaign to empower southern trade by revitalizing direct trade with Europe. A belief in the structural strength of their local economies, their commitment to slavery, and continued faith in laissez-faire policies preempted radical proposals. Instead, visionaries assumed that internal improvements coupled with mild legislative encouragement, sound business decisions, and some overseas assistance would revitalize the southern economy and lead to greater commercial independence from the North. Rather than a complete transformation reformers wished to foster economic rejuvenation that would resurrect once-promising colonial ports by making them the gateways linking an expanding West to the world.

These goals led planters to embrace the projects that artisans and merchants had been arguing for, including increased investment in mills, ironworks, and, most centrally, railroads. While planter-politicians like McDuffie and South Carolina Representative James Hammond invested in local manufacturing efforts, the general tone of early economic reform sought to foster a wider base of consumers that would better attract European suppliers.[18] Northern and southern critics of

18. For efforts at manufacturing, see Landers, *Textile Industry*, 50. In Georgia from 1831 to 1838, ten textile manufacturers received state charters: Milton Sydney Heath, *Constructive Liberalism: The Role of the State in Economic Development in Georgia to 1860* (Cambridge: Harvard University Press, 1954), 306, table 21. For specific efforts in Athens, Georgia, see Ernest C. Hynds, *Antebellum Athens and Clarke County, Georgia* (Athens: University of Georgia Press, 1974), 22–25; and Michael Gagnon, "Transition to an Industrial South: Athens, Georgia, 1830–1870" (Ph.D. diss., Emory University, 1999). For pre-1840 efforts in Alabama see Randall Martin Miller, *The Cotton Mill Movement in Antebellum Alabama* (New York: Arno Press, 1978), 9–24.

nullification alleged that southern commercial decline had resulted less from a protective tariff than from the region's diminutive demand for European goods compared with the demand from more populous northern ports. To remedy this, planters joined southern merchants in projects aimed at broadening the market potential of port cities. Though slavery probably limited regional demand for European finished goods, enthusiasts seemed unconcerned with this structural problem, and none, of course, proposed abandoning a system perceived as the primary source of regional wealth. Instead, they focused on efforts to link inland markets to Atlantic ports through more aggressive internal improvements.

The grandest of these schemes was former nullifier Robert Hayne's effort to link Charleston to the Ohio River at Cincinnati. The railroad was to be the largest in the world and on July 4, 1836, just under four hundred delegates from nine states gathered in Knoxville, Tennessee, to hail a project that Carolinians hoped would increase the "ties of mutual interest and dependence" between the West and South.[19] Despite considerable subscriptions from South Carolinians and a sizable loan from British investors, the project failed to attract the necessary capital. Instead hopes for more open markets and an economic marriage between the West and South came to rest on various state-sponsored efforts in Georgia, Alabama, Mississippi, and Tennessee to open trade between the Tennessee and Mississippi river valleys and Atlantic ports. Georgia also turned to more aggressive state projects, and between 1833 and 1839, the legislature incorporated twelve steamboat companies and twenty-two railroad companies. The most ambitious of these was a state-owned railroad aimed at tying the Tennessee River Valley to a terminus convenient to several private railroad companies (decided at a later point to be Atlanta). After steady initial progress, the economic depression of the early forties temporarily halted the project. Completion in 1850, however, eventually led to considerable profits and made Atlanta one of the fastest-growing inland commercial towns in the country. Moreover, a branch line from Atlanta to Augusta ultimately gave Charleston better access to the western markets that had been envisioned fifteen years earlier. Alabama and Mississippi efforts remained more defensive and focused on rechanneling a greater portion of their state's own crops away

19. *Memorial in Relation to the Charleston & Cincinnati Railroad,* cited in Charles Schultz, "Hayne's Magnificent Dream: Factors Which Influenced the Efforts to Join Cincinnati and Charleston by Railroad" (Ph.D. diss., Ohio State University, 1966), 24.

from New Orleans and Savannah and to Natchez, Vicksburg, and Mobile. Still, boosters in Alabama and Mississippi imagined a railroad system, eventually started in the 1850s, that would unite Gulf ports with northwestern and Atlantic markets.[20]

These early projects were conceived as part of a larger economic plan to revitalize southern commerce and find empowering economic (and, it should be added, political) ties to both the western states and Europe. The Panic of 1837, though devastating to the credit systems of the southwestern states, ironically elevated optimism in Georgia and South Carolina. According to a meeting of Athens, Georgia, entrepreneurs, the crisis created conditions "the most favorable that has occurred since the formation of the American government, to attempt a new organization of our commercial relations with Europe."[21] The resulting call for a "convention of Southern and Western merchants" in October 1837 triggered a series of commercial conventions. Known by contemporaries as the "Direct-Trade Conventions," their purpose has often been ignored or distorted by historians who view them simply as predecessors for later conventions that stressed the need for southern manufacturing. Though the conventions were primarily attended by Georgians and South Carolinians, subsequent meetings in 1838 and 1839 sparked interest from communities in Alabama, North Carolina, Tennessee, and the Florida territory.[22]

20. The history of South Carolina and Georgia projects are traced in U. B. Phillips, *Transportation in the Eastern Cotton Belt* (New York: Macmillan, 1913); Heath, *Constructive Liberalism*, 254–92; Charles Schultz, "Hayne's Magnificent Dream"; Alexander Blanding, *Address of Col. A. Blanding to the Citizens of Charleston: Convened in Town Meeting on the Louisville, Cincinnati, and Charleston Railroad* (Columbia, S.C.: A.S. Johnson, 1836); *Niles' Register*, 55, Oct. 27, 1838, 129 and Nov. 17, 1838, 178; John C. Calhoun to Robert Hayne, Nov. 17, 1838, *The Papers of John C. Calhoun*, 14, 465–66. For efforts in the Southwest, see R. S. Cotterill, "The Beginnings of Railroads in the Southwest," *Mississippi Valley Historical Review* 8, 4 (Mar. 1922): 318–26. Edwin A. Miles, *Jacksonian Democracy in Mississippi* (Chapel Hill: University of North Carolina Press, 1960), 120–22.
21. *Niles' National Register*, 55, 43, 189.
22. W. M. Davis, "Ante-Bellum Southern Commercial Conventions," *Transactions of the Alabama Historical Society*, 5 (Montgomery: Alabama Historical Society, 1904), 153–203; Herbert Wender, *Southern Commercial Conventions, 1837–1859* (Baltimore: Johns Hopkins Press, 1930); John Van Deusen, *The Antebellum Southern Commercial Conventions* (Durham: Duke University Press, 1926). For an excellent study of the later conventions, see Vicki Vaughn Johnson, *The Men and the Vision of the Southern Commercial Conventions, 1845–1871* (Columbia: University of Missouri Press, 1992).

These assemblies, like preceding railroad conventions, stressed commercial outreach and regional financial empowerment. "The disruption of the existing channels of trade," a resolution passed at the 1838 Augusta convention suggested, "affords an opportunity of breaking down the trammels which have so long fettered our commerce and of restoring the South to its natural advantages."[23] While participants understood the problem of overinvestment in cotton and slavery, they continued to perceive both as natural structural strengths. Indeed, economic theorists in the Cotton South defined their objectives as capturing a larger percentage of the wealth made from the international cotton trade and directing it toward the goal of broader commercial empowerment. Though participants placed significant blame on the "unequal" operations of protection, they were careful not to condemn northern merchants nor did they encourage discriminatory measures against them. Instead a unanimously approved committee report written by McDuffie suggested that in addition to the "involuntary tribute" necessitated by the tariff cotton southerners paid a "voluntary tribute" (estimated to be $10,000,000 a year) in service fees and transportation costs for unnecessary indirect trade through northern cities.[24] Ending this tribute would, it was believed, provide the capital necessary to expand internal improvements and commercial ventures thus allowing southern merchants and planters to become their own carriers and to supply an expanding West: "If Georgia and South Carolina . . . would bring their individual energies and resources to the completion of those lines of communication connecting their atlantic [sic] cities with the navigable waters of the West the day would not be distant when our most ardent hopes and sanguine anticipations would be realized."[25] To further inspire merchant and planter associations the first convention in October 1837 petitioned state legislatures to pass limited liability laws for copartnerships, a policy quickly enacted by Georgia, South Carolina, Alabama, and Tennessee.[26]

Finally, the conventions encouraged southern banks to form direct

23. *Georgia Messenger* (Macon), Apr. 12, 1838.

24. McDuffie's report, along with other reports of the early commercial conventions, was reprinted in *De Bow's Review* in the 1840s. See "Direct Trade of Southern States with Europe," *De Bow's Review* 3, 6 (June 1847): 557–59 and 4, 2 (Oct. 1847): 208–26.

25. *Georgia Messenger* (Macon), Oct. 26, 1837.

26. Robert Russell, *Economic Aspects of Southern Sectionalism, 1840–1860* (1924; reprint, New York: Russell & Russell, 1960), 26; Heath, *Constructive Liberalism,* 312; *Georgia Messenger* (Macon), Nov. 23, 1837.

connections with European banks, and even establish agencies in major European financial centers. The widespread financial chaos created throughout the nation in 1837 gave hope that European investors would invest in the relatively conservative and less-affected banks of Georgia and South Carolina. The near half-million in specie that lawyer, politician, and entrepreneur James Hamilton Jr. acquired in 1838 for the Charleston to Cincinnati Railroad represented one example that fueled confidence. Even in the fiscally devastated regions of the Southwest, optimism for Anglo-southern partnerships initially flourished. In late 1837, executors for the Planters and Merchants Bank of Mobile charged the British consul, James Baker, with attracting London capital for their fledging bank.[27] Little is known about the results of Baker's efforts, but his confidential correspondence with the British Foreign Office reflects both the initial enthusiasm for Anglo-American financial connections and the limits of British official support.

As southerners had hoped, Baker accepted "the political and commercial importance of countenancing the Southern section of the United States in their present efforts of opening a direct trade and intercourse with Great Britain," and Baker sought to induce London banks "to cooperate with the Southern States in bringing about this beneficial arrangement." Citing the 1837 Augusta Convention and subsequent passage of favorable bankruptcy laws, Baker told Viscount Palmerston's assistant that he believed British merchants would find southern ports attractive places to do business, and suggested that London capitalists had "greatly aided" his efforts on behalf of the Mobile bank. Accepting the anti–National Bank position of many southern Democrats, Baker decried what he saw as the Philadelphia Bank of the United States's efforts to monopolize Anglo-American commerce by buying up cotton and opening a London agency. He urged the British government to guard against such developments by encouraging direct trade in goods and capital to the American South.[28] The precise reply cannot be found, but according to Baker, "Lord Palmerston did not enter into my views with regard to American Affairs."[29]

27. William H. Brantley, *Banking in Alabama*, 2 vols. (Birmingham: Birmingham Printing, 1961), 1:320.

28. James Baker (confidential) to John Backhouse, Jan. 13, 1838, and Mar. 8, 1838, P.R.O., Foreign Office (FO), 5/236.

29. James Baker (private) to John Backhouse, Mar. 26, 1838, FO, 5/236. Palmerston may have abhorred the thought of more British subjects being placed in a posi-

If official government support was not forthcoming, an extraordinary cotton crop and decent prices in 1838 did lead private British merchants to expand their contacts and investments in the cotton trade. The London-based Baring Brothers, who previously had provided only credit, contacted Mobile, Augusta, Savannah, and Charleston firms in 1837 hoping to purchase cotton, "the great staple by which we hope to make up for all . . . losses" created by the panic. Baring's primary financial competitor, the Baltimore and Liverpool–based Alexander Brown and Company, also expanded its cotton operations in 1838. In spring 1839 McDuffie traveled to Manchester in pursuit of a more modest scheme for Anglo-American cooperation. Associations of twenty-five to thirty planters each would pool their cotton and buy directly from English manufacturers, eliminating middlemen and reducing prices by up to 25 percent.[30]

As with much of southern commercial history the results of the attempts have not been seriously explored. Historians have assumed them to be failures but have not explained why or what their impact was on southern economic thought. All of the same structural arguments used to explain retarded growth in southern manufacturing might also apply to the region's failure to create a stronger southern commercial sector: comparative advantage in agriculture, social and political biases against commerce, the inability to transfer slave capital into other types of capital, limited market size, or income distribution. In fact some aggressive proponents of southern manufacturing in the 1840s increasingly believed one or more of these systemic problems must be overcome for development to occur. In addition to these structural arguments, however, we might also consider a more specific and historicized argument,

---

tion to receive slaves or money from the sale of slaves as payment of debts. In a March 1847 circular, Palmerston declared that any subject would be punished for violating laws related to the slave trade should he be found complicit "either by receiving and becoming owners of slaves in payments of Debts due him; or by selling such slaves, and exchanging them for the money in lieu of which they were received" (Wilkins, *History of Foreign Investment*, 71).

30. Quoted in Wilkins, *History of Foreign Investment*, 255. See also, Ralph Hidy, *The House of Baring in American Trade and Finance* (Cambridge: Harvard University Press, 1949), 254–59; Edwin J. Perkins, *Financing Anglo-American Trade: The House of Brown, 1800–1880* (Cambridge: Harvard University Press, 1975), 101. McDuffie to J. H. Hammond, Mar. 31, 1839, *J. H. Hammond Papers*, Library of Congress, cited in Russell, *Economic Aspects*, 28–29n.

focusing on the role that the near-decade-long depression in cotton prices played in forestalling these efforts. Just as planters, legislatures, and many farmers intellectually and to a considerable degree financially invested themselves in the prospects of commercial development, their endeavors were devastated by circumstances they felt were beyond their control.[31]

If the Panic of 1837 heightened optimism for direct trade and attracting capital, the aftermath of the Panic of 1839 temporarily ended European investment in the South while simultaneously undercutting local efforts to raise capital. Baring, Brown, and others withdrew from investing in cotton or state bonds. Granting of corporations all but ceased from 1840 until 1845. "Wild-cat" banking ventures from the 1830s went bankrupt, and those stable enough to survive, including most Georgia and South Carolina banks, chose survival over potentially risky commercial investments.[32] The Panic of 1839 and subsequent depression in cotton prices fueled planter-entrepreneurs to embrace a movement for southern industrialization that would continue up to the Civil War. Yet the ambiguous nature of the panic and depression prevented agreement on solutions and widespread questioning of the desirability of free trade. In the 1850s the rise of cotton prices along with a return in foreign investment renewed southerners' faith that, within the context of global interdependence and international free trade, a slave-based, cotton economy could modernize.

The broad consensus for free trade achieved during the 1820s and general unity over the desirability of commercial empowerment discussed in the 1830s fragmented in the midst of an economic depression that left the Cotton South reeling. The worsening economic situation in

31. Like contemporaries, historians have not reached agreement on what caused the Panics of 1837 or 1839. Reginald C. McGrane, *The Panic of 1837* (Chicago: University of Chicago Press, 1924); Peter Temin, *The Jacksonian Economy* (New York: Norton, 1969), 113–71; Larry Schweikart, *Banking in the American South from the Age of Jackson to Reconstruction* (Baton Rouge: Louisiana State University Press, 1987), 48–90.

32. On Baring, see Mira Wilkins, *History of Foreign Investment*, 66–75. On charters, see Heath, *Constructive Liberalism*, 307, chart 2; J. Mills Thornton III, *Politics and Power in a Slave Society: Alabama, 1800–1860* (Baton Rouge: Louisiana State University Press, 1978), table on 292; Schweikart, *Banking in the American South*, 91–120; James Rogers Sharp, *The Jacksonians versus the Banks: Politics in the States after the Panic of 1837* (New York: Columbia University Press, 1970), 274–84.

the early 1840s made a previously maligned Whig agenda more attractive. With state finances in shambles or retrenched and some Democrats crusading against banks of any kind, a Whig platform promising federal support for internal improvements and continued support for banks gained new adherents. The continuing dismal performance of cotton in international markets gave merit to the idea that more proactive measures, including even protective tariffs and a new national bank, were needed to re-create regional economic prosperity. Even as some elites reconsidered the economic positions of the previous decade many others—including most Democrats—continued to believe that natural developments would lead to a balanced economy suitable for the South's needs. Consensus over what policies best served the goal of regional prosperity was never reached, but the deepening political crisis over slavery redoubled the efforts of supporters of diversification to remove the South from economic dependence on the North. Disagreement over particular policies remained considerable, but by the late 1850s a large number of political and economic leaders in the Cotton South felt that political union provided as many obstacles as opportunities.

Unlike after the panics of 1819 and 1837, the depression that followed the 1839 panic could not easily be attributed to normal economic cycles. Continually worsening conditions led some to more thoughtfully reexamine the foundations of the cotton economy, concluding that cotton had reached the stage when production might continually outstrip demand. As a result, leaders suggested that the South must turn toward manufacturing. Unlike Whigs in the Upper South, those in the Lower South never fully embraced the principle of protection. They did, however, soften their opposition, and after passage of the 1842 protective tariff they sought to minimize political damage by praising it as a revenue measure. Eyeing the 1844 elections and seeing some improvement in the national economy, an increasing number of Whigs in the Lower South tempered their opposition and, with one exception, united in opposing congressional Democrats' 1844 push to reduce the tariff.[33] Leaders in Georgia, the cotton state with the strongest Whig party, proved particularly important as party leaders John Berrien, Robert Toombs, and Alexander Stephens all came out strongly against southern Democrat proposals to raise revenues through direct taxation instead of tariffs. In

33. Only one Whig, a Georgia states-righter, voted for the bill.

so doing, they occasionally supported the positive effects that tariffs had for assisting manufacturing. Similarly, South Carolinian William Gregg, heralded as the most successful manufacturer in the South, chastised Democrats for investing energy in opposing the tariff rather than using it to advance southern industrialization.[34]

Such individuals were, by their own admission, in the minority and at odds with most of their constituents. Antitariff positions remained wildly popular throughout the Lower South. It would be a gross mistake, however, to equate opposition to tariffs with hostility to manufacturing. For example, South Carolina's James H. Hammond, a leader of the radically antitariff Blufton Movement, believed that southern industrialization was politically and economically desirable. He and others rather easily fit the development of manufacturing within their vision of natural economic progress. The South's bountiful raw cotton supply and ready access to waterpower were seen as natural advantages that would enable southern manufacturers to rapidly catch up with their northern neighbors. They assumed that fostering southern textile manufacturing would then trigger wider investment in other industries necessary for its support, like metalworking. The supposedly poverty-inducing urban mills of Manchester were undesirable, but Hammond and his followers believed it was possible to "reconcile industry with free trade, slave labour, agricultural advancement & Southern tone."[35]

The natural development of manufactures was thought completely compatible with commercial agriculture and the goal of attracting more direct trade with Europe. Supporters suggested that products of southern textile mills could not directly compete with the fine goods produced in Europe, but they could compete well against coarser fabrics then

34. Michael Holt, *The Rise and Fall of the Whig Party* (New York: Oxford University Press, 1999), 167; Donald A. DeBats, *Elite and Masses: Political Structure, Communication, and Behavior in Ante-Bellum Georgia* (New York: Garland Publishing, 1990), 87–88; Anthony Gene Carey, *Parties, Slavery, and the Union in Antebellum Georgia* (Athens: University of Georgia Press, 1997), 58–63; William Gregg, *Essays on Domestic Industry: or, An Inquiry into the Expediency of Establishing Cotton Manufactures in South Carolina* (1844; reprint, Graniteville: Graniteville Co., 1941); Broadus Mitchell, *William Gregg: Factory Master of the Old South* (Chapel Hill: University of North Carolina Press, 1928), 15–32.

35. Hammond, *An Address Delivered before the South Carolina Institute* (Charleston: Walker & James, 1849); Russell, *Economic Aspects*, 35–36. Quoted in Drew Faust, *James Henry Hammond and the Old South: A Design for Mastery* (Baton Rouge: Louisiana State University Press, 1982), 275–76.

produced in the North. Some even envisioned that the South would one day become an exporter of simple cloth, a vision that led many to seek direct trade with markets in South America. High tariffs on European iron especially hindered southern efforts to build manufacturing firms and railroads. Such product distinctions allowed economic reformers in the Lower South to continue to embrace the importance of regional manufacturing while also stressing the desirability and attainability of commercial interdependency. Economic reformers, even those support-ing tariffs on some items, did not want to restrict international trade.[36]

In the fifties efforts to pursue direct partnerships between British merchants and bankers and the Atlantic and Gulf ports of the Lower South intensified southerners' hopes of breaking what one commenta-tor called the "chain of commercial thralldom" binding the South to New York.[37] Again the perceived receptivity of free trade in Britain served as a model for commercial and industrial development. "Standing as Great Britain does at the head of the great movement of civilization adminis-tered as her government is with such profound wisdom," W. W. Boyce indicated that "her example, in this particular [free trade] commands our attention, and her remarkable success invites our cooperation." He further suggested that direct and unexploitative international trade would provide enough capital to develop southern industrial resources. Prais-ing the formation of associations in Mobile that pooled and directed commercial capital toward industrialization, he proposed, "Free trade virtually gives us this capital, because it gives us the fruits of capital. . . . Freedom of exchange gives us the benefit of a vast foreign capital."[38] Optimism about direct trade with Europe rose with international cot-ton prices. Excepting the years 1855 to 1856, demand for raw cotton outpaced supply from 1849 through the Civil War. In Britain, still by far the largest consumer of raw cotton, intensified efforts to diversify sup-ply failed, and the American South continued to supply 80 percent of Britain's supply trade, giving it a near monopoly. Additionally, increased

36. Even William Gregg ultimately supported the cause of direct importation: Gregg, "Southern Patronage to Southern Imports and Domestic Industry," *De Bow's Review*, 29:1 (July 1860): 77–83; 29:2 (Aug. 1860): 226–32; 29: 4 (Oct. 1860): 495–500; 29:5 (Nov. 1860): 623–31; 29:6 (Dec. 1860): 771–78; 30:1 (Jan. 1861) 102–4; 30:2 (Feb. 1861) 216–23.

37. John Forsyth, "The North and South" *De Bow's Review*, 17: 4 (Oct. 1854): 375.

38. Boyce, "Direct Taxation and Free Trade," *De Bow's Review*, 25:1 (July 1858) 23.

cotton textile manufacturing on the Continent offered diversified markets, a reality demonstrated by increased cotton shipments from southern ports to France and Germany, particularly from Mobile. All of these developments furthered the belief that southern cotton was indeed king.[39]

In part because credit and capital networks in the Lower South flowed through merchant houses or individual factors that have not received systematic study, it is difficult to assess international trade's effect on capital development and industrialization. Anecdotal evidence, however, suggests that the presence of European trade houses in the Lower South should not be overlooked. Even prior to the 1850s cotton boom, 43 percent of British mercantile houses in the United States (58 of 134, including all 14 shipping merchants) operated in the cotton ports of Charleston, Savannah, Mobile, and New Orleans.[40] Perhaps more important, the outbreak of revolutions in Europe in 1848 and higher cotton prices made United States financial markets more favorable places to invest. An analysis of foreign investment in 1853 may give some indication of the importance of overseas capital for a South which, not surprisingly, lagged behind the North in the accumulation of financial capital. Nationally, foreign investors provided only 2.5 percent of bank capital, but two major exceptions to this trend were Alabama and Louisiana, where 27.3 percent and 27.9 percent, respectively, of bank capital came from foreign sources. A more widespread trend emerges when the percentage of foreign holders of state stock is considered. With the exception of South Carolina, all of the cotton states came in well above the national average, estimated to be 58 percent. Foreigners owned 100 percent of Mississippi's bonds, 97.7 percent of Alabama's, 83.4 percent of Louisiana's, and 75 percent of Georgia's. Overseas investment was critical for the nearly sixfold jump in railroad mileage in the Southern states between 1848 and 1860.[41] Southern legislatures and

39. Fogel and Engerman, *Time on the Cross*, 92, fig. 28; Albion, *Rise of New York*, 399, appendix 8 demonstrates that by 1860 53 ships left Mobile for France, 21 from Charleston and 6 from Savannah.

40. According to consular returns from that year New York had 37 houses, Philadelphia 34, followed by New Orleans (24), Charleston (16), Mobile (13), Savannah (5), Boston (2), Baltimore (2), Alexandria (1). See Mira Wilkins, *The History of Foreign Investment in the United States to 1914* (Cambridge: Harvard University Press, 1989), 74.

41. Calculated from table 3, "Report of the Secretary of Treasury in Answer to a Resolution of the Senate Calling for the Amount of American Securities held in

entrepreneurs, it seemed, sought to sell stock to European investors, who, in turn, seemed willing investors. The eagerness with which such investments were sought was a far cry from the early national period when such transactions were seen as unpatriotic. The comparatively worse effects of the Panic of 1857 on the North and West than on the Cotton South suggested that cotton growth and production proved a more enduring form of wealth than previously thought. Even northern contemporaries believed that after the panic, the South held a higher percentage of national specie than it ever had before.[42]

These gestures toward fostering international free trade, internal improvements, and southern manufacturing, however, did not, indeed could not, solve the dilemma of how to prevent southern consumers from purchasing northern goods from northern merchants. Protective tariffs against foreign goods would do nothing to defend southern manufacturers from competition with northern products. The constitutional guarantee for free trade within the Union ensured that northern comparative advantage remained a serious obstacle in the pursuit of a competitive market. The apparent failure of efforts to rely strictly on nature and internal improvements forced many prophets of free trade to also argue for special legislation designed to defend against what they perceived as a northern commercial monopoly. State legislatures and politicians, earnestly seeking to accelerate southern economic diversification and development, scrambled to find legislative policies that would be effective and constitutional. In the mid-1840s, South Carolina and Alabama attempted to overcome this perceived monopoly by exempting articles manufactured within the state from state taxes. When some northern states refused to enforce the fugitive slave law, contributing to a political crisis in 1850, more drastic, unconstitutional efforts such as nonintercourse or import taxes on northern goods were

---

Europe and other Foreign Countries, on the 30th June 1853," U.S. Senate, Executive Document, No. 42, 33rd Congress, 1st sess., Washington D.C, 1854, reprinted in Mira Wilkins, ed., *Foreign Investments in the United States* (New York: Arno Press, 1977). Only 48.7 percent of South Carolina bonds were foreign owned. On railroad investment see Cleona Lewis, *America's Stake in International Investments* (Washington, D.C.: Brookings Institution, 1938), 29–30; P. L. Cottrell, *British Overseas Investment in the Nineteenth Century* (London: Macmillan Press, 1975), 19–29.

42. *Hunts Merchant's Magazine,* v39, 459; v42, 157; v43, 455 cited in Russell, *Economic Aspects,* 205.

proposed both for their political effect and to encourage southern industrial efforts. In Georgia, Senator Berrien attempted to negotiate the constitutional obstacles by suggesting that once northern goods were delivered into the hands of merchants in Georgia they fell under state jurisdiction and could be charged a high discriminatory tax. Similarly, Hammond proposed doubling the property tax on nonresidents. Opponents argued that such policies were hypocritical and violated the very free-trade axioms that southerners had heralded. Supporters, however, invoked their stilted version of history, citing that a long train of mercantilist measures by the North necessitated such remedies. The arguments followed the logic employed against Britain in the Jeffersonian period. An unnatural northern mercantilist system had made the South unnaturally dependent on northern manufacturers.[43]

Achieving international interdependency and the free-trade ideal also necessitated interventionist measures that would reroute direct trade to the South. To encourage southern shipbuilding, Louisiana's legislature offered a bounty of five dollars per ton for every ship over one hundred tons built in the state. Restrictions on foreign ships' participation in the coastal trade had presumably diminished European involvement in the shipment of cotton. In 1858 Alabama Senator C. C. Clay worked to repeal navigation acts that many felt guaranteed a northern monopoly on the coastal trade and raised freight rates. At an 1856 commercial convention Robert Toombs proposed that foreign imports be exempted from state taxes as a means of encouraging direct trade, a policy that the Alabama legislature enacted. Leaders elsewhere supported a plan whereby directly imported goods were released from paying state license fees.[44]

While most shared the goals of increased economic independence from the North and increased interdependence with Europe, disparate groups could not easily agree on specific policies. Even when they could agree on minor policies, tensions persisted between the need for truly discriminatory policies and the intellectual commitment to laissez-faire economics. Broad consensus within the Lower South could be reached regarding federal land grants to support rail lines and the continued

43. These arguments are catalogued by Robert Russell, ibid., 156–61.
44. See Robert Toomb's proposal to 1856 Savannah Convention, *De Bow's Review*, 22:1, 102–4.

economic profitability of slavery. At times the Lower South appeared convinced that westward expansion into the Southwest and a southern railroad to California would assist industrial and commercial efforts. Still, disagreements ranging from the economic impact of reopening the slave trade to the role of the federal government stymied attempts to provide a clear vision for regional economic reform. The fact that division rather than consensus dominated southern economic thought on the eve of the Civil War must prevent us from believing economic factors, per se, caused secession. Unionist-minded individuals, particularly in the Upper South, provided an equally reasonable and more positive interpretation, stressing that southern wealth advanced precisely because of a healthy mutual dependency with the North. As has been repeatedly demonstrated, the threat to slavery presented by a Republican-led North provided the framework, the spark, and the fuel for the formation of the Confederacy.[45]

This does not, however, mean we should write economics out of the secession story. Nor need we embrace an essentialized economic understanding of the sectional crisis as an unavoidable one between slavery and capitalism. Even if we believe that slavery and free-labor capitalism are incompatible, there remains plenty of evidence that they could and indeed had coexisted. What then might we say about the relationship between the story told here and the political crisis that culminated in war? First, the long debates over national and sectional economic policy had forced southern elites to contemplate their economic situation in a regionally defined way and had heightened their perception that they were being exploited by the North. This undoubtedly increased outrage over the more gravely feared threat: a North united behind antislavery measures. We might also think of it in another way. Whereas southerners had embraced the constitution in 1787 with the belief that a national union of interests existed, the debates of the antebellum period had convinced a majority in the Lower South that this union no longer provided the economic bonds that made continued compromise worthwhile.[46]

45. See, for example, Charles Dew, *Apostles of Disunion: Southern Secession Commissioners and the Causes of the Civil War* (Charlottesville: University Press of Virginia, 2001); William Freehling, *The Road to Disunion*, vol. 1, *Secessionists at Bay, 1776–1854* (New York: Oxford University Press, 1990).

46. Cathy Matson and Peter Onuf, *A Union of Interests: Political and Economic Thought in Revolutionary America* (Lawrence: University Press of Kansas, 1990).

In addition, developments in the 1850s heightened optimism about the South's potential regional strength and the opportunities that might develop internationally. Though the South was still considerably behind the North, the increase in southern industrial development and rail-roads and a growing perception of self-sufficiency in the 1850s provided faith that a southern confederacy was economically sound enough to support independence and the war effort necessary to ensure it. Just as critically, secessionists counted on the continued global importance of slave-produced cotton to ensure that their new nation would be recognized and guaranteed a prominent place within the Atlantic world. Some individuals overseas shared their expectation and funneled illicit support to the Confederate cause, most notoriously in a guns-for-cotton trade through the Mexican port of Matamoros. Yet, after much debate in European capitals, southern hopes were not realized. Trading partners failed to intervene. King Cotton and free trade were not quite as mighty as its advocates had thought. The fate of the Confederacy and the system of slavery supporting it moved beyond the rhetoric of "peace and harmony" and onto the harsh realities of the battlefield.[47]

47. Gavin Wright's important work provides convincing evidence of the general economic optimism of the 1850s and of the fear that Republican control would lead to a drop in cotton prices, *Political Economy of the Cotton South*, 128–157. For the highly lucrative nature of the wartime cotton trade through Matamoros see James W. Daddysman, *The Matamoros Trade: Confederate Commerce, Diplomacy and Intrigue* (Newark: University of Delaware Press, 1983). There are many British authors emphasizing the desirability of an independent Southern Confederacy. For one written by a Member of Parliament see George McHenry, *The Cotton Trade: Its Bearing upon the Prosperity of Great Britain and Commerce of the American Republics* (London: Saunders, Otley, 1863); Howard Jones, *The Union in Peril: The Crisis over British Intervention in the Civil War* (Chapel Hill: University of North Carolina Press, 1992).

Industrialization and Economic Development
in the Nineteenth-Century U.S. South

Some Interregional
and Intercontinental
Comparative Perspectives

Shearer Davis Bowman

Most historians of the U.S. South in the nineteenth century, especially when discussing the Civil War era, employ a comparative method,
at least in the classroom, when they address questions about regional
patterns of economic development, social structure, political perspective, and cultural values in the North versus the South.[1] And there is
ample evidence and testimony from contemporaries and scholars alike
that the southern slave states possessed a much more "backward" economy than the northern free states according to numerous measures of
"development," from manufacturing output to urbanization rates to
transportation infrastructure. To cite but one frequently invoked statis-

---

1. For a fine recent review of the literature juxtaposing the South and the Northern "UnSouth" since the eighteenth century, see Peter Kolchin, *A Sphinx on the
American Land: The Nineteenth-Century South in Comparative Perspective* (Baton
Rouge: Louisiana State University Press, 2003), ch. 1. For a very helpful introduction to interregional understanding of northern and southern economic development, see David L. Carlton and Peter A. Coclanis, *The South, the Nation, and the
World: Perspectives on Southern Economic Development* (Charlottesville: University
of Virginia Press, 2003), 1–23.

tic, according to the 1860 census the South contained 36 percent of the U.S. population, but "contributed less than 11% of the country's industrial output."[2] Several valuable recent monographs confirm and amplify this evaluation of southern "backwardness" by focusing on railroads. Examining these studies will set the stage for an excursion into the realm of international and intercontinental comparative history, where the South's relative "backwardness" vis-à-vis the North throughout the nineteenth and early twentieth centuries appears in a very different light.

John Majewski's *A House Dividing: Economic Development in Pennsylvania and Virginia before the Civil War* (2000) juxtaposes two counties of the Atlantic Piedmont: Cumberland in the Keystone State and Albemarle in the Old Dominion. The author suggests that contentious debates over whether or not the slave South was "capitalist" have overshadowed the more concrete and historical question, "Why did the North and the South develop differently?" Focusing on his two counties, Majewski concludes that eastern Virginia failed to develop "a large commercial city" like Philadelphia "that could provide investors, traffic, and passengers for major transportation projects, especially 'intersectional trunk lines' linked to towns and markets in the Ohio Valley west of the Appalachian Mountains." Although during the decade before the Civil War "Virginians invested in more miles of railroad per capita than did Pennsylvanians," and the state government purchased over 60 percent of the stock of the Virginia Central Railroad that ran through Albemarle Country, the Virginia General Assembly never succeeded in overcoming intrastate town rivalries that pitted "Richmond, Norfolk, Petersburg, and Lynchburg in a battle for commercial supremacy." In contrast, in the late 1830s Philadelphia financiers delivered most of the capital invested in the Cumberland Valley Railroad (CVRR) that linked Cumberland County to the state capital at Harrisburg on the Susquehanna River. Subsequently, the Pennsylvania Railroad, whose corporate financing came from either Philadelphia capitalists or city governments, integrated systems like the CVRR into major trunk lines that extended to Chicago and beyond. But why did Virginia fail to develop a

2. Walter Licht, *Industrializing America: The Nineteenth Century* (Baltimore: Johns Hopkins University Press, 1995), 36. "In 1860 the South produced one-fifth the value of manufactures per capita as the Middle Atlantic states and only one eighth that of New England" (Jeremy Atack and Peter Passell, *A New Economic View of American History*, 2nd ed. [New York: Norton, 1994], 317).

metropolis comparable to Philadelphia? The answer lies in the state's combination of staple-crop commercial agriculture and slavery, which encouraged "the growth of largely self-sufficient plantations that limited population density and town growth," thereby placing severe limits on the intrastate market for manufactured goods. "Philadelphia's densely populated countryside," by providing both foodstuffs to the metropolis and a market for the products of the city's workshops and factories, "spurred industrialization well before the arrival of interregional railroads."[3]

This conclusion seems to echo a judgment familiar to British economic historians, who contend that a prominent port city like Bristol began to fall behind Liverpool and Glasgow during the eighteenth century because Bristol lacked "an extensive hinterland" that underwent both "rapid economic and demographic growth."[4] At the same time, Majewski's work seems to illuminate the necessity to distinguish clearly between the microeconomic profitability of individual slave plantations to their proprietors and the macroeconomic impact of plantation agriculture and slavery on antebellum southern society. As Morton Rothstein observed in 1970, it is one thing to discuss "whether slavery was on the whole profitable for individual plantation entrepreneurs," as in eastern Virginia, and another to discuss "whether a society which encouraged and protected slavery did not inescapably create institutions and barriers to long-term growth" of the kind experienced by southeastern Pennsylvania.[5]

When the secession crisis of 1860–1861 transformed the national "house dividing" into a long and devastating civil war, the Confederate

3. John Majewski, *A House Dividing: Economic Development in Pennsylvania and Virginia before the Civil War* (Cambridge: Cambridge University Press, 2000), 3, 9–11, 171–72.

4. Kenneth Morgan, *Slavery, Atlantic Trade and the British Economy, 1660–1800* (Cambridge: Cambridge University Press, 2000), 89–90.

5. Morton Rothstein, "The Cotton Frontier of the Antebellum United States: A Methodological Battleground," *Agricultural History* 44 (1970): 151–52. This essay is included in the special Jan. 1970 issue of the same periodical edited by William N. Parker and entitled *The Structure of the Cotton Economy of the Antebellum South.* Cf. Harold D. Woodman, "The Profitability of Slavery: A Historical Perennial" (1963), in *Did Slavery Pay? Readings in the Economics of Black Slavery in the United States,* ed. Hugh G. J. Aitken (Boston: Houghton Mifflin, 1971), 3; and Robert William Fogel, *Without Consent or Contract: The Rise and Fall of American Slavery* (New York: Norton, 1989), 108–9.

South's poorly integrated and managed railroad system proved a major liability in the Richmond government's military efforts to repel invasion by Union armies. As William Freehling points out in *The South vs. the South* (2001), his panoramic "tale of the southern house divided" against itself, the Confederacy's industrial and demographic strength was hamstrung from the outset by the loyalty of the border slave states—Maryland, Kentucky, and Missouri in particular—to the United States. Not only did the three largest cities in the loyal slave states—Baltimore, Louisville, and St. Louis—contain more inhabitants than the fourteen largest cities together in the eleven seceded states; losing the border states deprived the Confederacy of half its factory capacity and crippled "its capacity to make and repair ships and railroads."[6]

Freehling has long insisted on distinguishing among several "subregions" in the slave South: in particular, the seven states of the Lower South (which seceded before Lincoln's inauguration in March of 1861), versus the Middle South (the four states that seceded after the Confederacy's bombardment of Fort Sumter in April and Lincoln's call for troops to suppress the "rebellion"), versus the loyalist Border South that never joined the Confederacy (including West Virginia, which "seceded" from Virginia during the war). His work demonstrates clearly that historians should be extremely wary of any argument that the "Old South" was somehow monolithic economically, socially, or politically. As Freehling demonstrated well over a decade ago, by 1850 slaves made up 43 percent of the Lower South's population, 30 percent of the Middle South's, and only 17 percent of the Border South's. "The farther north the southern state, the cooler the clime, the fewer the slaves, and the lower the relative commitment to perpetuating slavery."[7] In light of John

6. William W. Freehling, *The South vs the South: How Anti-Confederate Southerners Shaped the Course of the Civil War* (New York: Oxford, 2001), xiii, 61.

7. William W. Freehling, *The Road to Disunion*, vol. 1, *Secessionists at Bay, 1776–1854* (New York: Oxford, 1990), 17–18. In 1860 the slave population in the seven "early seceders" of the Lower South was 46 percent, in the four "late seceders" of the Upper South, 28.6 percent, and in the four "loyal states" of the Border South, 10.9 percent (Kolchin, *A Sphinx on the American Land*, 16). Barbara Jeanne Fields observes of Maryland on the eve of the Civil War that "however independent of slave society Baltimore and the northern counties might be in terms of their economic pursuits, they remained subaltern where political power was concerned" (*Slavery and Freedom on the Middle Ground: Maryland during the Nineteenth Century* [New Haven: Yale University Press, 1985], 20).

Majewski's analysis, therefore, it is hardly surprising that Virginia, North Carolina, Kentucky, and Tennessee seem to have possessed "a greater capacity for structural transformation" than did most of the Deep South, where many farms also enjoyed a comparative advantage in growing cotton. Hence after the Civil War these four Upper South states "moved further and faster away from an agrarian economy."[8]

Freehling's *The South vs. the South* highlights the Union's gain during the Civil War, and the Confederacy's corresponding loss, of the nation's third largest metropolis in 1860 after New York and Philadelphia, Baltimore. The Baltimore and Ohio Railroad shops around Mount Clare "became the Civil War hospital for Yankee railroads."[9] The military importance of the Union's superior manufacturing capacity and rail system is developed in John E. Clark, Jr.'s *Railroads in the Civil War: The Impact of Management on Victory and Defeat* (2001). Starting from the premise that the Civil War, arguably "the first modern war," was in truth "a railroad war," Clark focuses on two particular movements of troops by rail from the Virginia theater of the Civil War into northern Georgia and eastern Tennessee in the fall of 1863. (Looming large here is Kentucky's reluctance to secede in 1861, and the occupation of the state by U.S. military forces.) Clark's first troop movement was the transfer of Longstreet's corps of 13,000 men from the Army of Northern Virginia to reinforce Bragg's Army of Tennessee at what became the Confederate victory at Chickamauga, which the Confederate command failed to exploit. The second transfer was the Union command's response to defeat at Chickamauga by shifting 23,000 men from the Army of the Potomac to assist Rosecrans's Army of the Cumberland at what became the more momentous Union victory of Chattanooga. This latter battle, in turn, set the stage for stunning Federal successes at Lookout Mountain and Missionary Ridge in November, which drove the Confederates out of East Tennessee, thus making possible Sherman's 1864 advance against Atlanta. Clark's two logistical transfers "provide a unique opportunity to compare and contrast the quality of war management exercised by Union and Confederate leaders," business as well as political.

8. Patrick O'Brien, *The Economic Effects of the American Civil War* (Atlantic Highlands, N.J.: Humanities Press International, 1988), 23.

9. Freehling, *The South vs the South*, 61–2. Freehling emphasizes that in the loyal border slave state of Missouri "St. Louis factories transformed finished iron into paralyzing warships. The resulting gunboats exemplified how the South's most advanced cities helped fashion a more advanced Union military machine" (63–64).

That only half of Longstreet's troops arrived in time to fight at Chicka-mauga—including the Seventeenth Mississippi, which spent eleven days covering a 950-mile circuitous route through Atlanta—was due to dila-tory decision-making, flawed communications, many separate trans-fers, and numerous delays. The Longstreet movement illustrates how the Confederacy "never took the most rudimentary steps to improve the condition of its rails to best exploit its interior lines" of communication. The Union response also took eleven days but delivered several times as many infantry across more than 1,230 miles spanning nine railroad companies' tracks. The Union's much greater transport efficiency arose from much smoother cooperation between the central government and the railroad companies; the effective management of the U.S. Military Railroad (authorized in January of 1862) under the leadership of Daniel McCallum and Herman Haupt; far superior civilian railroad managers, especially John Garrett, Tom Scott, and Preston Smith; and the much greater industrial capacity supporting construction and maintenance of Union railroads. Also of critical importance were quick decisions by Lincoln and Secretary of War Stanton to reinforce the Army of the Cumberland, versus Jefferson Davis's "glacial" process of ordering the transfer of troops from Virginia to the Army of Tennessee. The Lincoln administration "secured northern railroads' cooperation with carrot and stick," while Davis's government "never made a serious try with ei-ther." Clark takes special aim at "the Davis administration's ignorance of, and contempt for business." The final chapter addresses the general question of southern attitudes toward business entrepreneurship, in the process citing what leading economic historians like Stuart Bruchey and Fred Bateman and Thomas Weiss have written on the subject. Clark concludes judiciously that "southern planters demonstrated sound managerial instincts and a bias toward risk-taking in the business of growing cotton." At the same time, "the mismanagement of southern railroads" clearly illustrates how "the southern economy produced too few people with management expertise adequate for the trials the Con-federacy faced."[10]

10. John E. Clark Jr., *Railroads in the Civil War: The Impact of Management on Victory and Defeat* (Baton Rouge: Louisiana State University Press, 2001), 2–4, 126, 229, 227, 69, 223. This is a volume in the series Conflicting Worlds: New Dimen-sions of the American Civil War, edited by T. Michael Parrish. Clark's mentor at Princeton, James M. McPherson, has emphasized that the "Puritan work ethic was strongest among New Englanders in general, and among Congregationalists,

Clark's analysis accords with what seems to be the current consensus among historians about the economy of the antebellum South and the economic outlook of the planter elite.[11] Slaveholding proprietors of commercial farms (the larger ones generally denominated plantations, whose principal cash crops could be cotton, tobacco, wheat, corn, hemp, rice, or sugar) were by and large successful agricultural businessmen responding to market forces—the most important being the impressive growth of the British textile industry and transatlantic demand for cotton after the 1790s. Slavery proved at the same time profitable and viable: profitable because investment in slave labor was quite lucrative though evidently less so than riskier investments in alternative ventures like factories; and viable in the long-run sense that slaveholders garnered capital gains from biological reproduction among slaves, and hence the slaveowner was economically better off *not* manumitting his infant slaves.[12] Between 1800 and 1860, even as the cultivation of upland, short-staple cotton expanded geographically beyond the Piedmont of South Carolina and Georgia south toward the Gulf of Mexico and west across the Mississippi River, the monetary value of cotton output per hand seems to have increased about fivefold, and the average price of a prime field hand tripled. Hence a recent observation by Kenneth Pomeranz seems particularly relevant to the Old South: "Where production and elite incomes can be increased by driving bound laborers harder and/or bringing unused land under the plow, elites are not very likely to

---

Unitarians, Presbyterians, and Quakers in particular. It is no coincidence that New England was at the cutting edge of American modernization or that a disproportionate number of entrepreneurs and inventors were New England Yankees of Calvinist background" (*Ordeal By Fire: The Civil War and Reconstruction* [New York: Knopf, 1982], 14). See the fascinating autobiography by Henry Merrill (1816–1873), a businessman of Presbyterian background in upstate New York—an area heavily settled by New England natives—and termed by *De Bow's Review* "one of the shrewdest Yankee manufacturers," who built and operated important textile factories in Georgia and Arkansas from the late 1830s to the early 1860s. James L. Skinner III, ed., *The Autobiography of Henry Merrill: Industrial Missionary to the South* (Athens: University of Georgia Press, 1991).

11. For an excellent review of the relevant literature, see Mark M. Smith, *Debating Slavery: Economy and Society in the Antebellum South* (Cambridge: Cambridge University Press, 1998).

12. See Robert Margo, "The South as an Economic Problem: Fact or Fiction?" in *The South as an American Problem,* ed. Larry J. Griffin and Don H. Doyle (Athens: University of Georgia Press, 1995), 165. Cf. the discussion of profitability and efficiency in Smith, *Debating Slavery,* 60–61.

invest in attempts to develop new production processes."[13] We need also recall the importance for "Western" agricultural history until the twentieth century of what Susan Archer Mann has termed "the unpredictability and capriciousness of nature"—that is, drought and flood, insects and disease. Thus farms confronted more formidable natural obstacles than factories to the "predictability and standardization" associated with industrial capitalism and its use of advanced technology operated by wage labor. "It seems clear," concludes Mann, "that the industrial revolutions of the late eighteenth and nineteenth centuries, while sufficient to industrialize industry, were not sufficient to industrialize many spheres of agriculture."[14]

Only temporary downturns interrupted the growth of the antebellum southern economy, except for the depression that followed the Panic of 1837 and extended into the late 1840s.[15] Free whites saw their average real incomes rise by over 40 percent during the last two decades before the Civil War, and slave property made the average white person

13. Kenneth Pomeranz, *The Great Divergence: China, Europe, and the Making of the Modern World Economy* (Princeton: Princeton University Press, 2000), 214; and O'Brien, *Economic Effects of the Civil War,* 15. According to Stanley Lebergott, overall slave prices almost quadrupled from the de jure end of the foreign slave trade in 1808 to the eve of the Civil War in 1860. "Underlying that increase was the quadrupling by 1860 in Southern crop production per slave" (*The Americans: An Economic Record* [New York: W. W. Norton, 1984], 213–14).

14. Susan Archer Mann, *Agrarian Capitalism in Theory and Practice* (Chapel Hill: University of North Carolina Press, 1990), 127, 139. With regard to the Old South, Clement Eaton points out that the harvesting of cotton might last from late August until early January. Because the cotton bolls ripened unevenly, it might be necessary to pick over a field at least three times. "This unequal ripening was the most important reason for the failure until the 1930s to develop a successful mechanical picker" (*The Growth of Southern Civilization, 1790–1860* [1961; reprint, New York: Harper Torchbooks, 1963], 28). According to Robert C. McMath Jr., "The [mechanical] cotton picker more nearly resembles the mechanical tomato harvester, developed in the 1960s, than does the machinery that revolutionized grain harvesting before the Civil War" in the North. That is, the mechanical cotton picker involved a much higher degree of technological sophistication than did McCormick's reaper. McMath, "Variations on a Theme by Henry Grady, Technology, Modernization, and Social Change," in *The Future South: A Historical Perspective for the Twenty-first Century,* ed. Joe P. Dunn and Howard L. Preston (Urbana: University of Illinois Press, 1991), 89.

15. See the concise discussion of economic trends in William J. Cooper Jr. and Thomas E. Terrill, *The American South: A History,* 3rd ed. (Boston: McGraw-Hill, 2002), 1:185–86.

in the South considerably wealthier than in the more diversified and "developed" North. Although on the eve of the Civil War the South's average per capita income (free and slave) remained far behind that of the North, between 1840 and 1860 per capita income in the slave states rose by 39 percent, as opposed to 29 percent for the free states and 33 percent for the nation as a whole.[16] Outside the cotton belt that stretched from several southeastern Virginia counties into eastern Texas, lesser slaveholders in central Missouri (i.e., those owning fewer than ten slaves) found slave labor well suited to raising a wide variety of food crops in addition to tobacco and hemp, while many large slaveholders in eastern Virginia (those owning at least twenty or thirty slaves) shifted successfully from tobacco to wheat. The wealthiest among these Upper South planters might buy Deep South lands suitable for cotton or sugar and send their "surplus" slaves to work those fields.[17] Slaves could be and were employed effectively in industrial enterprises, particularly iron

16. Kolchin, *A Sphinx on the American Land,* 26; O'Brien, *Economic Effects of the Civil War,* 22; and Lebergott, *The Americans,* 208–9. Mark Smith, after evaluating the complex debate over these oft-cited per capita income statistics (first published by Robert Fogel and Stanley Engerman in 1974) has concluded, "the South's high per capita income reflects the growing wealth not [of] a region but of a small class of planters who themselves had to move westward to maintain their level of income." Smith, *Debating Slavery,* 85. Per capita income was generally higher in the Lower than in the Upper and Border Souths; and the western cotton belt, particularly the alluvial soils of the Mississippi River valley, contained more fertile and productive land than did the eastern cotton belt. Per capita income in the seven states of the Lower South averaged $97 in 1860, led by Louisiana's $131. In the four states of the Upper South the average was $91, led by $95 for Arkansas. For the Border South, per capita income in Kentucky came to $83, while the estimates for Missouri and Maryland are $90. O'Brien, *Economic Effects of the Civil War,* 15. According to Donghu Yang, "the inequality of wealth distribution in the rural South at the eve of the Civil War was far higher than the inequality of the rural North; and southern wealth distribution lies somewhere between the position of the planter dominance thesis and the simple view that there was a prospering middle class" ("Recent Findings on the Distribution of Wealth, on Social Structure, and on Economic Mobility among Free Southerners during the Late Antebellum Era," in *Without Consent or Contract: The Rise and Fall of American Slavery,* vol. 2, *Evidence and Methods,* ed. Robert W. Fogel, Ralph A. Galantine, and Richard L. Manning [New York: Norton, 1992], 244).

17. On cotton cultivation in southeastern Virginia counties along the North Carolina border, see Daniel W. Crofts, *Old Southampton: Politics and Society in a Virginia County, 1834–1869* (Charlottesville: University Press of Virginia, 1992), 78–81. On cotton and slavery in Texas, see Richard G. Lowe and Randolph B. Campbell, *Planters and Plain Folk: Agriculture in Antebellum Texas* (Dallas: Southern Methodist University Press, 1987), esp. 169: "With the exception of small slave-

manufacture and tobacco processing, but in 1860 large slaveholders seem to have owned only 12 percent of the South's manufacturing stock.[18] Northern industrial and railroad executives had assumed important roles in the ranks of northern business and political elites and could contribute immensely to the northern war machine, but the southern elite was dominated by agricultural businessmen and their allies in the learned professions and could provide significantly less industrial capacity and management expertise to the Confederate war effort. As Fred Bateman and Thomas Weiss suggested in 1981, even if a "planter ethos" that emphasized land and slaves as sources of wealth and status had not caused "the region's comparative advantage" in large-scale, staple-crop agriculture to be "overindulged," the Old South's "factor endowment would have still led to an industrial sector . . . small relative to that of the [Northeast]."[19]

---

holders (1–9 slaves), all groups [of slaveholding cotton farmers] enjoyed rates of return (i.e., profits as a percentage of investment) of approximately 6 percent or better in 1850 and 1860." On Missouri, see especially R. Douglas Hurt, *Agriculture and Slavery in Missouri's Little Dixie* (Columbia: University of Missouri Press, 1992), ch. 9. On Upper South planters investing in Deep South lands for surplus slaves, see Lebergott, *The Americans*, 207; and Shearer Davis Bowman, "Conditional Union ism and Slavery in Eastern Virginia, 1860–61: The Case of Dr. Richard Eppes," *Virginia Magazine of History and Biography* 96 (1988): esp. 42–44; and Crofts, *Old Southampton*, 25–33. At the Virginia Secession Convention of 1861, the only delegate to whom the 1860 census ascribed the ownership of more than 100 slaves (134 to be exact) was 54-year-old James Coles Bruce in Halifax County, in the southern Piedmont. Bruce told his fellow delegates that after returning to Virginia from a visit to New Orleans in 1844, "I advised my friends who were also large planters to carry a portion of their negroes South, where their profits were great, and not keep them here where our profits were small. To show my sincerity in the belief, I went to Louisiana, and became a cotton and sugar planter" (George M. Reese, ed., *Proceedings of the Virginia Convention of 1861, February 13–May 1, in Four Volumes* [Richmond: Virginia State Library, 1965], 2:241–44); and Ralph A. Wooster, *Secession Conventions of the South* (Princeton: Princeton University Press, 1962), 144–45.

18. See Fred Bateman and Thomas Weiss, *A Deplorable Scarcity: The Failure of Industrialization in the Slave Economy* (Chapel Hill: University of North Carolina Press, 1981), 163–65; and James C. Cobb, *Industrialization and Southern Society, 1877–1984* (Chicago: Dorsey Press, 1984), 8–9. A helpful study of the most industrialized city in the Confederate South is Midori Takagi, *"Rearing Wolves to Our Own Destruction": Slavery in Richmond, Virginia, 1782–1865* (Charlottesville: University Press of Virginia, 1999), esp. p. 4. See also Charles B. Dew, *Bond of Iron: Master and Slave at Buffalo Forge* (New York: Norton, 1994).

19. Bateman and Weiss, *A Deplorable Scarcity*, 162–63. For a trenchant argument against exaggerating slaveholding's "seignurial pleasures" versus its "monetary return," see Lebergott, *The Americans*, 214. Consider the famously successful New

The Northeast is the standard of comparison here. But we need always to keep in mind that the northeastern states in 1860 constituted the industrializing vanguard of a northern economy that would within half a century establish itself as "the preeminent economy in the Western world," a political economy and culture that would help drive the United States down the road of overseas territorial and imperial expansion at the turn of the century.[20] The Old South looks much more prosperous and "developed" if we juxtapose it to another contemporary society in the transatlantic "West," whether the Old Northwest region of the United States, Italy or Spain, or a Latin American country with plantation slavery. As Walter Licht reminds us, had the late antebellum slave states become a separate and independent nation, "it would have then ranked in the top five or six of industrial nations, and not just in textiles, but iron-making, mining, milling of grains and timbers, sugar refining

---

Hampshire native Daniel Pratt, who lived for fourteen years in Georgia before moving to Alabama in 1833. See Curtis J. Evans, *The Conquest of Labor: Daniel Pratt and Southern Industrialization* (Baton Rouge: Louisiana State University Press, 2001), 205.

20. Margo, "The South as an Economic Problem," 171. In 1860 per capita income in the Northeast was $141, versus $89 in the north-central states of the Old Northwest. Kolchin, *A Sphinx on the American Land,* 26. When the U.S. Senate voted 57 to 27 in favor of annexing the Philippines in February of 1899, 41 of the favorable votes came from Republicans, and 22 of the negative votes came from Democrats, mostly southerners. To be sure, South Carolina's John Lowndes Mc-Laurins (1860–1934) spoke strongly in support of an "open-door policy" in China so that the United States could "command equal trade rights with other nations in China." As historian Patrick J. Hearden has concluded, by 1899 "the New South's rapidly growing China trade promised to keep the entire American cotton industry in a healthy condition." But McLaurin insisted with regard to the Philippines that "'imperialism' . . involves the incorporation into our body politic as American citizens of millions of semi-barbarous inhabitants [i.e., Filipinos] of a tropical country. I do not believe such a thing is intended, possible or desirable; nor is such a result necessary to secure such commercial expansion as we want." No doubt McLaurin was well pleased by the Supreme Court's rulings in the several Insular Cases, 1901–1904, that the Constitution did not necessarily extend to annexed and "unincorporated" territory, that the inhabitants did not necessarily become U.S. citizens, and that "the Constitution did not automatically 'follow the flag,' as many Americans had long believed" (Walter LaFeber, *The American Age: United States Foreign Policy at Home and Abroad since 1750* [New York: Norton, 1989], 201–2, 205, 211, 198–99); and "Senator McLaurin Demands an Open Door in China, 1899," in James J. Lorence, ed., *Enduring Voices* (Lexington, Mass: D. C. Heath, 1990), 294–95.

and leather tanning as well."[21] Historian Richard Graham has given us a remarkable pair of essays comparing the southern economy with that of the mid-nineteenth century's second largest slave society, Brazil. Although the percentage of slaves in the South's population was twice the figure for Brazil, the slave states far outstripped Brazil in transportation infrastructure, industrial manufacturing, and agricultural technology. How to explain much greater southern "development" relative to Brazilian "backwardness"? Graham points briefly to significant differences in social structure, the different roles played by southern cotton and Brazilian coffee in the growth of industrial capitalism, and dissimilar cultural legacies from a more enterprising England and an Iberian Portugal whose elites held commerce and industry in lower esteem.[22]

The South's historical experience in the nineteenth and early twentieth centuries also looks very different if juxtaposed against the experiences of what Americans and western Europeans in the twentieth century came to regard as "underdeveloped" or "developing" countries in Africa, Asia, and Latin America. "Measured against the experience of the developing world," concluded Robert Margo in 1995, "the southern economy is a success story of major proportions." Furthermore, from an intraregional perspective within the United States, "the evidently slow pace at which the South converged" on the national average of per capita income between the Civil War and World War II "was not all that unusual in the American experience" if you also examine the midwestern states as composing a region distinct from the Northeast.[23] Between 1920 and 1940 the South's per capita income held steady at about 60 percent of the national average, and the region's rate of convergence on

21. Licht, *Industrializing America*, 36. Later Licht observes that "economists estimate that had the South seceded without resistance [in 1860–61], it would have joined the ranks of independent nations as the world's fourth richest nation" (117). Cf. Smith, *Debating Slavery*, 84. Measuring wealth is, of course, different from, though related to, measuring industrial development.

22. Richard Graham, "Slavery and Economic Development: Brazil and the United States South in the Nineteenth Century," *Comparative Studies in Society and History* 23 (1981): 620–55; and Graham, "Economics or Culture? The Development of the U.S. South and Brazil in the Days of Slavery," in *What Made the South Different?* ed. Kees Gispen (Jackson: University Press of Mississippi, 1990), 97–124. When the United States abolished chattel slavery in 1863–1865, about four million slaves were emancipated. When Brazil enacted formal abolition in 1888, about 1.5 million slaves were freed.

23. Margo, "The South as an Economic Problem," 171–76.

the nation exceeded the Midwest's rate of convergence on the northeastern average. Of course, thanks to federal government spending during
World War II and then the Cold War, combined with "the twentieth-
century revolution in agricultural technology" (especially machines for
stripping and picking cotton) and with the much better public schools
that accompanied the dismantling of formal, institutionalized segregation, by 1990 southern per capita income had reached 90 percent of the
national average.[24]

As Margo suggests, what really made the late-nineteenth-century
southern economy "backward" and problematic relative to the rest of
the United States was the magnitude of the "adverse economic 'shock'"
that the region experienced as a consequence of the Civil War.[25] This
fundamental point is often overlooked amid explanations that may em-
phasize the agricultural inefficiency of postbellum sharecropped plantations as compared with consolidated antebellum plantations worked
by gang labor, or the decelerating growth rate of the British textile industry and its demand for cotton even as the emergence of a global
market brought India's agriculture into the equation, or a regional labor
market that served to exclude southerners from the emerging international labor market (i.e., foreign immigrants filling jobs in northern industries), or a poor system of education and an unskilled labor force.
Although Margo himself does not explore in detail the economic costs
of the Civil War for the South, we can turn to British economic historian Patrick O'Brien for a concise summary of the war's devastating impact on the regional economy. To be sure, the abolition of slavery brought
both de jure liberty and clear gains in "leisure and job satisfaction" to
some four million former slaves. Yet the Confederate South, with 27 per-

24. McMath, "Variations on a Theme by Henry Grady," 87–90. McMath quotes
William Faulkner's lamentation in 1956: "Our economy is no longer agricultural.
Our economy is the Federal Government." Before World War II "poor midwestern
states did not converge much faster on the richer Northeast than the South converged on the national average." But the Midwest's average per capita income
reached 92 percent of the Northeast's average in 1950 (Margo, "The South as an
Economic Problem," 174, 179 n. 26).

25. Margo, "The South as an Economic Problem," 174. Cf. Harold D. Woodman,
"Economic Reconstruction and the Rise of the New South, 1865–1900," in *Interpreting Southern History: Historiographical Essays in Honor of Sanford W. Higgin-
botham,* ed. John B. Boles and Evelyn Thomas Nolen (Baton Rouge: Louisiana State
University Press, 1987), 263–67.

cent of the U.S. population and 20 percent of the national income, suffered almost two-thirds of the war's short- and long-term costs. These
costs translate into a decline in the per capita income of white southerners of well over 40 percent below the level of 1860, as opposed to
about a 7 percent decline in the average per capita income of northerners. Although in 1860–1861 only a small number of radical abolitionists
envisioned an end to slavery without compensation to slaveholders, the
aggregate cost of uncompensated emancipation to white southerners
came to some $2.7 billion (in 1860–1861 dollars) after ratification of
the Thirteenth Amendment in 1865.[26] Granted, only one-third of the
free population in the Confederacy had belonged to the families of
slaveholders. But as C. Vann Woodward pointed out, "no ruling class of
our history ever found itself so completely stripped of its economic
foundations as did that of the South in this period"; perhaps the only
other propertied elites in modern history to undergo such expropria-
tion were slaveholders in Haiti at the end of the eighteenth century and
landowners in European or Asian countries that experienced Communist revolutions in the war-torn years of the twentieth century.[27] Add to
the $2.7 billion figure for lost slave property another $1 billion worth of
military expenditures plus the estimated costs of destroyed or damaged
persons and properties, and the total cost of the Civil War to the white
South adds up to at least $6 billion. And this excludes the dramatic fall
in the valuations of southern lands that reflected a decline in agricultural productivity resulting from the sudden termination of enslaved
and coerced labor.[28] Is it any wonder that the postbellum South suffered
from a shortage of indigenous capital and skilled labor, realities that do
much to explain what James C. Cobb calls "the colonial nature of much
of late nineteenth-century southern industrial development?" Promoters
of an industrialized "New South" sought to attract outside investors
with the lures of "an ample supply of unskilled but dirt-cheap labor

26. O'Brien, *The Economic Effects of the Civil War*, 28, 13, 21. O'Brien draws many
of these statistics from essays, listed on p. 172, by Claudia Goldin. Seen another
way: "while the North was recording a 9 percent gain in commodity output during
the Civil War decade, southern per capita income slipped by 39%" (Atack and
Passell, *New Economic View*, 378).

27. C. Vann Woodward, *Origins of the New South, 1877–1913* (Baton Rouge:
Louisiana State University Press, 1951/1971), 29; and O'Brien, *Economic Effects of
the Civil War*, 26.

28. O'Brien, *Economic Effects of the Civil War*, 12–13.

and abundant natural resources." The sort of "labor-intensive, extractive, and processing operations" that experienced the most rapid expansion during the post-Reconstruction decades, and that pushed the region's rates of industrial growth consistently ahead of national averages (albeit from a far smaller base), appear to have been "typical of an underdeveloped economy."[29] Much research over the past quarter-century has clearly demonstrated that the postbellum South's economic and political elite was neither dramatically different from nor identical to the antebellum slaveocracy. As Harold Woodman noted in 1985, "Hindsight allows us to see the growth and consolidation of a new dominant class made up of some elements of the old planter aristocracy and some newcomers who were able to capitalize on the new conditions."[30] These new conditions included a long-term decline in cotton prices, which encouraged some merchants and landowners to invest in Piedmont textile mills;[31] the new "miracle crop" of bright flue-cured to-

29. Cobb, *Industrialization and Southern Society, 1877–1984*, 16–20. Cf. Dewey W. Grantham, *The South in Modern America: A Region at Odds* (New York: HarperPerennial, 1994), 5–6; and Edward L. Ayers, *Southern Crossing: A History of the American South, 1877–1907* (New York: Oxford University Press, 1995), 58.

30. Harold D. Woodman, "The Reconstruction of the Cotton Plantation in the New South," in *Essays on the Postbellum Southern Economy*, ed. Thavolia Glymph and John J. Kushma (College Station: Texas A&M University Press, 1985), 11. Four monographs that have been especially helpful in illuminating the South's postbellum elite are Dwight B. Billings Jr., *Planters and the Making of a "New South": Class, Politics, and Development in North Carolina, 1865–1900* (Chapel Hill: University of North Carolina Press, 1979); Michael Wayne, *The Reshaping of Plantation Society: The Natchez District, 1860–1880* (Baton Rouge: Louisiana State University Press, 1983); Laurence Shore, *Southern Capitalists: The Ideological Leadership of an Elite, 1832–1885* (Chapel Hill: University of North Carolina Press, 1986); and Douglas Flamming, *Creating the Modern South: Millhands and Managers in Dalton, Georgia, 1884–1984* (Chapel Hill: University of North Carolina Press, 1992), pt. 1. Newer research demonstrates that elite white southerners "embraced" the 1867 Bankruptcy Act passed by Congress, finding it "a well-time[d] source of relief and opportunity" to escape the burdens of debt, including debt that had been secured by slave property abolished in 1863–1865. See Elizabeth Lee Thompson, *The Reconstruction of Southern Debtors: Bankruptcy after the Civil War* (Athens: University of Georgia Press, 2004).

31. Ayers, *Southern Crossing*, 59: "The textile mills were built with local capital and employed local [white] people. Until after the turn of the century, Northern capital played only a small roll in building the Southern factories." It is also important to note that in North Carolina—whose textile mills made it "the acknowledged industrial leader of the New South"—"It has been documented several times that textile mills use their power to keep high-wage industries out of their communities," since the coming of high-wage industries "might have meant unionization."

bacco grown north of the cotton belt along the Virginia–North Carolina border; and the diffusion of commercial phosphate fertilizers across the Southeast. Most important was the fundamental fact, in the succinct phrase of Atlanta editor Henry Grady, that planters were "still lords of acres, though not of slaves."[32]

Thus far I have painted in broad strokes an economic portrait of the nineteenth-century South that highlights, first, an antebellum prosperity spearheaded by agricultural slaveholders, and then a relative postbellum poverty wrought first and foremost by the devastating impact of the Civil War. We need also look for an intercontinental as well as an interregional context or perspective that may serve to "normalize" the different developmental patterns of the South and the Northeast throughout the nineteenth century, even apart from the exogenous and contingent impact of the Civil War. Keep in mind that the growing volume of transatlantic trade, the driving force behind an emerging global market, seems to have rendered David Ricardo's law of comparative advantage (now some 180 years old) highly relevant to understanding different patterns of regional development on both sides of the Atlantic Ocean. As William Parker has explained, the nineteenth-century international economy "arranged itself with heavy concentrations of industry in Northwestern Europe and the Northeastern United States," in part because almost all the new transportation techniques developed between

---

Billings, *Planters and the Making of a "New South,"* 42, 227–28. We find an antebellum analogue to the postbellum development of textile mills in the example of fourth-generation North Carolinian Edwin Michael Holt, a planter who responded to collapse of cotton prices after the Panic of 1837 (when he was thirty-four) by borrowing money and traveling to the Northeast to purchase machinery for a small spinning mill, later known as the Alamance Factory, "built on his family's land along the Haw River in rural Orange County." According to Bess Beatty, "[A]fter 1837 the Holts were fundamentally capitalists committed to industrial development." Edwin's seven sons "became successful industrialists in their own right." Edwin's slaves, of whom he owned fifty-one in 1860, "helped construct the mill buildings and mill houses and they may have worked in the dye house, but there is no evidence that they ever tended the spindles and looms." Those who worked the machinery seem to have been entirely white and three-quarters female. Beatty concludes that Holt "needed all of his slaves to perform myriad agricultural and construction tasks" (*Alamance: The Holt Family and Industrialization in a North Carolina County, 1847–1900* [Baton Rouge: Louisiana State University Press, 1999], xiii-xv, 30–31, 61–62).

32. Quotations from Robert C. McMath Jr., *American Populism: A Social History, 1877–1898* (New York: Hill & Wang, 1993), 35, 30.

1770 and 1870, especially the railroad and the ocean-going steamship, "promoted the geographical concentration of industry."[33] As for the perennial question of why England became the first nation to experience an Industrial Revolution in "its two most important and dynamic sectors: textiles and the coal/steam/iron complex," I will defer to the perceptive synthesis formulated by J. R. and William McNeill, which, in turn, reflects the influence of the insightful "world-historical" argument set forth in 2000 by Kenneth Pomeranz. "A short answer," conclude the McNeills, "is that internal characteristics (lots of coal and iron) and developments (the sociopolitical environment after 1688) combined with the tightening of the web [that is, the intensification and expansion of communication and trade] both within Britain (roads, canals, railways, postal service) and the international context (overseas trade and colonies, and population growth) to create the necessary conditions for industrialization growth), ones in which both the freedom and incentive to innovate attained unusual proportions."[34]

33. William N. Parker, *Europe, America, and the Wider World: Essays on the Economic History of Western Capitalism*, vol. 1, *Europe and the World Economy* (Cambridge: Cambridge University Press, 1984), 144–46.

34. J. R. McNeill and William McNeill, *The Human Web: A Bird's Eye View of World History* (New York: W. W. Norton, 2003), 234. Like John Majewski, the McNeills avoid discussion of the contentious concept of "capitalism." At the risk of oversimplification, Kenneth Pomeranz emphasizes the English combination of colonies and coal under a regime that was "the most pro-mercantile of Europe's national states." In the late eighteenth and early nineteenth centuries England led western Europe in breaking through "the fundamental [ecological] constraints of energy use and resource availability that had previously limited *everyone's* horizons." Easily accessible coal deposits provided a ready substitute for scarce fuel wood, and coal became essential to "Britain's breakthroughs, especially in iron, steel, steam, power, and transport." At the same time, England's "ability to take advantage of a new world of mineral-derived energy" depended on substantial colonial inputs of fiber, especially cotton, and calories in the form of cheap sugar and tea, both of which "tend to act as appetite suppressants" (*The Great Divergence*, 175, 207, 61, 218–19). After carefully reviewing the extensive literature responding to the seminal argument presented in Eric William's *Capitalism and Slavery* (1944), Kenneth Morgan has recently concluded "that transatlantic trade and slavery were indeed significant for British economic development between 1660 and 1800, especially after 1750, but as much for their stimulus to manufacturing production in textiles, metalware and hardware, receipts from the sale of invisibles, financial intermediation and business improvements as for their direct impact on capital investment and national income" (Morgan, *Slavery, Atlantic Trade and the British Economy*, 98).

The analyses offered by William Parker, Kenneth Pomeranz, and the McNeills seem easily compatible with the conceptual framework of an evolving "world economy" whose driving force from the sixteenth century was transatlantic trade. (Whether or not this globalizing economy and its regional participants should be denominated "capitalist" is a contentious issue, pregnant with meaning that is beyond the scope of this essay.)[35] In the nineteenth century this nascent "world system" became characterized by industrializing and free-labor "core" societies at one end of the developmental spectrum, and at the other end a variety of more backward "peripheries" yielding agricultural commodities and other raw materials, often with some form of coerced or "unfree" labor. This conceptual framework also helps to illuminate what Györky Ranki has termed "the dialectic of development and backwardness" as it operated within as well as between particular countries[36]—to wit, the very different paths of economic development evident in the northeastern and southern regions of the United States. As Charles Maier pointed out in a 1989 evaluation of the pathbreaking work of economic historian Alexander Gerschenkron (1904–1978), in more recent economic history "regions and sectors have tended to displace undifferentiated national economies as the appropriate units of analysis."[37]

The peripheral status of both the antebellum and postbellum Souths can be illuminated by comparing these states to the peripheral region of

---

35. Shearer Davis Bowman, *Masters and Lords: Mid-Nineteenth-Century U.S. Planters and Prussian Junkers* (New York: Oxford University Press, 1993), ch. 3, entitled "Contentious Concepts," which sees much merit in historical sociologist Immanuel Wallerstein's concept of an evolving "capitalist world-system." The best introduction to Wallerstein's argument is his "The Rise and Future Demise of the World Capitalist System: Concepts for Comparative Analysis," *Comparative Studies in Society and History* 16 (1974): 387–415; reprinted in his *The Capitalist World Economy* (Cambridge: Cambridge University Press, 1979), 1–36. For a balanced and sensible review of the scholarly debate over the "capitalist" and "modern" characteristics of the slave South, see Smith, *Debating Slavery,* esp. 87–94. A very helpful introduction to "capitalism as an historical process that has changed over time" is Richard Grassby, *The Idea of Capitalism before the Industrial Revolution* (Lanham, Md.: Rowman & Littlefield, 1999). This is a volume in the series "Critical Issues in History," edited by Donald T. Critchlow; the quotation is from p. vii of the foreword.

36. Györky Ranki, "Probleme der komparativen Geschichtsschreibung," *Jahrbuch für Geschichtswissenschaft,* 1978, pt. 2, 141.

37. Charles S. Maier, foreword to *Bread and Democracy in Germany,* by Alexander Gerschenkron (1943; reprint, Ithaca: Cornell University Press, 1989), xxix.

Europe that I happen to know best: the six East Elbian provinces (i.e., those situated entirely or in part to the east of the Elbe River) in the Kingdom of Prussia, under whose military and political leadership the German Empire was forged between 1866 and 1871.[38] Juxtaposing the U.S. South and East Elbia seems particularly appropriate since, by the eve of World War I, both the United States and Germany had surpassed Great Britain in industrial might.[39] By the same logic that identifies the South and East Elbia as agrarian peripheries, the U.S. Northeast appears to have been an emerging core region analagous in some respects to Prussia's two western provinces, the Rhineland and Westphalia, which in-

38. The idea of comparing the plantation South and its elite with Prusso-German East Elbia and its elite is hardly original with me. The pioneering work is Barrington Moore Jr., *Social Origins of Dictatorship and Democracy: Lord and Peasant in the Making of the Modern World* (Boston: Beacon Press, 1966), esp. xiv-xv, 115. Theodore S. Hamerow observes that "throughout the region of the latifundia, primarily Prussia, Russia, Austria-Hungary, southern Italy, and many parts of Spain, the modernization of agriculture failed to end the traditional dominance of the aristocratic landowner over the countryside" (*The Birth of a New Europe: State and Society in the Nineteenth Century* [Chapel Hill: University of North Carolina Press, 1983], 34). Peter Kolchin offers a masterful comparative study in *Unfree Labor: American Slavery and Russian Serfdom* (Cambridge: Harvard University Press, 1987). Maier, foreword to *Bread and Democracy,* xxvii-xxviii, offers a brief overview of literature on the Italian South as a peripheral economic region analogous in some ways to East Elbia. For a discussion of regional analogies between the Italian South and the American South that focuses on issues of culture and nation, see Don H. Doyle, *Nations Divided: America, Italy, and the Southern Question* (Athens: University of Georgia Press, 2002). See also Enrico Dal Lago and Rick Halpern, eds., *The American South and the Italian Mezzogiorno: Essays in Comparative History* (Houndsmill, Eng.: Palgrave, 2002).

39. As of 1913, "In comparative terms the index was USA 298.1, Germany 137.7, Britain 127.2" (Michael Stürmer, ed., *The German Empire: A Short History* [New York: Modern Library, 2000], 88). As David Blackbourn pointed out in 1997, "The starkly uneven regional chararacter of German industrialization has deservedly become a central theme of research in the last fifteen years" (*The Long Nineteenth Century: A History of Germany, 1780–1918* [New York: Oxford, 1997], 189). Hamerow emphasizes that "Industrialization and urbanization became possible because, to put it simply, far fewer people in the rural economy were producing far more grain, meat, butter, cheese, and eggs." Hence it is not surpising that in 1900 "the most efficient system of farm labor [in Europe] was to be found in the United Kingdom with 225 [according to an index for the development of agriculture in various European countries] and Germany with 220." Yet on the eve of the First World War, only 8 percent of the British working population was engaged in agriculture, versus 35 percent in Germany! (Hamerow, *The Birth of a New Europe*, 55, 49, 53).

cludes the Ruhr Valley of mining and metallurgical fame. To wit, consider Wolfgang Mommsen's description of "the deep-seated structural tensions that existed [in Prussia] between the western parts of the state, which were middle-class and industrial, and the agricultural provinces in the east."[40] Of course, we cannot any more posit a monolithic Prussian East Elbia than we can a monolithic American South; and we must recognize that particular developments within each region often reflected internal differences in geography and rivalries among provinces or states, towns, and even families. The eastern province of Silesia included a miniature analogue to the mountainous Appalachian South, hilly Upper Silesia, where significant mining and smelting operations had first appeared in the 1780s, although Upper Silesian coking coal proved inferior in quality to that of the Ruhr. Hence we find in Upper Silesia a vibrant "tradition of aristocratic involvement in industrial activity, a tradition that bore fruit in the post-1850 development of metallurgy" exemplified in the operations of Count Franz von Ballestrem.[41] North of Silesia, the province of Brandenburg included the metropolis

40. Wolfgang Mommsen, *Imperial Germany, 1867–1918: Politics, Culture, and Society in an Authoritarian State*, trans. Richard Deveson (London: Arnold, 1995), 54–55. Cf. Frank B. Tipton, *A History of Modern Germany since 1815* (Berkeley: University of California Press, 2003), 30–33. For a marvelous overview of agriculture and landownership, society and culture in an important nineteenth-century East Elbian province, Pomerania, see Shelley Baranowski, *The Sanctity of Rural Life: Nobility, Protestantism and Nazism in Weimar Prussia* (New York: Oxford, 1995), 17–38.

41. Lawrence Shofer, *The Formation of a Modern Labor Force: Upper Silesia, 1865–1914* (Berkeley: University of California Press, 1975), 8, 29, 42–43. In the more remote Appalachian South, "small quantities of coal were mined and marketed in parts of western Virginia as early as the 1790s." However, it was only after the Civil War that serious development of Appalachian coalfields commenced in tandem with the postbellum railroad boom. If we recall John Majeski's work, it seems less ironic that Philadelphia investors, in response to the urgings of former Confederate major and New York native Jedidiah Hotchkiss, financed construction of the Norfolk and Western Railroad, which, in turn, transformed the Flat Top Mountain region in southern West Virginia into "one of the most productive coal fields in the world" (Ronald D. Eller, *Miners, Millhands, and Mountaineers: Industrialization of the Appalachian South, 1880–1930* [Knoxville: University of Tennessee Press, 1982], 4, 50). For a sophisticated monograph that places the nineteenth-century development of eastern Kentucky within the context of a "capitalist world system" where "capitalist development occurs evenly across geographical space and historical time," see Dwight B. Billings and Kathleen M. Blee, *The Road to Poverty: The Making of Wealth and Poverty in Appalachia* (Cambridge: Cambridge University Press, 2000); quotation from p. 40.

of Berlin, which saw its population climb from less than 200,000 in 1800 to over 400,000 at midcentury to over two million in 1910. (The nineteenth-century South's largest city, New Orleans, had fewer than 120,000 inhabitants in 1850.) As "the prime rail node in Europe," and with a handful of joint-stock banks centered in the city acquiring "almost undisputed sway over the German capital market," by the 1870s imperial Berlin combined most of the functions played by Chicago, New York City, and Washington, D.C., in the United States.[42] Of course, political decisions and developments exerted tremendous influence over regional and national patterns of economic development in both countries. Indeed, the creation of an interstate U.S. free-trade zone under the Constitution of 1787 found a later analogue in the 1834 formation of the German Customs Union under the leadership of Prussia and with the support of anti-Austrian, anti-Hapsburg proponents of a unified "Small Germany" [Kleindeutschland].[43] Thanks in part to Berlin's sta-

42. For Berlin's growing population, see Blackbourn, *Long Nineteenth Century,* 33, 199–200. On New Orleans, which at midcentury began "its long decline" as an export city relative to New York, see David R. Goldfield, *Cotton Fields and Skyscrapers: Southern City and Region, 1607–1980* (Baton Rouge: Louisiana State University Press, 1983), 30, 126. On Berlin as "the prime rail node in Europe," at the intersection of eleven main railroad lines radiating from the city, see Alexandra Richie, *Faust's Metropolis: A History of Berlin* (New York: Carroll & Graf, 1998), 140. On Berlin's "almost undisputed sway over the German capital market," see Helmut Böhne, *An Introduction to the Social and Economic History of Germany: Politics and Economic Change in the Nineteenth and Twentieth Centuries,* trans. W. R. Lee (New York: St. Martin's Press, 1978), 64; and also Richie, *Faust's Metropolis,* 148–49. Germany adopted a law of free incorporation in 1870. Frank B. Tipton Jr. has computed that by 1882, the German Empire's "group of industrial regions," with a quarter of the population, "included the urban centers of Berlin and the Hanse cities (Bremen, Lubeck, and Hamburg) on the one hand and the Kingdom of Saxony [distinct from the Prussian province of Saxony] and the Prussian provinces of Westphalia and the Rhineland on the other" (*Regional Variations in the Economic Development of Germany during the Nineteenth Century* [Middletown, Conn.: Wesleyan University Press, 1976], 45–46).

43. A concise and persuasive case for the importance of the Prusso-German Customs Union, which by 1848 included twenty-eight of the thirty-nine German states, and which encouraged the growth of a German railroad network even before the creation of the Prusso-German Empire in 1871, has recently been made by Hagen Schulze in his wonderfully illustrated *Germany: A New History,* trans. Deborah Lucas Schneider (Cambridge: Harvard University Press, 1998), 139–40. See also Eric Dorn Brose, *German History 1789–1871: From the Holy Roman Empire to the Bismarckian Reich* (Providence: Berghahn Books, 1997), 117–18; and Richie, *Faust's Metropolis,* 141.

tus as the capital of both the Kingdom of Prussia and the German Empire, East Elbia remained the preponderant heartland of the Hohenzollern monarchy throughout the nineteenth century. In marked contrast, during the 1860s the South became subordinate to an economic, political, and military alliance between the free states of the Northeast and the Midwest, whose citizens saw themselves as the political, economic, and cultural heartland of the U.S. republic.[44]

Beginning in the sixteenth and seventeenth centuries, respectively, East Elbia and the South had developed something of a symbiotic economic relationship with northwestern Europe, Britain in particular, by using unfree labor (i.e., serfs and slaves) to produce cash crops (grain, tobacco, rice) for which population growth and mercantile sophistication in the Netherlands as well as England created a growing demand. Beginning in the late eighteenth century, England's textile-based "First Industrial Revolution" accelerated consumption of East Elbian grain and wool even as it created a dynamic new market for southern cotton. In both peripheral regions the principal beneficiaries of this foreign demand were landed elites: the "Junker" proprietors of legally privileged "knight's estates" (*Rittergüter*) and the slaveholding proprietors of plantations.[45] However, accelerating British demand for East Elbian and southern staple crops affected the regions' labor systems very differently. Whereas southern slavery received a new lease on life as plantations expanded generally westward from the Atlantic seaboard, the particular demographic, geographic, ethnic/racial, and military complexion of East Elbian society meant that de jure serfdom (i.e., hereditary bondage to the soil) was abolished during Prussia's "Reform Era" of 1807–1819, although the obligations of smallholding peasants to perform labor services (if they could manage to hold onto their farmland) remained in force until after the Revolution of 1848. Well before mid-century,

---

44. Steven Hahn, "Class and Status in Postemancipation Societies: Southern Planters in Comparative Perspective," *American Historical Review* 95 (Feb. 1990): 75–98, emphasizes "the swift and dramatic decline in the fortunes of the Southern planter class" after the Civil War, in contrast with the enduring power of the Prussian Junkers in the wake of the Stein-Hardenberg era and German national unification.

45. It is both easy and tempting to exaggerate the class unity of the planter and Junker elites, but both landed classes were, of course, internally split by local, state/provincial, ideological, and personal differences. See Bowman, *Masters and Lords*, esp. 7–10, 206–16.

however, most labor on Junker estates was being performed by resident cottagers (often termed *Insten*), whose legal status as a species of "day-laborers on annual contracts" was analogous to that of sharecroppers as defined by post-Reconstruction southern state legislatures.[46] Because Junker estate owners retained local judicial authority over their laborers until 1849, and the right to exercise community police power until 1872, the East Elbian knight's estate retained much of the authoritarian character of the slave plantation insofar as both constituted what a late-nineteenth-century observer labeled an "almost completely independent governmental authority [*Herrschaftsverband*], a state within a state."[47]

As we have seen, a plantation economy based on slavery did have a decidedly negative effect on the rate of urban and industrial growth in the South vis-à-vis the Northeast. Heywood Fleisig has argued that slavery, by relaxing the labor constraint that planters would have faced under a system of free labor, served to retard diversified economic development by increasing the amount of capital that could be invested profitably in commercial agriculture.[48] *Rittergut* agriculture seems to have acted as a similar brake on the rate of East Elbian industrialization; in the words of Hannah Schissler, "agriculture itself absorbed labor power, attracted entrepreneurial talent, and required capital."[49] After 1807 affluent nonnobles could, and many did, purchase knights' estates along with the aristocratic privileges and status that accompanied them. Though the expansive planter elite was much larger and more fluid than was landlocked Junkerdom at midcentury, in 1856 untitled commoners owned nearly 45 percent of the approximately 11,500 knight's estates in the East Elbian provinces, helping to effect what Reinhard Koselleck has

46. Ibid., 18, 221.

47. August Meitzen and Friedrich Grossman, *Der Boden und der landwirtschaftlichen Verhältnisse des preussischen Staates,* 8 vols. (Berlin: Paul Parey, 1868–1908), 6:286–87. See also Bowman, *Masters and Lords,* 18–19.

48. Heywood Fleisig, "Slavery, the Supply of Agricultural Labor, and the Industrialization of the South," *Journal of Economic History* 36 (1976): 581–83. See also William N. Parker, "Capitalism: Southern Style," in *Europe, America, and the Wider World: Essays on the Economic History of Western Capitalism,* vol. 2, *America and the Wider World* (Cambridge: Cambridge University Press, 1991), 87–100.

49. Hannah Schissler, *Preussische Agrargesellschaft im Wandel: Wirtschaftliche, gesellschaftliche, under politische Transformationsprozesse von 1763 bis 1847,* Kritische Studien zur Geschichtswissenschaft, vol. 33 (Gottingen: Vandenhoeck & Ruprecht, 1978), 187.

termed "the creeping transformation of the landed nobility/*Ritterstand* into an entrepreneurial class of manorial lords/*Gutsherren*."[50] Even the proud aristocrat Otto von Bismarck (1815–1898) studied soil chemistry at the Eldena Agricultural Institute in the late 1830s, during his mandatory year of military service. Living at the family's Pomeranian *Rittergut* Kniephof from 1839 to 1845 (when he inherited the more famous Brandenburg estate Schönhausen upon his father's death), Bismarck became involved in the Pomeranian Economic Society at Regenwalde, filling his account book with entries about crop yields. Hence he wrote to an old friend in 1844 that for five years he had devoted himself "with some success to the improvement of my [crop] rotation."[51]

Although the great majority of mid-nineteenth-century planters and Junkers saw no compelling incentives to make substantial and risky investments in business ventures unrelated to agriculture, a significant number did. East Elbia's far greater population density and more diversified agriculture meant that extractive rural industries such as distilling potato whiskey or refining beet sugar could yield substantial profits for entrepreneurial Junkers like Bismarck and the commoner Johann Friedrich Leberecht Pistorious, a Berlin liquor merchant who purchased the Brandenburg estate Weissensee in 1821. Across the Atlantic, some planters, from Southside Virginia to the South Carolina Upcountry to the Natchez District of Mississippi, compiled diversified investment portfolios that included holdings in railroads, mines, and even factories.[52] Consider the fascinating example of ardent states' rights advocate

50. The figure of 45 percent is based on figures in Karl Friedrich Rauer, *Hand-Matrikel der in sämtlichen Kreisen des preussischen Staats auf Kreis- und Landtagen vertretenen Rittergüter* (Berlin: Durch die Herausgeber, 1857), 451. The quotation is from Reinhard Koselleck, *Preussen zwischen Reform und Revolution: Allgemeines Landrecht, Verwaltung, und sociale Bewegung von 1791 bis 1848,* 2nd corrected ed. (Stuttgart: Ernst Klett Verlag, 1975), 507.

51. Erich Marks, *Bismarck: Eine Biographie, 1815–1851* (Stuttgart & Berlin: Cotta, 1915), 179–80; Ernst Engelberg, *Bismarck: Urprusse und Reichsgründer* (Berlin: Sideler, 1985), 149, 166–69, 180–81.

52. See Bowman, *Masters and Lords,* 102, 56. On late antebellum planters as diversified investors in Warren County, Mississippi, see Christopher Morris, *Becoming Southern: The Evolution of a Way of Life, Warren County and Vicksburg, Mississippi, 1770–1860* (New York: Oxford, 1995), 164–68. Across the Atlantic, by the 1870s Bismarck's political successes in engineering German unification had made him a wealthy man. As the owner of several dispersed estates, Bismarck found that agriculture pure and simple could no longer yield a profit, and "attacked his financial problem by becoming a petty rural industrialist," establishing potato

and secessionist Richard T. Archer (1797–1867), a Virginia native who attended William and Mary College before migrating in 1824 to the Natchez District, where in 1860 he owned five plantations in two counties and some five hundred slaves. In October of 1856, Archer wrote happily to his wife, Ann, from New York City that he had been reelected to the board of directors of the Southern Pacific Railroad, in which he owned almost six thousand shares. He expected the shares to be worth one hundred dollars apiece before the end of 1857, and thereby to "provide a good estate for each of our children." However, in the aftermath of the Panic of 1857, he wrote to his eldest son, Abram, in May of 1858: "I expect we will be swindled out of all that we have invested in the SPRR Co." It is significant that the Natchez District's slaveholding elite also included many professionals born and educated in the Northeast: men like lawyer/judge George Winchester (1793–1851) of Massachusetts, a Yale graduate, and physician John C. Jenkins (1809–1855) of Pennsylvania, who studied medicine in Philadelphia. Hence, as William Shade has concluded, "it is difficult to imagine any group of [antebellum] Americans more cosmopolitan in their tastes and connections than these Natchez nabobs."[53]

We have briefly discussed the debilitating impact of the Civil War on the wealth and economy of the postbellum South. It will be helpful to trace the historical trajectory of East Elbia's economy and society during the second half of the nineteenth century. The 1840s to the 1870s were something of a "golden age" for Junker agriculture, as the growth of urban markets in Berlin and in the Kingdom of Saxony, together with the gradual lowering of internal transport costs due to better roads and new railroad construction (coming after the formation of the Prusso-German Customs Union in 1834) kept domestic grain prices high even

---

distilleries and paper factories (Otto Pflanze, *Bismarck and the Development of Germany*, vol. 2, *The Period of Consolidation, 1871–1880* [Princeton: Princeton University Press, 1990], 67–77).

53. William G. Shade, "In Re Those 'Prebourgeois' Planters" in *Inside the Natchez Trace Collection: New Sources for Southern History*, ed. Katharine J. Adams and Lewis L. Gould (Baton Rouge: Louisiana State University Press, 1999), 173. Cf. in the same volume, Morton Rothstein, "Acquisitive Pursuits in a Slaveholding Society: Business History in the Natchez Trace Collection," 93–114. Richard T. Archer Family Papers, Boxes 2E646 and 2E647, Natchez Trace Collection, Center for American History at the University of Texas at Austin. Archer makes many appearances in the Adams and Gould essay collection.

though American grain started to penetrate the English market in the 1850s, and higher quality wool from Australia began to supply British woolen mills.[54] (Compare the dual impact on postbellum southern prosperity of English cotton mills' slowing growth rates in output along with competition from cotton growers on the Indian subcontinent.) During the post-1873 depression, and more dramatically in the mid-1890s (the peak of the Populist movement in the United States), eastern Prusso-Germany faced what Mommsen labels "a severe crisis in agriculture" due to "the long-term decline in farm prices." As the Junkers' economic position became ever more precarious, they accepted "an alliance with heavy industry" in the German legislature by means of "a pro-tariff coalition of 'rye and iron.'" At the same time they exploited all the more blatantly what Hans-Jürgen Puhle has termed their "privileged position next to the bureaucracy and the military" in the Prusso-German monarchical establishment. "To overstate the case somewhat," concludes Wolfgang Mommsen, "from now onwards Prussia degenerated into a welfare agency for needy landowners."[55]

Concurrently, as emigrants from rural East Elbia moved by the hundreds of thousands to German cities (including Berlin) and overseas, the expanding cultivation of sugar beets increased Junkerdom's demand for large numbers of seasonal laborers. Beginning in the 1880s, and despite legal obstacles from 1885 to 1891, Junker estate owners turned to the seasonal employment of low-wage migratory workers from the Polish districts of the Russian and Austro-Hungarian Empires. Also during the late nineteenth century, manorial lords were replacing their cottagers' fixed payment in kind (i.e., the *Deputat* customarily allotted to *Insten*) with cash wages whose level was determined by the wages

54. During the 1850s, "eastern landlords, western industrialists, and government bureaucrats, concluded a de facto truce whereby the government undertook to lessen the legal and financial impediments to western industrial growth while constructing railroads that would open the markets of central Germany to eastern agriculture" (Tipton, *Regional Variations in the Economic Development of Germany*, 53).

55. Mommsen, *Imperial Germany*, 68–69, 47–49; and Hans-Jürgen Puhle, "Aspekte der Agrarkapitalismus in 'Organisierten Kapitalismus,'" in *Sozialgeschichte Heute: Festschrift für Hans Rosenberg zum 70. Geburtstag*, ed. Hans-Ulrich Wehler (Göttingen: Vandenhoeck & Ruprecht, 1974), 547. Quotations on "an alliance" and "pro-tariff coalition" from Maier, foreword to *Bread and Democracy*, xvi. According to Michael Stürmer, Bismarck recognized that he had "the material to forge a solid and docile center-right coalition of *Rittergut und Hochofen*, the landed estate and the blast furnace" (*The German Empire*, 39).

paid to migratory Polish workers. This, in turn, encouraged more Prusso-Germans to leave the countryside, thereby accelerating the recruitment of seasonal Polish farmhands, whose numbers exceeded 430,000 in 1914 (about one-seventh of all German agricultural workers).[56] Across the north Atlantic, some German immigrants to the United States, along with millions of other "new immigrants" from eastern and southern Europe, took jobs in northern cities and factories. By encouraging kinsmen back home to make the transatlantic trek, they fostered integration of northern and transatlantic labor markets. Few southern sharecroppers and other manual laborers participated in a U.S. "national" labor market until the "Great Migration" north and west during the era of the First and Second World Wars.[57]

On both sides of the north Atlantic toward the end of the nineteenth century, commercial farmers raising grain and cotton for an increasingly integrated world market faced falling prices. As both the German Empire and the United States became powerful and expansive industrial nations, within their more rural backwaters it became clear "what backwardness was; backward regions were agricultural, and agriculture was in trouble." Both the United States and Germany produced agrarian revolts that called for an inflationary bimetallic currency and denounced the exploitative triad of big corporations, big banks, and big cities. In Germany the Farmers' or Agrarian League (*Bund der Landwirte*) blossomed in East Elbia in 1893 and took the lead in pushing the German Conservative Party (established in 1876, and dominated by Junkers) toward what Hans Rosenberg has termed "the recasting of 'aristocratic' into 'plebiscitary' conservatism." In the American South the agrarian revolt echoed the "passionate opposition to modern life personified as the City, Industry, Socialism, and the Jew" that infused "agrarian conservatism" in Prusso-Germany. After mobilizing in the Farmers' Alliances of the 1880s, southern agrarians joined with allied movements from the

56. Bowman, *Masters and Lords*, 110–11. "Rapid increases of population and industrial development in the Berlin-Potsdam district, on the one hand, and slow development and stagnating population in the eastern regions, on the other, were related phenomena" (Tipton, *Regional Variations in the Economic Development of Germany*, 109).

57. See Gavin Wright, *Old South, New South: Revolutions in the Southern Economy since the Civil War* (New York: Basic Books, 1986), esp. ch. 4; O'Brien, *Economic Effects of the Civil War*, 34; and Margo, "The South as an Economic Problem," 169–70.

Great Plains and the Mountain West to found the People's Party in 1892. But even after endorsing a free-silver Democrat in 1896, the agrarian revolt could carry a national election. Within the South the Populist movement ran afoul of both the entrenched Democratic party and a white Negrophobia which, shrewdly exploited by Democratic politicians, became translated into lynchings and state movements for segregation and disfranchisement.[58]

"Juxtapositions of the modern and the archaic constantly jarred" both the South and East Elbia.[59] But the Junker elite and its allies, including a far more substantial and vociferous class of independent artisans and small shopkeepers (*Mittelstand*) than existed in the United States, could muster the political clout in Prusso-Germany to win additional protective tariffs for agricultural commodities in 1887 in order "to save the landowners from bankruptcy," despite the high cost "not only to German industry and the growing number of urban consumers, but also in terms of foreign policy, especially toward Tsarist Russia."[60] The American South and trans-Mississippi West remained subaltern regions within the United States, which at the end of the century had a far less unified national elite than did the German Empire.[61] Hence industrial interests in the U.S. could maintain high protective tariffs on manufactured goods from the 1860s to the 1910s without having to make the kind of financial concessions to southern agrarians that German industrialists gave to East Elbian landowners. To be sure, "northern business

58. Hans Rosenberg, "Die Pseudodemocratisierung der Rittergutsbesitzerklasse," in his *Probleme der deutschen Sozialgeschichte* (Frankfurt am Main: Suhrkamp, 1969), 35. Other quotations from Tipton, *Regional Variations in the Economic Development of Germany,* 118. A marvelous overview of late-nineteenth-century southern politics is provided by Grantham, *The South in Modern America,* 8–22.

59. Quotation from Ayers, *Southern Crossing,* 110.

60. Stürmer, *The German Empire,* 40. According to Blackbourn, *Long Nineteenth Century,* "Agriculture was, along with the *Mittelstand,* one of the noisiest interest groups. It gained significant concessions, the Junker estates most of all, although the importance of protective tariffs in the pattern of favouritism has been exaggerated" (350).

61. In Germany "a new ruling class was emerging, which combined the formerly separate elements of industrial and agrarian wealth with the professional elites and cut across all provincial boundaries," drawing on the works and words of John R. Gillis and Nikolaus von Preradovich (Otto Pflanze, *Bismarck and the Development of Germany,* vol. 3, *The Period of Fortification, 1880–1898* [Princeton: Princeton University Press, 1990], 13).

interests anxious to maintain economic stability in the South," explains Dewey Grantham, did make political concessions to southern leaders by encouraging the U.S. Senate to block "the so-called Lodge Force Bill" adopted by the House of Representatives in 1890 so as to strengthen Republican party control of the national government by authorizing federal supervision of elections south of the Mason-Dixon line.[62] Six years later, however, the GOP's resounding defeat of Democratic and Populist presidential nominee William Jennings Bryan marked the national demise of the agrarian revolt fomented in the South and West.

Examining comparatively the historical trajectories of the American South and Prusso-German East Elbia over the course of the nineteenth century serves to illustrate the importance of differing regional patterns of economic development within countries as well as among nations, within as well as among continents. Instead of seeing some agricultural regions as simply "backward" relative to more "modern" industrializing and urbanizing areas, we can see how complementary as well as competitive relations among a variety of regional/local economies and social structures seem to have been part and parcel of both evolving nation-states and an emerging global market, the latter driven for most of the nineteenth century primarily by the dramatic growth of transatlantic commerce. Through comparisons across regions and continents, it becomes clearer that at least the transatlantic history of our "modern" world economy has involved both cooperation and conflict between less-developed, peripheral "southern" or "eastern" regions on the one hand, and more developed "northern" or "western" core areas on the other. While exploring these interregional and intercontinental interactions, students of the United States continue to address longstanding questions about America's or the South's "exceptionalism" within a much broader and more fertile historical context.

---

62. Grantham, *The South in Modern America*, 9. It is indicative of the different levels of political power or status enjoyed by East Elbia and the South in the late nineteenth century that southerners paid "far more" into the national treasury than they received, "with the region running an annual deficit of $9 per capita" (Ayers, *Southern Crossing*, 85).

The Idea of Southern Economic Backwardness

A Comparative View of
the United States and Italy

Susanna Delfino

The southern regions of the United States and Italy, so profoundly different in many aspects of their historical experience, have shared a similar indictment for backwardness.[1] An overview of the two Souths'

1. Apart from the obvious difference constituted by the presence of slavery in one of the two southern societies under consideration, the most glaring contrast between them appears to be that concerning political-institutional arrangements. The U.S. South was part of a larger national entity within which it enjoyed political preeminence up to the Civil War. Thanks to the large middle-class composition of the population, white southerners had access to a broad political participation. During the 1830s, participation was extended to the lower classes in many states through constitutional revisions. None of this applied to the Italian South, which was a centuries-old independent kingdom swinging between a more or less enlightened absolutism and a constitutional monarchy with no established pattern of evolution. Here, despite some participatory concessions to the upper-middle strata of the society, the lower classes were barred from politics.

The Italian South is usually referred to as the *Mezzogiorno,* a definition suggesting interregional opposition and laden with the same value judgments as the words *North* and *South* came to conjure in the United States. For reasons of expediency, the two southern regions under discussion will be called the Italian and the United States', or American, South, respectively, throughout the essay. With these designations I mean to indicate all the slave states as far as the American case is concerned, and all the territories belonging to the Kingdom of Naples, which was renamed the Kingdom of the Two Sicilies following the monarchical restoration of 1816.

historical course points to the 1850s as crucial in the elaboration of this idea of their being underdeveloped. Moreover, at the end of that decade, both Souths were shattered by momentous events: the American Civil War and the Unification of Italy, respectively.

Although the American case never gave rise to the formalization of a "southern problem" comparable to the Italian one, there too a debate on the economic conditions of the South unfolded from the 1830s and culminated, a century later, in an official acknowledgement of its being "the nation's No. 1 economic problem."[2]

Recent historiography has cogently argued that ideas of both Souths appear to be intellectual constructs, largely built upon cultural/ideological assumptions, measured against a standard of reference: the North.[3] In this way, notions of "difference" and "distinctiveness" inevitably acquire derogatory meanings, usually construed as amounting to outright inferiority. Ideas of the South as backward seem firmly rooted in the economic dimension, whereby negative evaluations of a region's economic performance are sought as a confirmation for allegedly deep-seated structural deficiencies. The economic realm should therefore provide us with the clearest ground for investigation, if we wish to test the validity of those indictments of backwardness that so powerfully shaped negative images of both the American and the Italian Souths.

Exploring the boundary between the "real" and the "imagined" in constructing ideas of the two Souths would reveal much about both the northern and the southern societies. It would add new insights to our understanding of the traits of a supposed southern distinctiveness. The adoption of a comparative approach is also suggested by important work of the past half century, mainly conducted by economic historians

2. In a prefatory letter to the *Report on Economic Conditions of the South,* appearing in 1938, Franklin Delano Roosevelt wrote: "It is my conviction that the South presents right now the nation's No. 1 economic problem—the nation's problem, not merely the South's" (Frank Friedel, *Franklin Delano Roosevelt: A Rendezvous with Destiny* [Boston: Little, Brown, 1990], 283).

3. David L. Carlton, "How American is the American South?" in *The South as an American Problem,* ed. Larry J. Griffin and Don H. Doyle (Athens: University of Georgia Press, 1995), 33–56; Susan Mary Grant, *North over South: Northern Nationalism and American Identity in the Antebellum Era* (Lawrence: University Press of Kansas, 2000), 19–36; John A. Davis, "Changing Perspectives on Italy's 'Southern Problem,'" in *Italian Regionalism: History, Identity and Politics,* ed. C. Levy (Oxford: Oxford University Press, 1996), 53–68.

such as Alexander Gerschenkron, Franklin Mendels, and Sidney Pollard,[4] that has enormously widened our sensibilities on issues of "development" and "backwardness" in a historical perspective. By making these two concepts more relative and flexible, these scholars have exposed the dogmatic nature of the interpretive framework subscribed to by a large majority of historians, especially in respect to the pre-1860 period. The emphasis these authors have placed on the necessity to look at economic transformation as a transnational and global phenomenon amply justifies comparison between the American and the Italian Souths, two regions that were deeply enmeshed in the rise and development of merchant capitalism and international trade.

The history of two staple-crop-producing, export-oriented regions such as the United States' and the Italian Souths shows a constant concern with dependency: a condition that was much enhanced during the second half of the eighteenth century by the ever-increasing spreading of capitalist market relations. At the beginning of the following century, the adverse effects of market fluctuations and international politics on their economic well-being constituted a pressing concern for southerners of both countries, who seemed to understand well the meaning and long-term implications of "unequal exchange."[5]

As a result, the need to abandon specialized agriculture in favor of diversification was already an old theme in southern economic discourse at the close of the Napoleonic Wars, when Great Britain emerged as the uncontested arbiter of seaborne trade. In the southern colonies of North America, one of the earliest advocates of diversification was Robert

4. Alexander Gerschenkron, *Economic Backwardness in Historical Perspective* (Cambridge: Harvard University Press, 1962); Franklin Mendels, "Proto-Industrialization: The First Phase of the Process of Industrialization," *Journal of Economic History* 32 (1972); Sidney Pollard, *Peaceful Conquest: The Industrialization of Europe, 1760–1970* (Oxford: Oxford University Press, 1981).

5. I am here referring to the theory set forth by the Latin American *dependistas* school of Raul Prebish and Theotonio Dos Santos. By investigating the relationship between "centers" and "peripheries" within the international capitalist system, this school of thought has much improved our understanding of the historical role and special problems of economies such as those under consideration. See Jesse Love, "Raul Prebish and the Origins of the Doctrine of Unequal Exchange," *Latin American Research Review* 15 (1980): 45–72; Andre Gunder Frank, *Lumpenbourgeoisie, Lumpendevelopment: Dependence, Class and Politics in Latin America* (New York: Monthly Review Press, 1972). This latter author tries to establish a comparison between Latin American countries and the southern United States.

Beverley who, in *The History and Present State of Virginia* (1705), warmly supported measures to foster urban growth and encourage manufacturing. In the Kingdom of Naples, economic diversification was urged by many "enlightened" reformers, notably Ferdinando Galiani in his treatise *Della Moneta* (1751). In continuity with the old Virginia mercantilists, George Washington and James Madison endorsed the development of a more diversified economy. The Neapolitan *Illuministi*, from Antonio Genovesi to Ferdinando Galiani and Mario Pagano, although sensitive to the appeal of economic liberalism, assigned great importance to the development of manufacturing, and were followed by a new generation of reformers of a mercantilist persuasion such as Domenico Grimaldi and Giuseppe Spiriti. The latter believed that "liberty is a powerful lever to uplift the arts, but the fulcrum of this lever must be protection by the government."[6]

The mercantilist vision, with its fear of competition and its attendant emphasis on economic specialization on a geographical basis, implied the notion of dependency. This awareness found expression in southern economic thought as a perennial wavering between adhesion to either the laissez-faire or the mercantilist philosophy. Regulation, so white southerners reasoned, produced exploitation of the agrarian economies; its lack engendered dependency. Many southerners, both in Italy and the United States, made of the Smithian economic theory a convenient theoretical instrument to vent their aspirations to independence and freedom. They especially appreciated Adam Smith's argument in favor of the primacy of agriculture over commerce as well as his plea for a balanced development led by an agricultural sector organized by relatively small, efficient holdings. It is not hard to recognize here the source of inspiration for early Jeffersonian thought.[7]

Other white southerners believed instead that a state-regulated, diverse economy was the surest means to deliver themselves from an increasing dependence on the whims of international politics and the vagaries of the markets. However, the boundary between supporters of free trade and mercantilists was not always so clear-cut. In the attempt

6. Giuseppe Spiriti, *Riflessioni economico-politiche relative alle due province di Calabria con un breve prospetto economico della città di Messina* (Naples: Vincenzo Flauto, 1793), 154. See also Domenico Grimaldi, *Osservazioni economiche sopra la manifattura e il commercio delle sete* (Naples: Giuseppe Maria Porcelli, 1780).

7. Jacob J. Persky, *The Burden of Dependency: Colonial Themes in Southern Economic Thought* (Baltimore: Johns Hopkins University Press, 1992), 1–27.

to reconcile their assertion of the principles of free trade with the avoidance of ultimate economic dependency, neither Thomas Jefferson nor James Madison escaped the influence of the mercantilist doctrine and, in 1793, urged vigorous measures of protection, especially directed against England. The slow but steady shift in Jefferson's economic thought was signaled, after the War of 1812, by his final resolve that the time had come "to place the manufacturer by the side of the agriculturalist."[8]

Despite the complexity of positions resulting from growing awareness of the apparent irreconcilability between two equally cherished aspirations—prosperity and liberty—mercantilists and libertarians alike could nonetheless agree on the primacy of agriculture. Stimulated by the growing European demand for foodstuffs and other staple commodities, during the second half of the eighteenth century southerners of both countries concentrated on the promotion of agriculture to attain qualitative and quantitative improvement of production through agricultural diversification and the adoption of new techniques. To this end, agricultural societies and planters' clubs sprang up; notable among them was the agricultural society of Charleston, South Carolina, founded in 1785. In late-eighteenth-century Virginia, the most influential agricultural reformer was John Taylor of Caroline, whose writings on soil conservation, diversification, and the rotation of crops were fundamental in encouraging a significant shift from tobacco to wheat as the major crop. Between 1768 and 1773, wheat and flour exports from Virginia and Maryland alone equaled 25 percent of total exports from Pennsylvania and New York. In 1784, prospects for southern agriculture seemed so rosy as to lead James Madison to admit that "this country [Virginia] has indirectly tasted some of the fruits of independence." His impressions were indeed correct, for in 1792 the South contributed to national exports with over 60 percent of the corn, 63 percent of the wheat, and 38 percent of the flour.[9]

8. Thomas Jefferson to Benjamin Austin, Jan. 18, 1816, in *The Writings of Thomas Jefferson*, ed. Andrew A. Lipscomb and Albert E. Bergh (Washington, D.C.: Thomas Jefferson Memorial Association of the United States, 1903–1904), 20 vols., 16:391–92; Frank W. Taussig, *The Tariff History of the United States* (New York: G. P. Putnam's Sons, 1931), 14–15.

9. Lewis C. Gray, *History of Agriculture in the Southern United States to 1860* (Washington, D.C.: Carnegie Institution, 1933), 2 vols., 1:780–84, 2:606–11, 678–81; Robert E. Shalhope, *John Taylor of Caroline: Pastoral Republican* (Columbia: University of South Carolina Press, 1980). The quotation from James Madison

In the Kingdom of Naples, Domenico Grimaldi, a disciple of Genovesi's, was a major apostle of agricultural improvement and of the founding of agricultural schools. An extensive landowner and a cosmopolitan man, attentive to foreign developments in agricultural methods, Grimaldi was a member of the economic societies of Paris and Bern and the founder of the Calabrian economic society. His commitment to modernization was not, however, confined to theory. He was, in fact, the initiator of a new technique in the manufacture of olive oil that he introduced in Calabria and helped disseminate in other parts of the South. Another reformer, Giuseppe Palmieri, writing in the early nineteenth century, was perhaps the major southern theorist of a capitalistic development of agriculture based on extensive landowning. He also advocated the kingdom's independence from foreign carrying trade (i.e., building a merchant fleet of their own).[10]

Generally speaking, free traders were not averse to manufacturing in and of itself, but they differed from mercantilists on the importance to be assigned to it within the economy. Even archagrarian John Taylor, who went so far as to openly embrace the physiocrats' theories, never rejected manufacturing in principle. Rather, he was extremely suspicious of moneyed capital and its power to subjugate all other economic interests. Nor was the free-trade philosophy, soon to become the creed of the agrarians of both Souths, theoretically opposed to some sort of state intervention to provide for a measure of protection aimed at forwarding agricultural interests and securing general economic independence.[11]

With capitalism largely established as a desirable system—the only one able to promote endless progress of nations—the economic debates that stirred the Western world in the early part of the nineteenth century mainly revolved around the relative weight and reciprocal role to

---

is found in Merrill Jensen, *The New Nation: A History of the United States during the Confederation, 1781–1789* (Boston: Northeastern University Press, 1981), 235. James A. Henretta, *The Origins of American Capitalism* (Boston: Northeastern University Press, 1991), 94–95.

10. Franco Venturi, ed., *Riformatori napoletani* (Milan and Naples: Ricciardi, 1962), 456–72; Giuseppe Palmieri, *Della ricchezza nazionale* (Milan: G. G. Destefanis, 1805), 205.

11. Shalhope, *John Taylor of Caroline*. The popularity of physiocratic doctrines in late-eighteenth-century New England is noted by Jonathan Prude, *The Coming of Industrial Order: Town and Factory Life in Rural Massachusetts, 1810–1860* (Cambridge: Cambridge University Press, 1983), 39.

be assigned to agriculture, commerce, and industry, respectively. In an age in which industrialization was still a new phenomenon, while agriculture and landed property retained their ascendancy as principal sources of human happiness, the appeal exerted by the physiocratic theories combined with the Smithian and Malthusian emphasis on the propriety of placing political power in the hands of the landed aristocracies to shape the economic mind of both Italian and American southerners.

The launching of the American Union, between 1787 and 1789, had taken place under the aegis of a Federalist philosophy that saw economic regulation by the central authority as a necessary means to secure national growth and, to white southerners especially, emancipation from the European powers with which they traded most: Great Britain and France. Whatever their views about the new political-institutional order, all white southerners agreed that their first priority was the building of their own economic independence. To nationalists like Washington and Madison, the still mild differentiation between regional economies appeared a reliable premise for a balanced development.[12] Other white southerners, however, like Richard Henry Lee and George Mason, foresaw the impending threat of the imposition of a new commercial system dominated by the northern states, which would do nothing but reproduce the same sort of dependency the southern colonies had suffered under the British. Despite Alexander Hamilton's contention that "with respect to cotton . . . the best way will be to manufacture it where it grows," they shivered at hearing him and other northerners talk about "a mutually advantageous regional division."[13] Consequently, they opposed centralization as represented by the federal form of government. Although the expectations of southern Federalists rested on the observation of present conditions and the evaluation of future perspectives, the fears of the Antifederalists proved correct in the long run. Some

12. According to the report prepared by Philadelphia-born political economist Tench Coxe, in 1810 there were no substantial disparities in the value of manufactures recorded by the southern states as compared with those recorded by northeastern and mid-Atlantic states. New York boasted a value of 25 million dollars, Massachusetts one of 22 million, and Virginia one of 15 million dollars. Connecticut, New Jersey, North Carolina, and Kentucky all reported values ranging between 6 and 7.7 million dollars. Carroll D. Wright, *The Industrial Evolution of the United States* (New York: Flood & Vincent, 1895), 138.
13. Ibid., 53; Persky, *The Burden of Dependency*, 33, 51.

major transformations were in fact under way that sharpened divisions not only between the regions, but also among white southerners themselves. While the northern economy was turning to manufacturing, thanks to the protection offered by the nonimportation and embargo acts of the 1807–1809 period, southern commercial agriculture was being revitalized by a soaring international demand for cotton, following the onset of a second phase in British industrialization after 1815. This fact coupled with major technological innovation in the harvesting of cotton[14] to trigger a wave of speculative expansion into fresh western lands, which accelerated that capitalistic transformation of southern plantation agriculture that was already under way. From the middle of the eighteenth century, many planters had in fact introduced new technology and crop rotation, and had begun to make a more efficient use of their labor force through the adoption of task work in place of the traditional gang system of slave labor organization.[15]

Through the 1810s and 1820s, a more rational and exploitative management and, not infrequently, absentee ownership, became characteristic of the new plantations in the Southwest. As a consequence, the relationship between master and slave became more impersonal, wiping away the last vestiges of a patriarchal/paternalist plantation system that had existed in some areas of the Atlantic seaboard during the colonial age.[16] In other words, as southern agriculture was becoming more capitalistic in character, the region's comparative advantage in this branch of the economy, which promised to generate great wealth, began to consolidate.

Evolutions in southern Italy do not seem to have been different in substance. The ascent to the Bourbon throne by Charles III in 1734 had ushered in an era of reform and economic development in the King-

14. The invention of the cotton gin in 1793 made for a shift in daily cotton preparation per hand from 1 to 350 pounds.

15. Philip D. Morgan, "Work and Culture: The Task System and the World of Lowcountry Blacks, 1770–1880," *William and Mary Quarterly* 39 (1982): 566–99; Philip D. Morgan and Michael L. Nicholls, "Slaves in Piedmont Virginia, 1720–1790," *William and Mary Quarterly* 46 (1989): 222–37; Henretta, *Origins of American Capitalism*, 280–83.

16. The changed nature of plantation agriculture and slavery was noted by Daniel R. Hundley in *Social Relations in Our Southern States* (New York: M. B. Price, 1860), 91, 131–32. See James Oakes, *The Ruling Race: A History of American Slaveholders* (New York: Vintage Books, 1982), 77–91, 129–30.

dom of Naples. The determination of the monarchy to promote commerce and manufacturing and, at the same time, erode feudal relationships, was signaled by the abolition of *enfitheusis*[17] in 1752, the liberalization of silk production in Sicily in 1781, and the progressive abolition of guilds. Wheat exports, which had been central to southern commerce for over a century, were now supplemented by new exports such as wine, citrus fruits, almonds, and, especially, olive oil. Oil exports more than doubled between 1760 and 1771 until they accounted for over a third of the kingdom's exports, according to economist Giuseppe Maria Galanti.[18] The considerable spurt in economic growth enjoyed by the kingdom during the second half of the eighteenth century was acknowledged by economists Grimaldi and Galanti and was later recorded by historian Vincenzo Cuoco in his essay on the Neapolitan revolution of 1799. "The Neapolitan nation," he wrote, "from the advent of Charles the Third began to breathe . . . agriculture resurrected, commerce revived. . . . In fifty years we had made such a fast progress that there were reasons to hope that more was possible."[19]

In 1806, the French régime of Joaquın Murat outlawed feudalism. Although scholars mostly agree that this act did not reflect a strongly articulated demand on the part of the civil society, coming rather as a measure imposed from above, it nonetheless sanctioned the existing situation. A revolution in agrarian relationship was, in fact, already under way. It was signaled by the rise of a new class of merchants/speculators

17. *Enfitheusis* was the leasing of a tract of land for a period longer than twenty years. Under this type of contract, the lessee could bequeath the contract to his own heirs or, if he so wished, sell the right to cultivate the land to somebody else.

18. Giuseppe Maria Galanti, *Nuova descrizione storica e geografica delle Sicilie* (Naples: presso i soci del Gabinetto Letterario, 1788–1789), 2 vols., 2:336–49; Bruno Caizzi, *Storia dell'industria italiana dal XVIII secolo ai giorni nostri* (Turin: UTET, 1960), 92. For a general description of the economic development of the Kingdom of Naples during the second half of the eighteenth century, see also Luigi Dal Pane, *Storia del lavoro in Italia, dall'inizio del secolo XVIII al 1815* (Milan: Giuffrè, 1958).

19. Vincenzo Cuoco, *Saggio storico sulla rivoluzione napoletana del 1799* (1801, ed. Pasquale Villani; reprint, Bari: Laterza, 1980): "La nazione napoletana . . . dalla venuta di Carlo Terzo incominciava a respirare . . . si vide risorgere l'agricoltura, animarsi il commercio. . . . In cinquant'anni avevamo fatto progressi rapidissimi, e vi era ragione di sperare di doverne fare anche di più" (43–44). As for the opinions expressed by Grimaldi and Galanti on the economic development of the Kingdom, see Piero Borzomati, ed., *La questione meridionale. Studi e testi* (Turin: 1996), 54, 66.

who leased estates from their feudal owners and managed them according to capitalistic criteria, (i.e., with a view to extracting the highest
possible profits from them). If this phenomenon made southern agriculture more fit to operate in a capitalist market economy, encouraging
the adoption of intensive systems of cultivation through the introduction of new techniques and an increased exploitation of the labor force,
it also caused estrangement of the landlords from their possessions,
stripping the institution of feudalism of its most qualifying interper-
sonal traits. So the law of 1806, which reduced the size of feudal estates
and provided for some redistribution of the land, accelerated the formation of a landed bourgeoisie. The *latifundium*,[20] though surviving as
a formal property unit for decades, was thus deeply transformed, losing
its original premodern connotation.[21] The capitalistic character of
southern Italian agriculture, as well as the formation of an agrarian
bourgeoisie, seems to have been in place before the middle of the nineteenth century. In 1845, economist Paolo Balsamo, who was a staunch
advocate of modernization, explicitly referred to a class of "bourgeois or
rentiers" in one of his writings. His remark was echoed, the same year,
by a report of an economic society of Caltanissetta, Sicily, which men-
tioned "a number of entrepreneurs, said bourgeois, who would lease the
former fiefs and cultivate them on their own."[22]

The same sort of transformation had occurred in the American
South, especially in Maryland and Tidewater Virginia, in the latter
decades of the eighteenth century, when, driven by market and profit
considerations, landowners had begun to lease their plantations to
prosperous tenants, thus becoming rentier-capitalists.[23]

The character of these changes in the countryside also led to the for-

20. The *latifundium* system consisted of very large landed properties concentrated in the hands of a few owners. The cultivation of these estates was extensive,
rather than intensive, and the technologies used were usually very backward.

21. Piero Bevilacqua, *Breve storia dell'Italia meridionale dall'Ottocento a oggi* (Rome:
Donzelli, 1993), 3–6; Marta Petrusewicz, *Latifondo: Economia morale e vita materi-
ale in una periferia dell'Ottocento* (Venice: Marsilio, 1989).

22. Paolo Balsamo, "Memorie inedite di pubblica economia ed agricoltura," in
P. Borzomati, *La questione meridionale* (Palermo: 1845), 205; Dal Pane, *Storia del
lavoro in Italia*, 232. "Borghesi o fittuari" is the definition provided by Balsamo, while
the second quotation reads, "un numero di imprenditori, detti borghesi, i quali
sogliono prendersi in fitto gli ex-feudi e coltivarli per conto loro."

23. Henretta, *Origins of American Capitalism*, 282–83.

mation of a new stratum of middle-class landholders. This has not been valued appropriately as a genuinely capitalistic transformation. Many historians have instead insisted on the adoption by the new propertied classes of the standards of social values and behavioral norms of their seignorial predecessors. However, other evidence indicates that while such borrowing of the more formal aspects of aristocratic demeanor by the new propertied classes expressed their need for self-legitimization, it was accompanied by a totally new, dynamic outlook on economic matters. On the other hand, Karl Marx himself had identified forms of "spurious" or "transient" capitalism in which the guiding principle of profit-making was realized by taking advantage of older institutions like slavery or feudal relationships and, consequently, capitalism presented an admixture of old and new forms of social relations and systems of values. Nonetheless, he had qualified these situations, with express reference to the southern United States, as capitalistic.[24]

During the early decades of the new century, governmental support for balanced economic development faded. The increasingly protectionist orientation of both the U.S. government and that of the Kingdom of the Two Sicilies gave rise to ever more vocal demands for free trade by agrarians of both Souths. Supported by the views of eminent economists such as Neapolitans Francesco Fuoco and Antonio Scialoja and southern Americans Jacob Cardozo and Thomas Cooper, the reinvigorated agricultural interests of both regions gave new emphasis to the movement for agricultural reform. This aimed at promoting the adoption of better farming techniques, the improvement of productive capacity, and even a more equitable land distribution through the division of large estates. Agricultural societies proliferated. They organized public discussions and country fairs, supported the publication of specialized

24. Karl Marx, *Capital: A Critique of Political Economy* (Chicago, C. H. Kerr, 1906–1913), 3 vols., 1:270, 822, 3:290. While historians Elizabeth Fox-Genovese and Eugene D. Genovese have argued that the southern plantation system was *within* the international capitalist economy, but not *of* it, James Oakes has urged us to reconsider the changing nature of American slavery as part of the evolving international capitalist economy. Elizabeth Fox-Genovese and Eugene D. Genovese, *Fruits of Merchant Capital: Slavery and Bourgeois Property in the Rise and Expansion of Capitalism* (New York: Oxford University Press, 1983), 5, 16–22; James Oakes, "Slavery as an American Problem," in *The South as an American Problem*, ed. Larry J. Griffin and Don H. Doyle, 84; id., *Slavery and Freedom: An Interpretation of the Old South* (New York: Knopf, 1990), 52–56.

journals and other printed materials to spread modern conceptions of land cultivation among farmers, founded agricultural schools, and sought financial support for the implementation of their programs.

The debates stimulated by these initiatives expanded beyond regional boundaries to involve the larger American and Italian scientific and learned communities through the diffusion of specialized magazines such as the *Southern Agriculturalist,* the *American Farmer,* Edmund Ruffin's *Farmer's Register,* and the *Southern Cultivator* and the *Annali della Cala-bria Citeriore,* the *Giornale di economia rurale,* the *Giornale Economico* and *Il Progresso.*[25] Connections with major extraregional periodicals and other publications also helped promote the nationalization of an internal debate which often resorted to unmerciful, exaggerated descriptions of the backward state of southern agriculture to push home its point. In 1845, reformist planter Eli J. Capell of Mississippi wrote to the editor of New York's *American Agriculturalist:* "We are about one hundred years behind you in improvement."[26] At about the same time, Luigi Settembrini, who in 1835 had offered the most dire picture of the region surrounding his native Catanzaro, Calabria, reiterated his negative judgments on southern Italian agriculture, describing the southern kingdom as a place where "the people die of hunger, are in a state worse than beasts, the only law is caprice."[27]

During the 1850s, New York economic journal *Hunt's Merchants' Magazine* and New Orleans's *De Bow's Review* became national forums for discussion of the southern economy at large, pretty much like the Neapolitan *Giornale di Statistica* and the *Annali civili,* two publications that enjoyed relatively wide national diffusion. Increasingly, agrarian reformism merged with more general preoccupations of an economic nature, as is testified by the activities of the many economic societies existing in southern Italy, which included participation in the Italian scientific

25. Marta Petrusewicz, *Come il Meridione divenne una Questione. Rappresentazioni del Sud prima e dopo il Quarantotto* (Soveria Mannelli, CZ: Rubbettino, 1998), 63–83; Clement Eaton, *The Growth of Southern Civilization, 1790–1860* (New York: Harper & Row, 1961), 111–13, 179–80.

26. W. H. Stephenson, "A Quarter-Century of a Mississippi Plantation: Eli J. Capell of Pleasant Hill," *Mississippi Valley Historical Review* 23 (1936): 363, cit. in Eaton, *The Growth of Southern Civilization,* 113.

27. Luigi Settembrini, *Una protesta del popolo del regno delle Due Sicilie* (1847), quoted in Harry Hearder, *Italy in the Age of the Risorgimento, 1790–1870* (London: Longman, 1983), 125.

conferences. In the United States, desire for public discussion manifested itself in the organization of yearly conventions, which, from 1837
to 1859, brought together hundreds of delegates (845 at the Charleston
Convention of 1854) from the slave and midwestern states to discuss
free trade, direct commerce with Europe and the expansion of commercial routes, internal improvements, banking credit, the encouragement
of manufacturing, and many other related topics.[28]

Yet, despite the unquestionable fact that much more could be done,
neither Italian nor American southern agriculture was as backward as it
was portrayed. The favorable trend of development of southern Italian
agriculture, as well as its diversified cash-crop production of olive oil,
wines, cotton, grains, and citrus fruits for an ever-expanding international market had already been noted in 1832 by Jacques Millenet, a resident of the Neapolitan kingdom of French parentage. His impressions
proved correct; some thirty years later, the first statistics relating to the
newly created Kingdom of Italy reported that the provinces of southern
Italy produced almost half of the grains and legumes, 60 percent of the
oil, 20 percent of the wine and silk cocoons, and all the citrus fruits and
cotton of the country.[29]

In the southern United States, besides the typical staple crops (cotton,
tobacco, sugar, rice), agriculture was also extremely diversified, producing cereals, legumes, fruits, and vegetables in quantities which not
only ensured regional self-sufficiency in foodstuffs, but sustained a remarkable interregional export sector to the Northeast.[30] The absence of

---

28. Petrusewicz, *Come il Meridione divenne una Questione*, 48–49; John Van
Deusen, *The Antebellum Southern Commercial Conventions* (Durham: Duke Uni-
versity Press, 1926); Vicki Vaughn Johnson, *The Men and the Vision of the Southern
Commercial Conventions, 1845–1871* (Columbia: University of Missouri Press, 1992).

29. Jacques Millenet, "Agricoltura e industria del Regno di Napoli," *Antologia* (Florence), 45 (1832), in Borzomati, *La questione meridionale;* C. Correnti and P. Maestri,
Annuario statistico italiano (Turin: 1864), cit. in Edmondo Capecelatro and Antonio
Carlo, *Contro la 'questione meridionale'. Studi sulle origini dello sviluppo capitalistico
in Italia* (Roma: Savelli, 1975), 87–89.

30. William K. Hutchinson and Samuel H. Williamson, "The Self-Sufficiency of
the Antebellum South: Estimates of the Food Supply," *Journal of Economic History*
31 (1971): 591–609; Albert Fishlow, "Antebellum Interregional Trade Reconsidered," *American Economic Review* 54 (1964): 352–57; Lawrence Herbst, "Interregional Commodity Trade from the North to the South and American Economic
Development in the Antebellum Period," *Journal of Economic History* 35 (1975). The
1860 census for agriculture shows that the South produced twice as much wheat as

any serious gap in agricultural productivity between northern and southern Italy by the time of the Unification of Italy is confirmed by census reports and other statistics compiled soon after, as well as by the vivid description provided by Italian statesman Sidney Sonnino who, in his *Condizioni generali dei contadini in Sicilia* (1877), described the productivity of Sicilian land as superior to that of Tuscany. Confirming the findings of economist George Tucker twenty years earlier, New York journalist and merchant Thomas Kettell showed that, in 1860, agricultural productivity—both aggregate and per hand—in the southern United States far exceeded that of both the Northeast and the West, with an apparently even number of hands employed in each of the three regions.[31] Modern scholarship has determined that antebellum southern agriculture was at least as efficient and profitable as that of the North—a finding which would suggest the inappropriateness of describing the South as backward.[32]

Ultimately, even if the degree of modernization of southern agriculture were to be found modest, both in the Italian and the American cases, the relevance of this aspect is sharply reduced when these southern regions are placed in their respective, pre-1860 national contexts. Modernization, in fact, does not seem to have been a feature of northern agriculture either, at least not until the 1850s.[33]

---

the Northeast, although only about half that of the West. Its production of corn, however, was nearly double that of the West, and six times that of the Northeast. U.S. Bureau of the Census, *Agriculture of the United States in 1860* (Washington: Government Printing Office, 1864), xcvi and ff.

31. Thomas P. Kettell, *Southern Wealth and Northern Profits* (New York: G. W. & J. A. Wood, 1860), 45. Kettell, who aimed at dispelling wrong notions about southern economic lethargy, tried to provide evidence of work habits on the part of southern whites similar to those of northerners. For this reason, he endeavored to obtain figures for the productivity of white farm labor by excluding from the count the crops overwhelmingly raised by slaves. Even allowing for error in the elaboration of statistical data, it is difficult to imagine how dramatically favorable figures could be turned into unfavorable ones. See also George Tucker, *Progress of the United States in Population and Wealth* (Boston: Little, Brown, 1843).

32. Robert W. Fogel and Stanley L. Engerman, *Time on the Cross: The Economics of American Negro Slavery* (Boston: Little, Brown, 1974), 191–209; Fred Bateman and Jeremy Atack, "The Profitability of Northern Agriculture in 1860," *Research in Economic History* 4 (1979): 95, 116–17.

33. Piero Bevilacqua, *Tra natura e storia. Ambiente, economie, risorse in Italia* (Rome: Donzelli, 1996); Christopher Clark, "Rural America and the Transition to Capitalism," *Journal of the Early Republic* 16 (1996); Martin Clark, *Modern Italy,*

The booming thirties raised expectations among the internationally oriented agrarians of both Souths, even as they increasingly perceived the protectionist course of their respective national governments as a mighty constraint. The operation of protective tariffs was in fact believed to exact too heavy a toll on the agricultural interests, forcing them to subsidize the process of industrialization elsewhere. Free-trade opinions became loud in both Souths, acquiring a full political dimension. In the southern United States, grievances displayed a clearly political underpinning. In fact, a group of sovereign states that had long retained political preeminence at the federal level, and largely contributed to northern economic growth with their exports, felt now betrayed by the imposition of penalizing economic measures. South Carolina politician George McDuffie voiced this protest in a famous speech in the U.S. Congress in 1830. McDuffie subscribed to the Smithian assumption that taxes on agriculture are a burden to producers, rather than to consumers. He maintained that the operation of the tariff amounted to the transfer of a large share of southern-generated surplus to the federal government. He also denounced the unfair pattern of federal expenditures, which, despite the South's remarkable contribution to national wealth, disproportionately benefited the West.[34]

McDuffie's speech certainly strengthened the impression that farming must have been the South's only asset. Although emphasis on agriculture was wholly consistent with the terms of the intense debate then under way in the country about the desirability of encouraging an industrial system modeled after the British example, manufacturing was already an important part of the southern economy. By the end of the 1830s, even before the movement for large-scale industrialization in the South had gathered enough momentum to produce any appreciable results, the federal census reported an aggregate value for southern manufacturing one-third that of the Northeast but double that of the West. Investment in the southern cotton industry leaped from $290,000 to $9,840,000 between 1831 and 1860. Capital invested in cotton, woolen,

---

1871–1995 (New York: Longman, 1996); Paul David, "The Mechanization of Reaping in Antebellum Midwest," in The Reinterpretation of American Economic History, ed. Robert W. Fogel and Stanley L. Engerman (New York: Harper & Row, 1971), 217.

34. Persky, The Burden of Dependency, 259–63. For a more exhaustive discussion of the anti-tariff movement in the U.S. South as part of the larger debate on southern economy, see the essay by Brian Schoen in this collection.

and iron factories increased faster in the South, between 1840 and 1860, than in the U.S. as a whole. During the 1850s, several scholars have argued, manufacturing grew at a faster pace in the South than in the Midwest.[35]

Even though industrial performance in southern states paled in comparison with that of giants like Pennsylvania, New York, or Massachusetts, it nonetheless compared well with that of most other states of the Union. Virginia ranked seventh, even with Illinois, in the value of capital invested in manufacturing. Subregional data would be even more revealing, indicating areas of industrial concentration. In Georgia, the cotton industry gave work to thousands of white operatives, mainly females. During the 1850s, the Augusta Manufacturing Company and the Roswell Mills employed between 350 and 400 workers each, as many as the better known South Carolina Graniteville Manufacturing Company. In Georgia, the average number of hands per factory ranged between 75 and 200. Iron manufacturing, the third largest industry in Tennessee, employed perhaps up to 8,000 persons—whites and blacks, free and slave—in the 1850s. By the time of secession, only three American factories produced more iron than the Richmond's Tredegar Iron Works. The aggregate value of industrial production in cities like Richmond and Louisville exceeded that of Pittsburgh or Chicago.[36]

The case of southern Italy may appear even more striking, for the peninsula as a whole was, by 1860, one of the most industrially backward parts of Europe. Yet, with its numerous mechanized establishments employing over a thousand operatives each, notable among which were those located in and near Naples and Salerno, by 1860 the Campania

35. Kettell, *Southern Wealth and Northern Profits*, 44–46; Fogel and Engerman, *Time on the Cross*, 247–57; Viken Tchakerian, "Productivity, Extent of Markets, and Manufacturing in the Late Antebellum South and Midwest," *Journal of Economic History* 54 (1994). U.S. Bureau of the Census, *Manufactures of the United States in 1860. Compiled from the Original Returns of the Eighth Census* (Washington: Government Printing Office, 1865), 61–82, 560–78.

36. Susanna Delfino, *Yankees del Sud. Sviluppo economico e trasformazioni sociali nel Sud degli Stati Uniti, 1790–1860* (Milan: Franco Angeli, 1987), 19–20, 102–11; Michele Gillespie, "To Harden a Lady's Hand: Gender Politics, Racial Realities, and Women Millworkers in Antebellum Georgia," in *Neither Lady nor Slave: Working Women of the Old South*, ed. Susanna Delfino and Michele Gillespie (Chapel Hill: University of North Carolina Press, 2002), 265–69; Fred Bateman and Thomas Weiss, *A Deplorable Scarcity: The Failure of Industrialization in the Slave Economy* (Chapel Hill: University of North Carolina Press, 1981), 20–22.

region produced almost as much cotton sheeting as Lombardy. In the early 1840s, the Egg Cotton manufactory, located near Caserta, had a labor force of 1,300. Overall, the southern cotton textile industry compared favorably with that in other parts of Italy. The same pattern of concentration and mechanization was evident in the woolen and silk industries. By the time of Unification, the latter employed about 3,000 workers. Paper milling was another important industry in the South. The nine factories located in the Liri Valley employed over 200 hands each and exported their products abroad. But it was in shipbuilding, metal working and machine construction that the South excelled. The Castellamare and Naples shipyards gave work to 3,400 people; the Pietrarsa Ironworks and machine shops, with over 800 workers, was reputed to be the largest industrial complex of its kind in the whole peninsula, far outstripping the Genoese Ansaldo. Besides the Guppy plants, it was the only one able to turn out railroad tracks and locomotives in Italy.[37]

The few examples reported only highlight southern industrial realities in both countries; a full description would take much more space than is available. Nor is it my purpose here to determine the actual level of industrialization reached by the two southern regions by 1860, when their economies were on the brink of being radically altered by the consequences of the Civil War and Unification, respectively. Furthermore, the fact that only a geographically circumscribed area of the United States was experiencing accelerated industrial growth between 1840 and 1860 still reduces the significance of exploring the causes of a lag which was such only when compared with a few northern states, and even here only in terms of manufacturing, not of wealth or per capita income, and not compared with the international scene save for Britain.[38]

37. Capecelatro and Carlo, *Contro la 'questione meridionale,'* 71–74, 106–15; Bevilacqua, *Breve storia dell'Italia meridionale,* 20–32; Luigi De Rosa and Pasquale Villani, eds., *Iniziativa e capitale straniero nell'industria metalmeccanica del Mezzogiorno, 1840–1904* (Naples: Francesco Giannini e Figli, 1968).

38. Fogel and Engerman, *Time on the Cross,* 247–57. Considering the South as constituting a separate nation, Fogel and Engerman find that the per capita income grew 30 percent faster in the South than in the North between 1840 and 1860. According to these authors, the South showed an annual growth rate higher than those of Great Britain, France, and Germany (1.7 as against 1.5, 1.2, and 1.4, respectively). Besides, the South ranked sixth in cotton manufacturing, and second in railroad mileage per capita among the nations of the Western world.

As for Italy, its overall lag in industrial development compared with the other western European countries renders the gap between North and South even more trifling. Relevant to the present argument is the contrast between two realities, in which industry was neither economically nor culturally alien, and the image of them as uniformly rural regions, which came to be the mainstay in the construction of the idea of their being "backward." The imposed regional uniformity has also blurred the high degree of socioeconomic articulation achieved by these two societies by the mid-nineteenth century, reducing dynamic complexity to the representation of a stereotypical social landscape comprising chosen qualifying types: planters/slaves/poor whites and landlords/poor peasants, respectively. In this way, even the diversity of the agricultural world has been obscured, not to mention the significance of other economic pursuits to people's lives. As much as the rural world was the locus of the early phases of the industrial transformation, the pursuit of industrial or protoindustrial activities as a supplement to family income involved more members of the farming population than census records are able to represent.

In this light, it is indeed impressive to find that, by 1840, Virginia reported 32,336 individuals employed in manufacturing, putting the state fifth behind New York, Pennsylvania, Massachusetts, and Ohio (the four most industrialized states of the Union). In 1850, North Carolina had 20,613 persons engaged in commerce, manufacturing, and mining, a figure which soared to 30,017 ten years later. According to another estimate, one-fifth of the total white population of Virginia, North Carolina, South Carolina, and Georgia were manufacturing workers in 1860.[39] As for Italy, the general census of 1861 revealed that 51 percent of all workers employed in Italian industry were in the South.[40]

The importance of these data does not lie in any attempt to reproduce the old-fashioned competitive pattern of approach between North and South in the study of southern industrialization, either in the American or in the Italian case. Rather, it rests with the cultural domain. As

39. Kathleen Bruce, *Virginia Iron Manufacture in the Slave Era* (New York: Century Company, 1931), 84; Richard D. Connor, *North Carolina: Rebuilding an Ancient Commonwealth, 1584–1925* (Chicago: American Historical Society, 1929), 2 vols., 2:84–85; Wayne Flynt, *Dixie's Forgotten People: The South's Poor Whites* (Bloomington: Indiana University Press, 1979), 5.

40. Ministero Agricoltura, Industria e Commercio (MAIC), *Censimento generale al 31 dicembre 1861* (Florence: 1866), xiii.

Edward Ayers masterfully put it: "Whether or not southern industry in the aggregate measured up to standards achieved elsewhere under more favorable circumstances," does not appear to be the most important issue. What matters, instead, is to appreciate that the spreading of manufacturing "touched the lives of . . . people. The impact of industry . . . needs to be measured in people's experience, not merely in numbers, not merely by debunking inflated rhetoric."[41]

In the attempt to identify mechanisms through which ideas of southern backwardness were constructed in the United States, one cannot help concluding that, although modernization debates revolved around the relationship between southern agriculture and slavery, this sort of cancellation of the nonagricultural South stemmed from the need to resort to the argument of its failure to industrialize to give further weight to the assumption that slavery generally hindered southern economic development. This argument is fully articulated in Stanley Engerman's essay in this volume.

From the 1830s, abolitionists provided an economic critique of the American South. Adhering to the Calvinistic belief that economic achievement was a confirmation of God's benevolence and approval, abolitionists not only argued that the South was incapable of industrializing *because* of slavery, but also that the institution was detrimental to overall American economic growth. Abolitionist thought combined with a more generalized acceptance of industrialization as a sign of a healthy economic development to give rise to what was later denounced as the "self-glorification upon northern industry."[42] Statements such as that made by abolitionist Theodore Parker, who maintained that the South was "the foe to northern industry—to our mines, our manufactures, and our commerce . . . she is the foe to our institutions," suggested the agricultural nature of the southern economy. This argument was reiterated by an article that appeared in the *New York Tribune* early in 1860, which read: "manufactories scarcely exist at the South; mechanical industry, distinct from agriculture, has hardly any existence."[43]

Yet, although the very logic of the confrontation between abolitionists

41. Edward L. Ayers, *The Promise of the New South: Life after Reconstruction* (New York: Oxford University Press, 1992), 105.

42. Kettell, *Southern Wealth and Northern Profits*, 53; Thomas Cochran, "The Paradox of American Economic Growth," *Journal of American History* 61 (1975).

43. John L. Thomas, *Slavery Attacked: The Abolitionist Crusade* (Englewood Cliffs: Prentice-Hall, 1965), 149; *New York Tribune*, Feb. 13, 1860.

and proslavery advocates entailed emphasis on the functional relationship of the peculiar institution to agriculture and on the agrarian nature of the southern economy, the most sensible and realistic leaders of the antislavery movement did not dispute its capitalistic character and, in an 1843 pamphlet, Lewis Tappan described the large slaveholders as "great capitalists."[44]

Ultimately, disparaging notions of southerners as uncivilized, lazy half-barbarians sprang from what were deemed to be the long-term effects exerted on the people by the unnatural protraction of archaic institutions such as slavery and feudalism.[45] This connection was reinforced, during the 1840s and 1850s, by the increasing identification of liberty with civilization. Mounting political rivalries and ideological tensions in the developing sectional conflict exaggerated the use of the economic argument in the North/South confrontation. The rising tide of abolitionist sentiment in the northern United States combined with uninterrupted control of the national presidency by either southern or prosouthern men from 1844 to 1860 to give substance to the idea of a "slaveholders' conspiracy" by which, according to William H. Seward, the ideologist and founder of the Republican party (1854), the destinies of twenty million Americans were at the mercy of three hundred thousand slaveholders. The fashioning of an abolitionist/Republican image of the South rested on assumptions of a relapse into barbarism and decadence which threatened to infect the whole Republic, had the slaveholders been allowed to push through their expansionist schemes. A demonstration of the latter's being on the wrong side was to be found, according to Republicans, in the deranged state of the southern economy. Seward himself, who does not seem to have had any direct knowledge of the South, summarized this view: "an exhausted soil, old and decaying towns, wretchedly neglected roads . . . an absence of enterprise and improvement."[46]

44. Laurence Shore, *Southern Capitalists: The Ideological Leadership of an Elite, 1832–1885* (Chapel Hill: University of North Carolina Press, 1986), 31.

45. Sidney Pollard, *Peaceful Conquest,* 76–77, 192–201, points out that in certain parts of Europe the encroachment of the capitalistic market economy engendered relapse into pseudofeudal forms of labor relations. On this point, see also Immanuel Wallerstein, *The Modern World-System: Capitalist Agriculture and the Origins of the European World-Economy in the Sixteenth Century* (New York: Academic Press, 1974), ch. 2.

46. The quote is from Eric Foner, *Free Soil, Free Labor, Free Men: The Ideology of the Republican Party before the Civil War* (New York: Oxford University Press, 1970), 41.

Not all attacks on the state of the southern economy originated outside the region. South Carolinian George Fitzhugh and North Carolinian Hinton Rowan Helper, two staunch supporters of, respectively, slavery and its abolition in the 1850s, both portrayed quite gloomy pictures of their region's economy to forward their opposite aims. However, the complexities underlying their arguments were largely ignored. Fitzhugh's work was superficially interpreted as the quintessential exposition of the philosophy of a slave society adverse to manufacturing, while Helper's book was quite conveniently included with the Republican literature in the 1860 electoral campaign as a demonstration of southern backwardness by a southerner.[47]

The proliferation of travel literature from the 1830s to the 1850s also reinforced ideas of a backward South, largely revealing travelers' awareness of the debate going on about the southern economy. Modernist economic views certainly influenced the account French minister Michel Chevalier penned about his journey through the United States in the early 1830s. A disciple of Saint-Simon and a staunch believer in the primacy of industrialism as the spearhead of progress, he described the region south of the Potomac as "wholly agricultural . . . without mechanical industry, and having but little commerce" and defined the South as a "great cotton plantation, yielding *also* [italics mine] some subsidiary articles, such as tobacco, sugar and rice."[48] In this way, Chevalier revealed ignorance of the very southern agriculture before his eyes, for it is well known that extreme specialization in cotton production was a post–Civil War phenomenon. On the other hand, even such a famous traveler from within the States as Frederick Law Olmsted was unable to grasp the special relationships existing between the patterns of land settlement and improvement, and between agriculture and manufacturing, that were not only unique to the South's geography and distribution of resources, but also to each of its diverse subregions. Unable to free himself from a preconception of what a southern plantation and a planter should look like, he could not make sense of what he considered inexplicable discrepancies between appearance and substance. Thus, he missed

47. For an innovative discussion of George Fitzhugh's works, see Shore, *Southern Capitalists*. Hinton R. Helper, *The Impending Crisis of the South: How to Meet It!* (New York: 1857).

48. Michel Chevalier, *Society, Manners, and Politics in the United States* (Boston: Barton, Weeks, Jordan, 1839), 229, 400.

important points about the culture of the southern slave society and economy.[49]

In Italy, too, political and ideological reasons seem to have presided over the elaboration of negative images of the South and southerners. According to Jacques Millenet, these were already looming large in the early 1830s. In his optimistic description of the progress being made within the kingdom, both in agriculture and manufacturing, in which he illustrated the relevance and extent of exports to plead the cause of freedom of commerce and milder tariffs, he could not restrain himself from exhorting southerners to disprove what seemed to be an already established stereotype about them. "That it is high time," he wrote, "to wash away that taint which blames us for idleness and dearth of enterprise amidst such a lavishly generous nature."[50]

The reactionary measures enacted by the Bourbons after the failed revolution of 1848, in full view of the international community, coupled with growing disagreement between southern political exiles and local elites to embitter the former by making them see the impracticability of a radical political solution for the southern kingdom. Disappointment turned easily into reification. Exile Francesco Trinchera best expressed it: "nothing that may hint at the life of a civilized people . . . no roads . . . no communications . . . no exchanges, no commerce, no arts, no industry, no manufactures."[51] The striking similarity between this description and that offered by Seward about the American South marked the passage, in both countries, to a formulation of the concept of backwardness in terms of incivility which was to prevail in the 1860s and 1870s.

In a speech delivered in late 1863 before the Italian parliament, General

49. Frederick Law Olmsted, *A Journey in the Seaboard Slave States, with Remarks on Their Economy* (New York: Dix & Edwards, 1856); *A Journey in the Backcountry* (1860; reprint, New York: B. Franklin, 1970); *A Journey through Texas; or, A Saddle-Trop on the Southwestern Frontier with a Statistical Appendix* (1860; reprint, New York: B. Franklin, 1969). On the characteristics of the use of the land in the American South, and its implications in the development of manufacturing, see the essay by John Majewski and Viken Tchakerian in this collection.

50. Millenet, "Agricoltura e industria," 172. The quotation in Italian reads: "che tempo è ormai di lavar quella taccia che d'indolenti ci accusa e poveri d'industria in tanta dovizia di liberale natura."

51. The quotation is in Petrusewicz, *Come il Meridione divenne una Questione*, 145–46.

Govone maintained that "Sicily has not yet emerged . . . out of the cycle which leads from barbarism to civilization," as all the other Italian states had.[52] Even Italian statesmen Leopoldo Franchetti and Sidney Sonnino, who were the first serious students of the "southern problem" did not escape popular stereotypes. In his *Condizioni economiche e amministrative delle provincie napoletane* (1875), Franchetti blamed not only the peasants but also the "possessing classes" for ignorance, indicating its source in the long isolation to which they had been doomed by the Bourbon monarchy. This judgment stands in sharp contrast with the cosmopolitan outlook and leading intellectual role that, despite the authoritarian involutions following 1848, southern Italians continued to play both within the peninsula and internationally. Sonnino, on the other hand, did not hesitate to define Sicily as "thoroughly medieval," when even American consul William Boulware in the 1840s had described the Kingdom of the Two Sicilies in these flattering terms: "Its culture is admirable, as far as I have seen, and its peasantry active, sober & laborious."[53]

The same tendency to derive a measure for backwardness from the supposedly deranged traits of the southern character manifested itself in the United States too by the time of the Civil War. Aiming at demonstrating the inferiority of southern civilization, this outlook tried to dispel notions of southern refinement that had been widespread in the North during the 1850s, fuelled by a northern fictional literature which eulogized the southern plantation as the exemplar of an idyllic and pastoral ideal longed for by all Americans.[54] Junius Henri Browne, who was a wartime correspondent for the *New York Tribune* in the South, pronounced merciless judgments on white southerners, mocking their supposed "refinement" and describing them as "uneducated, coarse, ignorant, vulgar people" who lived in a medieval, semibarbarous state.[55]

52. Dennis Mack Smith, ed., *The Making of Italy, 1796–1860* (New York: Walker, 1968), 373.

53. Ibid., 374–79. William Boulware to Daniel Webster, June 5, 1842, in Howard R. Marraro, *Diplomatic Relations between the United States and the Kingdom of the Two Sicilies: Instructions and Dispatches, 1816–1861* (New York and Ragusa: S. F. Vanni, 1951), 2 vols., 1:529.

54. Patrick Gerster and Nicholas Cords, "The Northern Origins of Southern Mythology," *Journal of Southern History* 43 (1977): 567–82.

55. Junius Henri Browne, *Four Years in Secessia: Adventures within and beyond the Union Lines* (Hartford, Conn.: O. D. Case, 1865), 434.

These negative opinions anticipated more sophisticated interpretations of southernness in terms of ethnic, when not overtly racial or biological, inferiority. Italian political thinker Antonio Gramsci, in denouncing racist attitudes about southern Italians, fashioned his argument from clearly economic premises.

> The common people of northern Italy . . . thought . . . that if the Mezzogiorno did not progress after being freed from the fetters that the Bourbon's regime posed to modern development, this meant that the causes of their poverty were not external, to be looked for in objective political-economic conditions, but internal, ingrained in the southern people . . . only one explanation remained, that of the organic inability of men, of their barbarism, of their biological inferiority.[56]

Notions of ethnic and cultural inferiority of southerners—black and white—also developed in the United States as the Republican promise of economic development after the abolition of slavery was not fulfilled, and came to especially identify certain groups of whites, mainly the inhabitants of the Appalachians, whose abject poverty became proverbial as the nineteenth century wore on.[57]

The aftermath of the American Civil War and Italian Unification saw an increasing divergence between northern and southern economic performance in both countries. This fact seemed to confirm original inferences of backwardness. From these premises, subsequent analyses of the "southern problem" largely dismissed economic investigation relative to the pre-1860 period. By positing the lack of a bourgeois revolution as well as of a major capitalist transformation in the countryside, and by instituting an intimate connection between capitalism and industrialization, the Gramscian interpretation has given crucial aid to the predicament of both Souths' pre-1860 societies as precapitalist.[58]

56. Antonio Gramsci, *Quaderni del carcere* (Turin: Einaudi, 1975), 4 vols., 3:2021.

57. Flynt, *Dixie's Forgotten People;* John S. Reed, *The Enduring South: Subcultural Persistence in Mass Society* (Chapel Hill: University of North Carolina Press, 1974); George Tindall, *The Ethnic Southerners* (Baton Rouge: Louisiana State University Press, 1976).

58. The Gramscian theory of the hegemony of the ruling classes has been applied to the American case by Eugene D. Genovese. See *The World the Slaveholders Made: Two Essays in Interpretation* (New York: Pantheon Books, 1969) and *In Red and Black: Marxian Explorations in Southern and Afroamerican History* (New York: Pantheon Books, 1971).

Capitalism, however, is now widely perceived as a "slippery concept" by many scholars who agree that, if the adoption of "core values rooted in individualism, competition, and the arbitration of market mechanisms,"[59] must be the defining traits, rural America, including the part of it which was to experience industrialization first, was very slow to absorb them.[60]

In this light, a new understanding of economic rationality can be applied to interpret the mind of Americans in the first few decades of the nineteenth century, one that offers new insights toward an explanation of the relative slowness of the shift from agricultural to manufacturing investments in the antebellum South, notwithstanding the higher profitability of the latter, in terms less biased by hierarchical assumptions about cultures.[61] The economic behavior of entrepreneurs and merchants has also been reassessed. Judging from what we know of the northern entrepreneurial elites, both in Italy and the United States, before 1860, they hardly expressed an articulate class or a homogeneous philosophy of modernization. One scholar has aptly described these entrepreneurs as "cautious men backing into the future."[62] In Italy, after 1860, land ownership continued to confer respectability and power.[63] From these premises, the *mentalité* and economic behavior of southern entrepreneurs have begun to be reappraised.

Division of labor, rather than mechanization, as represented by the big factory, seems to have lain at the heart of the industrial revolution.[64]

59. Paul A. Gilje, "The Rise of Capitalism in the Early Republic," *Journal of the Early Republic* 16 (1996): 160.

60. See, in this regard, Michael Merrill, "Cash Is Good to Eat: Self-Sufficiency and Exchange in the Rural Economy of the United States," *Radical History Review* 9 (1977); Daniel Vickers, "Competency and Competition: Economic Culture in Early America," *William and Mary Quarterly* 47 (1990); Alan Kulikoff, *The Agrarian Origins of American Capitalism* (Charlottesville: University of Virginia Press, 1992).

61. Fred Bateman, James Foust, and Thomas Weiss, "The Participation of Planters in Manufacturing in the Antebellum South," *Research in Economic History* 1 (1976): 277–97.

62. Carlton, *How American Is the American South?* 43; Robert Dalzell Jr., *Enterprising Elite: The Boston Associates and the World They Made* (Cambridge: University of Massachusetts Press, 1987).

63. Clark, *Modern Italy*. In the 1880s, the industrial, commercial, and professional elites of the Veneto region, in Italy, embraced land ownership a symbol of social status. See also Silvio Lanaro, "Le elites settentrionali," *Meridiana* 16 (1993).

64. Pollard, *Peaceful Conquest*, 24–27, 63–68; Prude, *The Coming of Industrial Order*, 34–64; Richard Stott, "Artisans and Capitalist Development," *Journal of the Early Republic* 16 (1996).

Perspectives on the industrial development of the antebellum South have been transformed accordingly. Rather than following competitive patterns of approach to the subject, future research should be sustained by the acknowledgment of the existence of a plurality of paths and logics to economic development both within the United States and Italy.[65] Imagining the capitalist/industrial transformation as an open-ended series of moments of coexistence, mutual adaptation, and synthesis between old and new elements may offer a valid springboard toward the elaboration of a new conceptual framework. Leaving aside considerations of comparative performance, such an approach might contribute to a different understanding of the idea of backwardness as applied to these two southern regions. If our aim is to shed light on the traits constituting a distinctive southern culture, both in Italy and the United States, then we must explore all the aspects of their economies and their transformations over time to provide a reliable and enduring evaluation.

65. Lucy Riall, *The Italian Risorgimento: State, Society and National Unification* (London: Routledge, 1994), 57–60.

Markets and Manufacturing

Industry and Agriculture in the
Antebellum South and Midwest

John Majewski and Viken Tchakerian

In 1776, the Scottish economist and philosopher Adam Smith famously argued that the "wealth of nations" depended upon the division of labor.[1] To make his point, Smith gave the rather mundane example of pin manufacturing. A single person, Smith argued, could hardly have the skills to make twenty pins per day. To produce even this seemingly simple item, the lone worker would have to straighten the wire, cut it into tiny parts, make the heads, carefully attach the heads to the pieces of wire, and then package them for sale. A workshop, however, could make each task a distinct operation. Because workers specialized in each operation, productivity in the workshop rose dramatically; a single firm with ten employees might make 48,000 pins a day. There was, however, an important catch to Smith's argument: the workshop needed a market so that it could sell its 48,000 pins. With no market, there could be no division of labor and no corresponding increase in productivity. Conversely, it was the lure of large markets that induced entrepreneurs to invest time, energy, and capital into enterprises such as pin factories.[2]

1. The authors would like to thank Stanley Engerman, Sarah Case, Jay Carlander, Lisa Jacobson, several anonymous referees, and the volume editors for very helpful comments.
2. Adam Smith, *An Inquiry into the Nature and Causes of the Wealth of Nations,*

Economic historians have increasingly understood early American industrialization as a Smithian response to the growth of markets. In its simplest and most stylized form, the story goes something like this: In the colonial period, local markets tended to be small. The overwhelmingly rural population was highly dispersed, and transportation to inland areas was notoriously costly and uncertain. In the early nineteenth century, markets began to develop. Population, both from immigration and natural growth, dramatically expanded. Turnpikes, canals, and railroads allowed manufacturers to better reach potential consumers. In classic Smithian fashion, the growth of markets encouraged the growth of manufacturing.[3] Farmers became less self-sufficient, selling increasingly large surpluses and buying more manufactured goods. Workshops began to expand, subdividing work so that output increased and prices fell. Intense competition encouraged innovation and incremental technological advances, which further increased productivity. By the Civil War, large northeastern cities such as New York and Philadelphia had become full-fledged manufacturing centers producing goods for consumers throughout the nation.[4]

A key question for economic historians to answer is why most of these workshops and factories clustered in the North rather than the South. The relative failure of the South to industrialize is somewhat sur-

---

ed. R. H. Campbell, A. S. Skinner, and W. B. Todd, vol. 1 (1776; reprint, Indianapolis: Liberty Classics, 1981), 13–36.

3. We follow the census in adopting a broad definition of manufacturing, which includes resource processing (lumber, milling, mining), consumer goods (textiles, boots and shoes, wagons), and producer goods (foundries, machine tools). We define manufacturing workers as anyone employed in these industries, including slaves, women, and children.

4. See especially the work of Kenneth Sokoloff, including "Inventive Activity in Early Industrial America: Evidence from Patent Records, 1790–1846," *Journal of Economic History* 48 (1988): 813–50; "Invention, Innovation, and Manufacturing Productivity Growth in the Antebellum Northeast," in *American Economic Growth and Standards of Living before the Civil War,* ed. Robert E. Gallman and John Joseph Wallis (Chicago: University of Chicago Press, 1992), 345–78; "Productivity Growth in Manufacturing during Early Industrialization: Evidence from the American Northeast, 1820–1860," in *Long-Term Factors in American Economic Growth,* ed. Stanley L. Engerman and Robert E. Gallman (Chicago: University of Chicago Press, 1986), 679–736; and "Was the Transition from the Artisanal Shop to the Non-Mechanized Factory Associated with Gains in Efficiency? Evidence from the U.S. Manufacturing Censuses of 1820 and 1850," *Explorations in Economic History* 21 (1984): 351–82.

prising given the general characteristics of manufacturing before the Civil War. Although many contemporaries associated industrialization with large-scale textile factories, productivity increased in a wide range of industries and for small and large firms alike. Southerners could have entered into any number of rapidly expanding sectors—food processing, boots and shoes, farm implements, and many more—that required no great outlay of capital or infusion of sophisticated, expensive technology. One might argue that the absence of southern manufacturing simply reflected the South's comparative advantage. Southerners, the argument goes, could make far more money growing staples than manufacturing goods. Yet as the antebellum period progressed, states such as Virginia and North Carolina fell behind the national average in per capita income. Why, then, did these southern states fail to shift more resources to manufacturing?[5]

To better understand the inability of southerners to keep pace with the rest of the nation, we compare manufacturing in the South with that in the Midwest. What makes this comparison worthwhile is the similar structure of the two regions—both specialized in producing agricultural commodities (cotton, tobacco, and rice in the South; wheat, corn, and hogs in the Midwest) for national and international markets. Despite these broad similarities, the added-in manufactured goods (the final value of the manufactured good minus the cost of the initial raw materials) for 1860 in the Midwest were almost 100 percent higher than the South on a per capita basis.[6] Southern manufacturing, it is true, was hardly stagnant; output and productivity grew substantially during the 1850s. Yet on a relative basis, the South still found itself well behind the Midwest and even further behind the industrial northeast.

A long tradition of scholarship, echoing the critiques of contemporary observers, has stressed how slavery and the region's mountainous geography inhibited the growth of southern markets. Some historians argue that slavery encouraged an unequal distribution of income that limited mass consumption. Another interpretation suggests that slaveholders effectively utilized slave labor to achieve self-sufficiency on their plantations, which discouraged the growth of towns and local manufacturing.

5. Robert William Fogel, *Without Consent or Contract: The Rise and Fall of American Slavery* (New York: W. W. Norton, 1989), 85.
6. Viken Tchakerian, "Productivity, Extent of Markets, and Manufacturing in the Late Antebellum South and Midwest," *Journal of Economic History* 54 (1994): 500.

Still others have emphasized how the Appalachian Mountains isolated large areas of the nonplantation South from regional and national markets, creating a "dual economy" in the process. Taken together, these historiographical traditions suggest that southern manufacturing found itself between the proverbial rock and hard place. In areas suitable for commercial agriculture, slavery created inequality and encouraged plantation self-sufficiency; in areas without slavery, mountains stood as an imposing barrier to markets and industrialization.

Our comparison confirms that slavery and topography did indeed help limit the growth of southern markets. We also find another important factor that the literature has thus far overlooked: agricultural land-use patterns. Our comparison reveals that southern farms contained a much higher percentage of unimproved land than those in the Midwest; about 66 percent of land in southern farms was unimproved, compared with 44 percent for the Midwest. Southern land-use patterns led to a far more dispersed settlement pattern, which made it exceedingly difficult for southerners to build a viable transportation network. Southern canals and railroads had much lower levels of traffic, which reduced their profitability and effectiveness. Without much of a home market and with inadequate transportation to more distant markets, southern manufacturing remained highly circumscribed. Precisely why southerners held so much unimproved land is unclear, but the prime suspects include the generally poor quality of southern soils and the inability of cattle and forage crops to thrive in the South's hot, humid climate. Smithian industrialization, it appears, could not take root in the shallow soil and warm temperature of the South.

Mapping Manufacturing and Markets

If the Smithian emphasis on markets is correct, then we should logically expect to see most southern and midwestern manufacturing located near large markets. Access to markets, however, was not the only variable in determining the location of industry. The presence of key raw materials—especially if the raw materials were bulky and hard to transport—could also influence where certain industries located. Many isolated counties in Michigan and Wisconsin, for example, ranked high in per capita manufacturing because of the presence of lumber milling and iron and copper mines. Similarly, North Carolina manufacturers in isolated pine barrens processed tar and turpentine from abundant natural resources. In some cases, the relationship between raw materials and manufacturing was somewhat more complex. The proximity of Richmond to Virginia's tobacco crop, for example, allowed the city's tobacco manufacturers to carefully select the best-tasting leaves, which was a crucial determinant for success in producing plug tobacco. By 1860, fifty-two Richmond firms, collectively employing more than thirty-three hundred workers, dominated the market for plug tobacco.[7]

Crop selection also determined the location of manufacturing. Here the Midwest had a decided advantage over the South. The hundreds of thousands of midwestern farm families producing wheat and corn created a market for firms that milled grain and distilled liquor. Grain farming, with its short harvesting season, also created a strong demand for agricultural implements that could help farmers quickly bring their wheat from the fields. A vast number of small towns thus arose across the Midwest to service the needs of local farmers, and most of the manufacturing output of relatively isolated midwestern counties consisted of milling and distilling grain. On a larger scale, cities that served as transportation hubs often became large-scale processing centers for the grain and livestock that midwestern farmers raised in such abundance. Chicago, for example, owed much of its tremendous growth to its flourishing processing and livestock industries.[8] No southern city could match the tremendous growth of antebellum Chicago, but cities such as Richmond, Virginia, and Louisville, Kentucky, became regionally important processing centers.

Only a small portion of the Upper South, however, specialized in grain. Cotton, the most important southern staple, was processed in factories far more complex than typical flour mills. Such capital-intensive enterprises could not readily exist in isolated areas. Since cotton was easily transportable, there was no overwhelming incentive to locate cotton factories near cotton fields. Most cotton was thus processed in New England or Great Britain. The only element of cotton production that created a demand for locally manufactured goods involved cotton gins.

7. John Majewski, *A House Dividing: Economic Development in Pennsylvania and Virginia before the Civil War* (New York: Cambridge University Press, 2000), 164–65.

8. William Cronon, *Nature's Metropolis: Chicago and the Great West* (New York: W. W. Norton, 1991), 97–259.

Before shipping their cotton, planters used gins to remove the seeds from the raw fiber. Daniel Pratt, a transplanted New Englander, built and operated the largest cotton gin factory in the world at his sprawling manufacturing complex in Prattville, Alabama. Pratt's close proximity to the cotton belt and his network of agents, who provided superior sales and service, helped him to successfully compete against New England firms.[9] Pratt's success suggests that when markets presented southerners with opportunities in manufacturing, they readily took advantage of them.

Pratt was clearly exceptional, and cotton as a general rule generated little demand for other manufactured goods. To stimulate industrialization, southerners would have to depend upon what contemporaries called "nearness to markets." "Nearness to markets" reflects two important factors that create demand: local population densities and the ability to transport goods to other areas. Southern counties with the highest per capita manufacturing output generally had a city with a population greater than eight thousand. Firms in these urban counties tended to be larger and more likely to produce consumer goods such as clothing, leather goods, and boots and shoes. These firms epitomized Smithian industrialization—their greater productivity gave them the ability to produce ready-made goods far more cheaply than could traditional artisans and craftsmen.

Urban firms sold goods in their own cities, but they could also compete in regional, national, and even international markets. Relatively cheap transportation allowed them to do so. Not surprisingly, major manufacturing centers such as Cincinnati, Chicago, Detroit, Milwaukee, Richmond, and Louisville all had excellent access to navigable waterways. Indeed, counties bordering navigable waterways, whether urban or rural, tended to have relatively high per capita manufacturing. In the 1820s and 1830s, many midwestern states built canal systems that linked many areas to the Great Lakes. Although navigable waterways still dominated the transportation system, by the 1850s railroads had provided a viable alternative. Railroads strengthened the position of cities that already had access to water transportation while opening up isolated interior counties. Railroads, for example, provided low-cost transportation to otherwise remote communities throughout Ohio, Indiana, and Illinois.

9. Curtis J. Evans, *The Conquest of Labor: Daniel Pratt and Southern Industrialization* (Baton Rouge: Louisiana State University Press, 2001), 32–64.

At least some southern localities with access to markets managed to keep pace with midwestern manufacturing. Sometimes, in fact, they did significantly better. Table 1 compares the manufacturing output of rural counties in Kentucky and the Midwest that bordered the Ohio River. Rural manufacturing flourished on both sides, suggesting that access to markets encouraged industry in free-labor and slave-labor economies alike. The per capita value of manufactured goods produced in the Kentucky counties was nearly 11 percent higher than that produced in the midwestern counties. Neither crop selection nor the presence of natural resources can explain the superior performance of the Kentucky counties; resource processing accounted for only a slightly higher percentage of manufacturing output on the southern side of the Ohio. Although these Kentucky counties were hardly part of the black belt, slaves nevertheless constituted 20 percent of the population, slightly higher than the statewide average of 18 percent.

The success of rural manufactures in Kentucky belies the stereotype of the lazy slaveholder uninterested in economic progress. When traveling down the Ohio River, Alexis de Tocqueville compared Kentucky with Ohio. Focusing on the supposed impact of slavery on southern economic values, Tocqueville remarked that the slaveholder on the Kentucky side of the Ohio "scorns not only work, but all undertakings that work makes successful; living in idle ease, he has the tastes of idle men. . . . Slavery, therefore, not only prevents whites from making a fortune; it diverts them from wanting it."[10] Tocqueville could not have been more wrong; the "idle men" in Kentucky readily responded to market incentives. The catch is that incentives for Kentucky entrepreneurs were quite different from those for most other areas of the South. This example helps reframe the problem of southern industrialization. The key problem is not how southerners responded to market incentives, but why they generally lacked those markets in the first place.

Mountains, Slavery, and the Limitations of Southern Markets

As noted above, most of the literature stresses how a combination of slavery and mountainous geography limited southern markets. Our

10. Alexis de Tocqueville, *Democracy in America*, trans. and ed. Harvey C. Mansfield and Delba Winthrop (1835; reprint, Chicago: University of Chicago Press, 2000), 333.

Table 1

Comparison of Manufacturing in Rural Counties Bordering
Ohio River in Kentucky and the Midwest

	Kentucky (bordering Ohio River)	Kentucky	Border South	Midwest (bordering Ohio River)	Midwest
Per-capita output ($)	$39.21	$16.08	$18.34	$35.40	$24.64
Per-capita value added ($)	$15.38	$6.22	$6.86	$12.90	$9.44
Resource processing (% of value added)a	46.5%	50.8%	49.4%	42.5%	40.9%
Per-capita agricultural output ($)	$81.13	$77.63	$62.27	$47.96	$71.45
Value of wheat (% of agricultural value)	13.4%	11.1%	18.7%	22.8%	21.8%
Value of corn (% of agricultural value)	57.0%	62.2%	49.0%	51.0%	55.8%
Value of tobacco (% of agricultural value)	13.4%	8.7%	10.2%	4.9%	0.5%
Value of animal products (% of agricultural value)	15.5%	17.0%	19.2%	19.5%	19.4%

a. Resource processing includes flour milling, leather tanning, lumber (planed and sawed), liquor distilling, meatpacking (provisions), tobacco manufacturing.

Notes: The distribution of rural Midwestern counties bordering the Ohio River were as follows: Illinois, 5 counties; Indiana, 10 counties, and Ohio, 10 counties. There are 26 rural counties in Kentucky bordering the Ohio River. As a base of comparison, we included the southern states of Kentucky and Virginia for the South, and for the Midwest Ohio, Illinois, and Indiana. To obtain rural statistics, we dropped counties with a city of 5,000 or more inhabitants.

Sources: U.S. Bureau of the Census. Eight Census of the United States, Manufactures Washington, DC, 1865. U.S. Bureau of the Census. Eight Census of the United States, Agriculture. Washington, DC, 1865. U.S. Bureau of the Census. Eight Census of the United States, Population. Washington, DC, 1865. Arthur Cole, *Wholesale Commodity Prices in the United States, 1791–1865.* Cambridge: Harvard University Press, 1938. For the specifics of the data, see Kenneth Sokoloff and Viken Tchakerian, "Manufacturing where Agriculture Predominates," *Explorations in Economic History* 34, no. 3 (1997): 243–64.

evidence confirms the importance of these factors. Focusing on rural counties, table 2 classifies counties according to the proportion of slaves to the total population: "Low" counties fell into the lowest quartile; "High" counties, into the highest quartile; and "Middle" counties, into the other two quartiles. The per capita output and value added is decidedly lower in the two extremes. The middling counties did especially well in Upper South states such as Virginia and North Carolina. In regions such as Virginia's Shenandoah Valley, small slaveholding plantations mixed with yeoman farms produced a diverse output of tobacco, grains, and livestock. The Shenandoah Valley also had good access to markets through a system of roads, canals, and railroads. The combination of a diverse agricultural regime and an excellent transportation system supported a strong market for manufacturing. Conversely, areas with few slaves and those with many slaves supported very low levels of manufacturing. Explaining the poor performance of these two extremes can help uncover the factors that constrained the southern market for manufactured goods.

The absence of manufacturing in the counties with very small slave populations is perhaps the easiest to explain. As table 3 shows, most of the southern counties without many slaves were concentrated in the Appalachian region. The generally high cost of transportation in these areas created isolated settlements with low levels of commercial agriculture and local manufacturing. Historians have gone so far as to argue that the South was a dual economy composed of semisubsistence yeoman farmers in the upcountry and commercially minded slaveholders in the plantation belt. The mountain folk, some scholars maintain, resisted railroads and other improvements that would enmesh them in the world of capitalism. Other historians argue that residents of the southern upcountry enthusiastically embraced new commercial opportunities that came with the arrival of the railroad.[11] Our evidence does not speak directly to this debate because so much of the southern upcountry remained commercially isolated in 1860. While a thick railroad network already covered much of the lower Midwest, large swaths of

11. For a summary of the "dual economy" thesis, see Harry L. Watson, "Slavery and Development in a Dual Economy: The South and the Market Revolution," in *The Market Revolution in America: Social, Political, and Religious Expressions, 1800–1880* ed. Melvyn Stokes and Stephen Conway (Charlottesville: University Press of Virginia, 1996), 43–73.

Table 2

*Relationship between Per-Capita Manufacturing
and Slavery in the Rural South, 1860*

	Low		Middle		High	
	Output ($)	Value added ($)	Output ($)	Value added ($)	Output ($)	Value added ($)
South	12.67 (13.2%)	5.13	18.23 (13.2%)	7.41	11.80 (51.4%)	5.15
Alabama	5.03 (16.4%)	1.83	11.97 (38.1%)	5.52	11.75 (54.6%)	5.86
Georgia	6.65 (22.9%)	3.14	15.02 (43.7%)	5.98	12.54 (57.6%)	4.96
Kentucky	10.62 (8.7%)	4.33	20.80 (17.4%)	8.27	26.48 (26.0%)	9.93
Louisiana	10.41 (45.5%)	6.74	10.99 (45.5%)	7.75	7.17 (45.5%)	4.08
Mississippi	11.90 (34.1%)	6.24	11.01 (53.9%)	5.63	7.14 (66.9%)	3.89
N. Carolina	10.30 (18.3%)	3.41	20.75 (31.3%)	8.14	13.17 (44.4%)	5.62
S. Carolina	17.41 (39.8%)	6.30	11.50 (55.5%)	4.61	12.80 (65.4%)	3.46
Tennessee	13.10 (9.1%)	4.86	14.93 (16.5%)	6.88	14.52 (27.1%)	6.59
Virginia	14.25 (4.2%)	6.24	25.43 (4.2%)	9.47	13.46 (4.2%)	4.51

Notes: "Low" represents the lowest quartile of counties within the South or a specific state of the distribution of the ratio of slave population to total county population. "High" represents the top quartile of counties within the South or a specific state of the distribution of the ratio of slave population to the total county population. "Middle" represents counties not falling in either of the above categories. The figures in parentheses represent the percentage of the population that was enslaved.

Sources: See table 1.

Table 3

*Geographic Distribution of Counties in the Lowest Quartile of
Slave Population as Percentage of Total County Population*

State	Number of counties	Geographical description
Alabama	7	5 out of 7 (71%) located in the northern Cumberland plateau and Appalachians
Georgia	14	11 out of 14 (79%) located in the upcountry Appalachian region
Kentucky	36	16 out of 36 (44%) located in the eastern section, part of the Cumberland plateau. The only state with diffused pattern.
Louisiana	None	
Mississippi	1	
N. Carolina	11	10 out of 11 located in the westernmost part of the state, i.e., the Appalachian mountains
S. Carolina	None	
Tennessee	36	28 out of 36 (78%) in the eastern section of the state, the Appalachian mountains and the Cumberland plateau
Virginia	55	39 out of 55 (71%) located in present-day West Virginia and hence in the Allegheny mountains and plateau. The rest of the counties are predominantly located close to the border of present-day West Virginia and are also in the Appalachians.

eastern Tennessee, western Virginia, and western North Carolina remained without viable transportation to regional and national markets as the Civil War approached.

Slavery also limited the extent of markets in the South. Historians have put forward a number of explanations of how slavery itself—as a factor distinct from soils, climate, or crop choice—retarded southern markets. Eugene Genovese has advanced perhaps the most influential thesis, arguing that the low population growth and high inequality of the plantation economy depressed southern demand for manufactured goods. Genovese notes that not only did the South have a much lower population density than the North, but it also had higher levels of inequality. A large number of slaves and poor whites demanded little in the way of consumer goods, while a small number of wealthy plantation owners purchased luxury manufactures directly from the North or from abroad. With little market demand, Genovese argues, southerners could not reap the same benefits of economies of scale as northerner manufacturers. The South was thus caught in a frustrating quandary. It provided a market for outside industry, but that market was too small to sustain local industry that could compete with factories supplying wider markets.[12]

Genovese's general emphasis on market limitations is certainly on the right track, but he may exaggerate the degree to which inequality hindered the growth of southern markets. Genovese postulates that slaves and poor white farmers constituted an exceedingly small market. Slaves undoubtedly consumed far fewer consumer goods than midwestern farm families, and slaveholders generally purchased rather minimal provisions of clothing, shoes, and blankets from outside suppliers. A substantial literature, however, suggests that some slaves purchased supplementary goods with money earned for extra work or produce grown on their own small plots. The work required to purchase a few comforts came at an exceedingly high price for slaves, who faced an already grueling work regime. Such purchases, though, provided slaves with a measure of autonomy and independence.[13] As for the South's "poor whites," some local

12. Eugene D. Genovese, *The Political Economy of Slavery: Studies in the Economy and Society of the Slave South* (1961; reprint, Middletown, Conn.: Wesleyan University Press, 1989), 165.

13. See, for example, Fogel, *Without Consent or Contract,* 191–93; John Campbell, "As 'A Kind of Freeman'?: Slaves' Market-Related Activities in the South

studies indicate that many yeoman families residing in plantation districts participated in the agricultural boom of the 1850s. As the rising price of cotton, tobacco, and grain increased the incomes of these farmers, it seems likely that these households purchased more manufactured goods.[14] Inequality may well have contributed to the lag in southern manufacturing, but something else seemed to have been holding back southern manufacturing at the local level.

Land-Use Patterns and Southern Manufacturing

Perhaps that "something" was another important link in Genovese's argument: the far lower rural population densities in the South. Regardless of the distribution of income, areas with low population densities would have smaller markets and higher transportation costs that would severely limit Smithian industrialization.[15] The problem, though, is that historians have not explained why slavery necessarily lowered rural population densities. A comparison of land-use patterns provides a possible answer. The 1860 census reports the number of improved and unimproved acres in each county. Improved acres consisted of land cleared for cultivation; unimproved land consisted of uncleared acreage. Table 4, which reports the ratio of improved to unimproved land in midwestern and southern states, shows a significant difference in agricultural regimes. Midwesterners farmed their acreage much more intensely—on average, 56 percent of their acreage was improved. On southern farms, only 33 percent of the acreage was improved. Although there was significant variation among states in both regions, no southern

Carolina Up Country, 1800–1860," in *Cultivation and Culture: Labor and the Shaping of Slave Life in the Americas,* ed. Ira Berlin and Philip D. Morgan (Charlottesville: University of Virginia Press, 1993), 243–74; Roderick A. McDonald, "Independent Economic Production by Slaves on Antebellum Louisiana Sugar Plantations," in *Cultivation and Culture,* ed. Berlin and Morgan, 275–99.

14. Majewski, *House Dividing,* 65–70. Frank L. Owsley, *Plain Folk of the Old South* (Baton Rouge: Louisiana State University Press, 1949), challenges the stereotype of the poor, degraded southern yeoman farmer.

15. Southern cities—and southern workers employed in industry—would also add to the aggregate demand of the region. The South's urban and industrial population, while growing in the antebellum period, was nevertheless still dwarfed by agriculture. In 1860, only 10 percent of the South's population lived in cities. Fogel, *Without Consent or Contract,* 307.

Table 4A

*Ratio of Improved-to-Unimproved Farmland
in the South and Midwest, 1860.*

SOUTH		MIDWEST	
States	Ratio	States	Ratio
ALL	0.496	ALL	1.260
Alabama	0.504	Illinois	1.612
Georgia	0.487	Indiana	0.994
Kentucky	0.664	Michigan	0.983
Louisiana	0.359	Ohio	1.561
Mississippi	0.477	Wisconsin	0.848
N. Carolina	0.389		
S. Carolina	0.405		
Tennessee	0.502		
Virginia	0.592		

Sources: See table 1.

ratio of improved to unimproved land came close to exceeding the lowest ratio in the Midwest.

To highlight the impact these differing ratios had on local population densities and markets for local manufacturing, consider the following thought experiment. A southern manufacturer determined that the geographic scope of his market was 72 square miles, which consisted of plantations with 75 improved acres each. What sort of rural market would this manufacturer have? Using the 1860 southern ratio of improved to unimproved acres, the average plantation would contain 226 acres, which would mean a total of 204 plantations. If southern plantations decreased the ratio of unimproved to improved acres to the midwestern average—and maintained the same number of improved

Table 4B

Ratio of Improved-to-Unimproved Farmland in the
South across Percent-of-Slave-Population Categories, 1860

	LOW	MIDDLE	HIGH
SOUTH	0.315	0.504	0.637
Alabama	0.269	0.474	0.747
Georgia	0.252	0.441	0.764
Kentucky	0.265	0.692	1.351
Louisiana	0.285	0.326	0.500
Mississippi	0.323	0.426	0.733
N. Carolina	0.308	0.346	0.566
S. Carolina	0.266	0.487	0.375
Tennessee	0.349	0.400	0.820
Virginia	0.253	0.630	1.055

Notes and sources: See tables 1 and 2.

acres—the market size for our southern manufacturer would dramatically jump 68 percent, to 342 plantations. That would mean 138 additional plantations to purchase clothing, boots and shoes, wagons, and an array of other manufactured goods. Simply by decreasing the number of unimproved acres in their farms, southerners would have developed significantly deeper rural markets to encourage manufacturing.

The South's dispersed rural population also had a significant impact on the region's transportation system. Southern canals and railroads, weaving their way through a countryside in which most of the land was uncultivated, had significantly less traffic than midwestern projects. The low level of local manufacturing further accentuated the lack of potential traffic. Local manufacturers and merchants who might have supplied traffic and capital to ambitious projects did not exist to the same degree in the plantation South as in the Midwest or Northeast. With far less potential to generate significant revenue, expensive intersectional improvements were particularly risky endeavors. Not surprisingly, the prospect of low returns generated calls for southern state governments to subsidize or directly operate most of the region's railroads. Whereas the private sector financed railroad construction in the North and Midwest, southerners increasingly relied on state governments.

The efforts of southern states met with decidedly mixed results. Southern railroad mileage rapidly increased in the 1850s, but southerners invested significantly less capital in each mile of track. In quality and speed, southern tracks were decidedly inferior, and southern railroads had far fewer locomotives and freight cars. State legislatures found it especially difficult to fund more ambitious trunk lines that would reach the dense markets of the Midwest. Politically powerful planters often opposed funding trunk lines, supporting instead shorter lines that served their own plantation districts. Urban merchants and manufacturers aggressively lobbied for the ambitious lines, but boosters from each southern city naturally supported their own cause at the expense of rival projects, which further divided state legislatures. As a result of the divisions within state legislatures, a series of proposed trunk lines remained unfinished at the onset of the Civil War.[16]

If land-use patterns in the South had such negative consequences for the southern economy, then why did southerners leave such a large percentage of their land unimproved? Slavery is certainly a prime suspect. Many northerners suspected that slavery encouraged southerners to adopt slovenly agricultural practices in which planters ruthlessly exhausted the soil before moving on to virgin lands.[17] More recently, economic historians have argued that slavery gave southerners much less incentive to invest in land.[18] The more detailed breakdown in table 4b,

16. For an analysis of railroads in Virginia, see John Majewski, "The Political Impact of Great Commercial Cities: State Investment in Antebellum Pennsylvania and Virginia," *Journal of Interdisciplinary History* 28 (1997): 1–26; and Majewski, *House Dividing*, 111–40. For the example of Georgia, see David F. Weiman, "Urban Growth on the Periphery of the Antebellum Cotton Belt: Atlanta, 1847–1860," *Journal of Economic History* 48 (1988): 270–71.

17. Sarah T. Phillips, "Antebellum Agricultural Reform, Republican Ideology, and Sectional Tension," *Agricultural History* 74 (2000): 799–822.

18. Gavin Wright, *Old South, New South: Revolutions in the Southern Economy since the Civil War* (New York: Basic Books, 1986), 17–50.

however, suggests that slavery was not the primary reason southerners left so much of their land unimproved. Counties without many slaves actually had the lowest ratio of improved to unimproved land; counties with lots of slaves had the highest. To a large extent, this pattern made economic sense. The mountainous topography of the nonslaveholding counties encouraged a more pastoral economy that utilized unculti- vated land for swine and cattle. The relative commercial isolation of the nonslaveholding economies would also discourage aggressive efforts to clear the land to produce surplus crops.[19] On the other hand, the high prices for cotton and tobacco in the 1850s encouraged slaveholders to clear as much viable acreage as possible. It should be kept in mind, though, that even with this economic incentive to clear as much land as possible, the ratio of improved to unimproved land in the large slave- holding counties was still well below the midwestern average.

Several clues suggest that the problem for southern agriculture was a combination of geography and climate. The ratio of improved to unim- proved land tended to decline as one moved from North to South. Three of the four Upper South states (Kentucky, Tennessee, and Virginia) ex- ceeded the overall southern ratio of improved to unimproved acreage; all five cotton states fell significantly below the regional average. More- over, the South's peculiarly low ratio of improved to unimproved land characterized the region's agriculture well into the late nineteenth cen- tury. In 1890, the ratio of improved to unimproved land in the nine southern states covered in table 4 was .73. Although somewhat higher than the antebellum ratio, it was nevertheless still significantly worse than the midwestern average for 1860. The midwestern states, in fact, had an improved-to-unimproved ratio of 2.9 in 1890. Southern states, in other words, still cultivated a far lower percentage of their land rela- tive to the Midwest twenty-five years after the abolition of slavery.

The South's soils and climate had much to do with its nineteenth- century land-use patterns. Most southern soils lacked calcium, potassium,

19. One might suppose that these counties might have specialized in resource ex- traction and other industries. Calculating the value added in flour milling, leather, liquor distilling, lumber, tobacco manufacturing, and turpentine (crude and dis- tilled), however, suggests otherwise. The percentage of these resource-processing activities out of all manufacturing value added in counties with relatively few slaves was 43.2; the figure for the rural South as a whole was 48.2 percent. Even processing industries, it appears, depended upon rural demand or good access to commercial markets. Many counties with few slaves had neither.

phosphorus, and other nutrients essential for plant growth. Southern settlers soon learned that the best way of "fertilizing" their land was to burn forests and undergrowth, which would release the needed nutrients into the soil. This method of cultivation, though, brought only short-term results. After five or six years, crops such as tobacco and corn would exhaust the supply of nutrients, forcing farmers and planters to allow the land to lie fallow for decades, when another forest covering could eventually be burned. Historians have sometimes associated this form of shifting cultivation with "soil exhaustion," but that term is misleading. Most southern soils, simply put, never possessed natural fertility to be exhausted.[20] Southerners might have used fertilizers to bring more land under cultivation, but these tended to be untried and expensive in the antebellum period. As agricultural historian Julius Rubin writes, southern farmers practiced "a form of shifting cultivation because there was no technological alternative."[21]

The warm, humid climate of the South also discouraged intensive agricultural practices. Antebellum farmers knew that clover and other fodder crops returned nitrogen to the soil, while providing cattle with excellent pasture. Northern farmers could thus utilize improved pasture lands to raise cattle that could produce milk, cheese, and butter, while preparing the land for future cultivation of wheat and other crops. These fodder crops, though, did not grow well in the southern climate. To make matters worse for southern farmers, the heat and humidity created a hospitable environment for ticks, which spread a low-grade fever among southern cattle. Although southern cattle usually survived such infections, their growth was stunted and their milk supply decreased.[22] Under these adverse conditions, it made little sense for south-

20. For a superb overview on the impact of southern soils, see Douglas Helms, "Soil and Southern History," *Agricultural History* 74 (2000): 723–58. Helms attributes the higher population density of the Midwest to the region's better soils (728). More than seventy years earlier, Ulrich B. Phillips recognized the importance of soils in shaping agricultural regimes in the antebellum South. See especially his comparison of Kentucky Bluegrass country with other parts of the South in *Life and Labor in the Old South* (New York: Little Brown, 1929), 72–111.

21. Julius Rubin, "The Limits of Agricultural Progress in the Nineteenth-Century South," *Agricultural History* 49 (1975): 362–73.

22. On the importance of livestock to intensive land use among northern farmers, see Donald H. Parker, *The Agricultural Transition in New York State: Markets and Migration in Mid-Nineteenth-Century America* (Ames: Iowa State University Press, 1995), 94–98.

erners to invest heavily in improved pastures, which had done so much to enable northerners to bring a higher percentage of land into cultivation. Instead, southern planters allowed their swine and cattle to roam their large tracts of unimproved land.

If climate and geography made it economically rational for southerners to hold a large percentage of their acreage in unimproved land, slavery may have reinforced these decisions. Economic historians Ralph Anderson and Robert Gallman have noted that "[t]o own a slave was to have access to his entire labor and to be responsible for his full maintenance." Masters thus considered slaves "fixed capital," which they had to keep busy year-round, especially during slack periods in the cycle of cotton cultivation. Slavery thus encouraged planters to grow food crops as well as export staples, but in a manner far different from that of northern farms. With plenty of hands to keep busy outside of planting and picking seasons, southern masters used their slaves to clear more land, which may account for the higher percentage of improved land in counties with slaves. To the extent that slavery gave planters a comparative advantage in shifting cultivation, economists who argue that slavery discouraged investment in land may be correct. Why invest in expensive fertilizers when otherwise idle slaves could clear land? Warm southern winters, Anderson and Gallman argue, further encouraged masters "to undertake tasks of repair, maintenance, land clearing, and construction in time between fall harvest and spring land preparation."[23] The interaction of climate and slavery gave planters every incentive to keep large tracts of unimproved land, the clearing of which could occupy their enslaved labor force.

Conclusion

Our comparison of the manufacturing of the Midwest and the South highlights the importance of markets in spurring early industrialization. When southerners enjoyed the same access as northerners to rich, deep markets—as in the case of the Kentucky counties along the Ohio River—entrepreneurs quickly responded and manufacturing flourished.

23. Ralph V. Anderson and Robert E. Gallman, "Slaves as Fixed Capital: Slave Labor and Southern Economic Development," *Journal of American History* 64 (1977): 28.

A multiplicity of factors hindered the development of similar markets in most southern localities, including the relative isolation of the southern upcountry, the unequal income distribution of the South, and the incentives for planters to establish relatively self-sufficient plantations. This chapter identifies another important factor—the climate and typography of the South, which encouraged farmers and planters to hold large tracts of unimproved land. The resulting dispersion hindered the development of the southern transportation network and discouraged southerners from moving resources out of agriculture and into industry.

The long-term pattern of southern landholding and its impact on manufacturing had political as well as economic consequences. Historians have long known that the South's insatiable appetite for more land helped create intense, sometimes violent competition over the fate of the western territories. Competition over the western territories, in fact, would do much to bring about the Civil War.[24] It remains puzzling, though, why southerners invested so much political capital in acquiring new land for slavery when so much of their acreage remained unimproved. Instead of risking violent confrontation with the North, why not simply improve their current farms or diversify into industry? Our analysis of landholding patterns suggests that southern farmers had little economic choice but to hold unimproved land as part of a comprehensive regime of shifting cultivation. The South's climate and soils made fertilizers and other reforms uneconomical for the vast majority of southern agriculturalists. Without the ability to improve agricultural practices, southerners could not build a home market that would spur industrialization. Southerners thus strove to expand slavery and their agricultural regime as far as possible. However politically disastrous, such a policy made economic sense given the constraints of southern climate and geography.

24. James McPherson, *Battle Cry of Freedom: The Civil War Era* (New York: Oxford University Press, 1988), 78–116.

Southern Textiles in Global Context

David L. Carlton and Peter Coclanis

The world, of late, has been all too much with the southern textile industry. For over a generation industry leaders have complained about the inroads of foreign competition on American domestic markets, while frantically "restructuring" their operations to enhance labor productivity—in the process shedding actual laborers and frequently whole communities. In 1997–1998 a peal of "distant thunder," sounded by the Asian financial crisis, sent the industry into a tailspin; by 2000 old-line producers of over a century's standing were collapsing, their buildings increasingly emptied or demolished (the rare cases of condominium conversion aside). Hollowed-out mill towns throughout the South, filled with aging, undereducated former millhands, could testify to the impact of the gales of globalization.[1]

While "globalization" has become a modern buzzword (or a cussword),

---

1. Charles Gerena, "Threads Rewoven," *Region Focus* (Federal Reserve Bank of Richmond) 6 (Fall 2002): 8–13; "U.S. Textile Makers Unravel under Debt, Import Pressures," *Wall Street Journal,* Dec. 27, 2001, p. A2. The term "distant thunder," the title of a classic film about the Bengal rice famine of 1941 by the Indian director Satyajit Ray, has been appropriated by Peter A. Coclanis to characterize the impact of distant events on another historic southern industry, rice cultivation. Coclanis, "Distant Thunder: The Creation of a World Market in Rice and the Transformations It Wrought," in David L. Carlton and Peter A. Coclanis, *The South, the Nation, and the World: Perspectives on Southern Economic Development* (Charlottesville: University of Virginia Press, 2003), 49–72.

however, the actuality of globalization has been a presence in southern textiles since the modern industry arose out of the ashes of the plantation regime. Factory-based textile production has for much of its history been closely bound up with the process of its diffusion to new regions of the world and with the successive rise and decline of industrial complexes. Possessed from the late nineteenth century of a sophisticated, centralized marketing apparatus, and a technology readily transferable and adaptable to a variety of local conditions, the textile industry, especially its ubiquitous cotton branch, is uniquely suited to a global treatment comparable to the commodity histories increasingly common in recent years.[2]

To be sure, the uses of a global perspective for understanding the rise, as well as the apparent fall, of the southern textile industry have not been readily apparent. For reasons indicated below, the story of the industry can be, and accordingly has been, written without much note of events occurring beyond American borders. Furthermore, scholarly neglect of the world context is mirrored by the parochialism of the southern industry itself, which has been slow to recognize the full extent of its world entanglements, and has often, characteristically, reacted to those entanglements with bursts of xenophobia. But a focus on the purely domestic context of the development of southern textiles is inadequate to understanding the industry's trajectory and, especially, the deep historical roots of its current crisis. The American South, as a "developing country" enmeshed in a developed one, has been paradoxically both in the world and outside of it, with telling consequences.

To begin with, it is arguably no accident that the strong expansion of the southern textile industry in the late nineteenth century coincided with a major transition in the history of the industrialized world, from the so-called First to the Second Industrial Revolution. In the "First"

2. The most important of these is Sidney Mintz, *Sweetness and Power: The Place of Sugar in Modern History* (New York: Viking, 1985). Other representative examples include Victor G. Kiernan, *Tobacco: A History* (London: Hutchinson Radius, 1991); Noel Deerr, *The History of Sugar* (London: Chapman & Hall, 1949–50); Redcliffe N. Salaman, *The History and Social Influence of the Potato* (Cambridge: Cambridge University Press, 1949); Carl A. Trocki, *Opium, Empire and the Global Political Economy: A Study of the Asian Opium Trade* (London: Routledge, 1999); Sophie D. Coe and Michael D. Coe, *The True History of Chocolate* (New York: Thames & Hudson, 1996); and ongoing work by Peter A. Coclanis on rice and Sven Beckert on cotton.

Industrial Revolution, factory-made cotton textiles had been a leading sector. Commencing with the now-legendary eighteenth-century machinery developments that culminated with the construction of the first cotton factories, the British industry surged to world dominance in the first half of the nineteenth century, as its export trade penetrated successive markets and supplanted local handicraft production around the globe. At the same time, and despite mercantilist export controls on textile technology, the industry began to spread beyond Britain. The first offshoot took root in the northeastern United States, where a common language and culture facilitated exchanges of people and ideas; later, especially after the 1843 dismantling of export controls on British textile machinery, factory textile production spread to nearby northwestern Europe.[3]

The textile industry thus displayed its wanderlust ways from early in its history; however, up until the 1860s textile production remained highly concentrated in the two constricted zones—the U.S. Northeast and Britain/northwest Europe—that at that time constituted the core of the industrial world. As the economist Paul Krugman, among others, has noted, the textile industry, in some ways readily transferable, is in others among the most "gregarious," or prone to cluster, of all industries. During the First Industrial Revolution its gregarious tendencies were arguably at a maximum. The pioneer textile entrepreneurs had a great many basic problems to solve in the industry's early years. Not only did they have to develop the factory system, both its technology and its new forms of labor relations, but they also had to develop supply and marketing channels and the auxiliary institutions they needed to provide both financial capital (banks, securities markets, etc.) and human capital (journals, clubs, mechanics' institutes, etc.). These problems were best solved by concentrations of diversely skilled people working in close proximity to one another; indeed, the great British economist Alfred Marshall devised his concept of "external economies of scale" with the Lancashire cotton industry in mind.[4]

3. David J. Jeremy, *Transatlantic Industrial Revolution: The Diffusion of Textile Technologies between Britain and America, 1790–1830s* (Cambridge: MIT Press, 1981); Gregory Clark, "Why Isn't the Whole World Developed? Lessons from the Cotton Mills," *Journal of Economic History* 47 (Mar. 1987): 141–73, esp. 142.

4. Clark, "Why Isn't the Whole World Developed?" 143; David R. Meyer, "Formation of Advanced Technology Districts: New England Textile Machinery and Fire-

To be sure, such centripetal forces did not fully confine modern factory production to these locales; cotton factories began to appear at scattered sites outside its North Atlantic heartland, including India, Brazil, Russia, Mexico, and the American South, from early in the nineteenth century. However, these nascent factory industries remained minor players in the emerging world textile economy. Plagued by inadequate transportation, poorly integrated and shallow markets, and weak business institutions, peripheral producers found it difficult to achieve the critical mass necessary to rival core producers in the robustness of their institutions or the vitality of their entrepreneurial communities. Virtually all of them were dependent from the start on imports of textile machinery, especially from Britain, but such imports were constrained by the high costs and uncertainties of both overland transportation and shipping in the Age of Sail.[5]

Nor were actual transfers of core entrepreneurs and capital all that common prior to the 1860s. The American South, for example, saw some migration of small manufacturers from the Northeast into its interior regions in the early nineteenth century; however, for the most part these producers sought out constricted markets incapable of considerable growth but affording natural protection to enterprises remote from the dynamism of the core. Late in the antebellum period, merchant-entrepreneurs such as South Carolina's William Gregg would begin to introduce larger-scale bulk production on a model similar to that developed by the Boston Associates in New England. Such early entrepreneurs could be of considerable importance to subsequent developments,

---

arms, 1790–1820," *Economic Geography* (extra issue, 1998): 31–45; William Mass and William Lazonick, "The British Cotton Industry and International Competitive Advantage: The State of the Debates," *Business History* 32 (Oct. 1990): 9–65, esp. 10–18. On the theory of industrial districts, see Paul Krugman, *Geography and Trade* (Cambridge: MIT Press, 1991); Alfred Marshall, *Industry and Trade,* 4th ed. (London: MacMillan, 1923), 284–88, 599–619.

5. Stanley J. Stein, *The Brazilian Cotton Manufacture: Textile Enterprise in an Undeveloped Area, 1850–1950* (Cambridge: Harvard University Press, 1957), 1–19; Stephen H. Haber, *Industry and Underdevelopment: The Industrialization of Mexico, 1890–1940* (Stanford: Stanford University Press, 1989), 54–58; Ralph M. Odell, *Cotton Goods in Russia,* Department of Commerce and Labor, Bureau of Manufactures, Special Agents Series No. 51 (Washington: Government Printing Office, 1912), 7–9; S. D. Mehta, *The Cotton Mills of India, 1854 to 1954* (Bombay: Textile Association [India], 1954), 3–25; Ernest M. Lander Jr., *The Textile Industry in Antebellum South Carolina* (Baton Rouge: Louisiana State University Press, 1969).

for they brought into the receiving region essential skills that could be transferred to local citizens later on, when conditions were more propitious. However, there was at this time little incentive for massive industrial transfers; the greatest opportunities for profit and growth were concentrated in the core, where the costs of supply, marketing, and capital were lowest, and the access to skills and ideas was greatest.[6]

The basic environment within which the industry operated, though, had changed dramatically by 1880. To begin with, the 1860s and 1870s were tumultuous times for core producers, especially in Britain and the United States. The 1860s, of course, saw the American Civil War with its attendant "cotton famine," followed by the disruptions of Emancipation and the reconstitution of the cotton regime in the postbellum South. On the heels of these crises came the economic depression of the 1870s, which marked the start of the long-term deflation of the late nineteenth century. More deeply for our purposes, the 1870s divided the "First" from the "Second" Industrial Revolution. If textiles were a leading sector in the first, the industry had reached maturity by the beginning of the second; having by that time successfully supplanted local handicraft production around the globe, its growth rate dropped after the 1870s to a much lower trajectory.[7]

What did this mean? Among other things, it represented a potentially serious crisis for suppliers of capital goods to the industry. Early textile manufacturers in both Britain and America had had their machinery constructed by local mechanics or, increasingly, by employees in their own machine shops. However, as the industries of both places burgeoned, machine building increasingly left the textile factory to become the special province of independent, freestanding enterprises such as

6. Lander, *Textile Industry in Antebellum South Carolina*; Richard W. Griffin, "North Carolina: The Origin and Rise of the Cotton Textile Industry, 1830–1880" (Ph.D. diss., Ohio State University, 1954). On the larger picture of industrialization in the slave South, see Fred Bateman and Thomas Weiss, *A Deplorable Scarcity: The Failure of Industrialization in the Slave Economy* (Chapel Hill: University of North Carolina Press, 1981).

7. D. A. Farnie, *The English Cotton Industry and the World Market, 1815–1896* (Oxford: Clarendon Press, 1979), 135–205; Gavin Wright, *The Political Economy of the Cotton South: Households, Markets, and Wealth in the Nineteenth Century* (New York: W. W. Norton, 1978), 94–97; Mary B. Rose, *Firms, Networks, and Business Values: The British and American Cotton Industries since 1750* (Cambridge: Cambridge University Press, 2000), 168.

Platt Brothers and Company of Oldham, Lancashire, and the Lowell Machine Shop of Massachusetts. In the salad days of the textile industry, these firms garnered plenty of business; firms such as Lowell faced a "seller's market," and could rely on continuing business and referrals to do their marketing for them. However, the successive crises of the 1860s and 1870s not only jolted short-term business, but also left their future outlooks cloudy. Textile machinery as a rule was quite durable. While mills were happy to replace their equipment with technologically more advanced models when profits were strong and the future bright, the new slower-growth environment, with its narrow and less-certain margins, made mill managers more cautious about capital expenditures. In turn, machine builders found themselves facing a straitened market confined largely to spare parts for older equipment, while their newer, more innovative models went begging for sales.[8]

Increasingly, the machine makers realized that they had to develop new markets for their products. Fortunately, new avenues were at that time opening up on the periphery of the industrial world. The previous generation had seen a revolution in global transportation and communications, including the application of steam and steel-bottomed hulls to blue-water shipping, the opening of the Suez Canal, and the laying of the first transoceanic cables. Within the United States, a transportation network that had still been disjointed in 1860 was knit into a coordinated network permitting continuous through shipments over a continental land mass. In India, the British Raj extended the railroad network and dismantled internal barriers to trade. Imperial power was now being projected more forcefully than ever before, whether directly in India and (in a manner of speaking) the American South, or indirectly in Latin America and (with the "Black Ships") Japan. The dominance of British financial and marketing institutions facilitated industrial trans-

8. David R. Meyer, "Formation of Advanced Technology Districts"; Farnie, *English Cotton Industry and the World Market,* 54–57, 186–87; D. A. Farnie, "The Textile Machine-Making Industry and the World Market, 1870–1969," *Business History* 32 (Oct. 1990): 150–65, esp. 151; George Sweet Gibb, *The Saco-Lowell Shops: Textile Machinery Building in New England, 1813–1949* (Cambridge: Harvard University Press, 1950), 203–10, 240–41; Thomas R. Navin, *The Whitin Machine Works since 1831* (Cambridge: Harvard University Press, 1950), 132–33. On the early milieu in which the New England textile machinery industry arose, see also John William Lozier, *Taunton and Mason: Cotton Machinery and Locomotive Manufacture in Taunton, Massachusetts, 1811–1861* (New York: Garland, 1986).

fers to economically porous nations such as Brazil, while nations more resistant to Western penetration, such as Japan, sought to build indigenous business institutions on Western models.[9]

Moreover, textile technology had developed in a manner that facilitated its transfer to underdeveloped regions. British engineers had perfected the self-acting mule by the late 1860s, an event that, according to D. A. Farnie, "freed the industry from the fear of technical change as well as from the need for the constant application of inventive skill." However, the major developments of this sort occurred in the United States. Unlike Britain, which relied heavily on its ample supplies of skilled mule spinners and weavers, American producers suffered from a chronic dearth of skilled labor. As a result, American inventors and machine builders concentrated on developing labor-saving, and especially skill-saving, innovations. The ring spindle, for instance, dramatically extended the range of yarn counts that could be spun by unskilled labor, including young girls; a sharp increase in spindle speeds in the 1870s and 1880s to around 10,000 RPM sparked a sharp increase in ring adoption. Later, in the 1890s, the automatic loom segmented some of the weaver's tasks into less-skilled specialties and automated others. After the 1870s these technologies were taken up by British machine builders as well, though primarily, and tellingly, for export rather than domestic use. Essentially, textile technology, whose development had earlier been closely tied to the "local knowledge" of skilled workers and manufacturers, had become portable, capable of being set up virtually anywhere and operated by workers with relatively ubiquitous skills; ring spinning, in particular, was a technology with great "democratizing potential."[10]

Accordingly, the last two decades of the nineteenth century saw what

9. Rose, *Firms, Networks, and Business Values*, 168–69; George Rogers Taylor and Irene D. Neu, *The American Railroad Network, 1861–1890* (Cambridge: Harvard University Press, 1956); Stein, *Brazilian Cotton Manufacture*, 13–14; Mehta, *Cotton Mills of India*, 40, 46. A good survey of the period with these developments in mind is Eric J. Hobsbawm, *The Age of Capital, 1848–1875* (New York: Scribner's Sons, 1975), esp. ch. 3.

10. Farnie, *English Cotton Industry and the World Market*, 246–47; Farnie, "The Textile Machine-Making Industry," 154–56; Navin, *Whitin Machine Works*, 182–203; William N. Mass, "Technological Change and Industrial Relations: The Diffusion of Automatic Weaving in the United States and Britain" (Ph.D. diss., Boston College, May 1984). The phrase *democratizing potential* comes from Gary Saxonhouse and Gavin Wright, "Technological Diffusion in Cotton Spinning, 1878–1933," Stanford Economics Working Paper, Jan. 2000.

could be termed a global "breakout" of the textile industry, as factory production sharply expanded outside the original core regions of the industrial world. In 1875 nearly 70 percent of the world's spindleage lay within the boundaries of either Great Britain or the American North; by 1910, despite continued expansion in both regions, their proportion of the world total had dropped to just over half.[11]

In Brazil, the first cotton factories were established in the 1840s, but as late as 1866 the nation could still boast a mere nine mills with total spindleage of 15,000, or a mere 1,500 apiece; by 1885 the number of mills had risen to 48, and the spindleage to 66,466, or more than quadruple the earlier capacity. Truly massive growth was still to come, though, as the establishment of the Brazilian Republic and massive institutional reform sparked a major industrial boom. By 1905 the industry had expanded to 110 factories, with over 11 times the spindleage of twenty years before. Growth continued into the 1920s at a less-breakneck pace before stabilizing at 2.5 million spindles and well over 100,000 workers.[12]

In India, where British manufacturers had largely supplanted traditional handicraft production with factory-made yarn and cloth, British and Indian entrepreneurs began to develop spinning mills in the early 1850s, creating an industry that by 1876 could already boast over 1 million spindles. By 1900 Indian spindleage had nearly quintupled, and the number of looms had quadrupled. Even more spectacular was the nascent textile industry of Japan, which after several false starts began to expand spectacularly from 50,000 spindles in 1884 to 1.38 million in 1900. By the 1890s Japanese entrepreneurs, who had followed the practice of their British suppliers by using mules, were switching massively to the ring spindle, which could be worked easily by their labor force of migrant country girls, and were beginning to tap government assistance to open export markets.[13]

11. Calculated from U.S. figures cited in Melvin T. Copeland, *The Cotton Manufacturing Industry of the United States* (Cambridge: Harvard University Press, 1917), 34, 275, subtracting southern spindleage from the U.S. total; and world figures cited in Copeland and in Farnie, *English Cotton Industry and the World Market*, 180.

12. Stein, *Brazilian Cotton Manufacture*, 191; Stephen Haber, "The Efficiency Consequences of Institutional Change: Financial Market Regulation and Industrial Productivity Growth in Brazil, 1866–1934," National Bureau of Economic Research, Historical Paper No. 94, Nov. 1996.

13. A brief overview of the Indian and Japanese cases can be found in Keijiro Otsuka, Gustav Ranis, and Gary Saxonhouse, *Comparative Technology Choice in*

By and large, these emerging non-Western industries pursued developmental paths appropriate to their peripheral positions. Brazilian firms patterned their operations early on after the integrated mills of places such as northern New England, producing bulk quantities of cheap, staple goods for sale to low-end customers both within Brazil and in the neighboring River Plate region. India and Japan initially built their industries as yarn-spinning complements to their nations' persistent handloom weaving sectors, broadening into cloth production later on. Indian spinners further bolstered their position by exploiting the massive markets offered by Chinese handloom weavers; later, as the Japanese began targeting export markets, they did so with bulk production of plain goods produced in integrated mills.[14]

Most strikingly, all three relied almost exclusively on British machine builders for their equipment. While some early Brazilian manufacturers purchased machinery from American shops, they quickly came to rely on Lancashire engineering firms; the other countries did so from the outset.[15] The choice of British technical support had little to do with the differences between British technology (based on the self-acting mule) and American. Brazilian and Japanese firms overwhelmingly adopted rings, and while mules remained important in India until after World War I, Indian manufacturers were enthusiastic early adopters of the

---

Development: The Indian and Japanese Cotton Textile Industries (New York: St. Martin's Press, 1987), 5–20. The timing of textile industry extension to India was similar for another fiber, jute. In 1854 John Kerr of the Douglas Foundry (the leading maker of flax- and jute-preparing machinery in Dundee) provided preparing and spinning machinery for a planned mill in Bengal—the Rishra mill near Serampore, which opened in 1855. Bruce Lenman, Charlotte Lythe, and Enid Gauldie, *Dundee and the Textile Industry,* Abertay Historical Society Publication No. 14 (Dundee: Abertay Historical Society, 1969), 27.

14. Stein, *Brazilian Cotton Manufacture,* 23–24, 115–17; W. A. Graham Clark, *Cotton Goods in Latin America,* part 2, *Brazil, Colombia, and Venezuela,* U.S. Department of Commerce and Labor, Bureau of Manufactures, Special Agents Series No. 36 (Washington: Government Printing Office, 1910), 49–50; W. A. Graham Clark, *Cotton Goods in Japan and Their Competition on the Manchurian Market.* U.S. Department of Commerce and Labor, Bureau of Foreign and Domestic Commerce, Special Agents Series No. 86 (Washington: Government Printing Office, 1914), 114–30; Mehta, *Cotton Mills of India,* 46–48.

15. Stein, *Brazilian Cotton Manufacture,* 35–38, 48; Mehta, *Cotton Mills of India,* 43; Otsuka, Ranis, and Saxonhouse, *Comparative Technology Choice in Development,* 91.

American innovation.[16] The industrialists of all these countries, though, preferred British versions of American-style equipment.

The British advantage lay in their pioneering creation of an engineering industry geared toward the systematic extension of British industrial practice to the outside world. As early as the 1840s, Lancashire machine builders had devised techniques for "packaging" British technology for offering to would-be entrepreneurs in other parts of northwestern Europe. As the non-European world became available as an industrial site, Lancashire engineers took advantage of the new markets to build one of late-Victorian Britain's most important export industries. Purveying their products to the world, they enjoyed the advantage of massive economies of scale. Selling to far-flung foreign markets as well as to their neighbors, they developed highly standardized products that made repairs fairly easy and kept their costs the lowest in the world. The skilled workingmen of such engineering centers as Oldham followed the machinery across the globe to set up British equipment and introduce British know-how to the world. Platt Brothers and Company of Oldham became by far the leading textile machinery maker in the world, at one time outproducing the whole of the American industry.[17]

Such was the world in which the textile industry of the American South began its surge in the late nineteenth century. In 1880 the southern industry was by no means negligible, its total spindleage being well over half a million—lower than India, but well ahead of Brazil and Japan. Nonetheless, southern spindleage expanded dramatically after 1880; by 1910 11.2 million spindles were located in the South, giving a hypothetically independent Confederacy the third largest installed capacity in the world, behind only Britain and the American North. While the nonsouthern (or "northern") industry had also expanded during

16. Mehta, *Cotton Mills of India,* 43–44; Gary Saxonhouse and Gavin Wright, "Rings and Mules around the World: A Comparative Study in Technological Choice," in *Technique, Spirit and Form in the Making of the Modern Economies: Essays in Honor of William N. Parker,* ed. Gary Saxonhouse and Gavin Wright, Research in Economic History, Supplement 3, 1984 (Greenwich, Conn.: JAI Press, 1984), 271–300, esp. 275–86.

17. Kristine Bruland, *British Technology and European Industrialization: The Norwegian Textile Industry in the Mid-Nineteenth Century* (Cambridge: Cambridge University Press, 1989); Farnie, *English Cotton Industry and the World Market,* 246; Navin, *Whitin Machine Works,* 325.

this time, some 60 percent of the incremental growth in American spindleage had been directed to Dixie.[18]

Like that of the factories of Japan, India, and Brazil, the bulk of southern growth came in the most "portable" branches of the industry. While an indigenous colored-goods industry flourished in central North Carolina, massive firms arose in South Carolina and further south devoted to the bulk production of a narrow range of staple constructions. The markets for these generic, commodity-like products having been long established, southern mills had no need to take risks on novelty items; competition was primarily on price, providing bulk producers combining low-cost, low-skill labor with skill-saving machinery to decisive advantage. While the South had no traditional handloom industry of the sort found in India or Japan, numerous spinning mills arose to supply the weave sheds and hosiery and carpet mills of Philadelphia, clustering particularly in the region around Charlotte, North Carolina.[19]

By the 1890s, when recurrent depression began to afflict the New England cotton-textile industry, northern machinery makers began to see their future in developing the southern market—just as their British cousins had seen theirs in supplying the nascent cotton mills of the non-European world. Not only were low-cost southern producers better able to withstand hard times, but new-generation machines such as the high-speed, lightweight ring spindle and the automatic loom—both adaptable to the bulk production and fresh-off-the-farm labor of the South—were adopted there with greater alacrity than they were in the builders' traditional markets.[20] Traditional relationships and word-of-mouth referrals no longer worked in a slow-growth environment; one

18. Copeland, *Cotton Manufacturing Industry of the United States*, 34. For another view of the southern expansion of the late nineteenth century, see Beth English, "Beginnings of the Global Economy: Capital Mobility and the 1890s U.S. Textile Industry," in this volume.

19. Pamela Vadman Ulrich, "'Plain Goods': Textile Production in Georgia, the Carolinas and Alabama, 1880 to 1920" (Ph.D. diss., University of Oregon, 1991); David L. Carlton, "The Revolution from Above: The National Market and the Beginnings of Industrialization in North Carolina," in *The South, the Nation, and the World*, 73–98.

20. Mass, "Technological Change and Industrial Relations," 83–140; Melvin T. Copeland, "Technical Development in Cotton Manufacturing since 1860," *Quarterly Journal of Economics* 24 (Nov. 1909): 109–59, esp. 131.

had to grow by aggressively seeking out new customers eager for new equipment, and the great happy hunting ground for new customers was the South.

The confrontation of an overbuilt capital-goods industry and a region of capital-short, hard-bargaining customers sparked an upsurge of cutthroat competition, as producers slashed prices and accepted southern mill stock in payment for equipment, thus helping transfer capital as well as technology to the South. More enduringly, competition for southern business forced machine makers to enhance the portability of their technology. Whereas previously machinery had been shipped fully assembled, shops began sending machinery partially "knocked down," so that the larger machine makers began to maintain a force of "erectors" in the South. Advances in precision machining—the fruits of the "American System" of manufactures—minimized the need for "fitting" at the erection site.[21]

Important institutional innovations further lubricated the southward transfer of technology. The depressed years of the 1870s had already seen the rise of the independent consulting engineer, providing aspiring but unknowledgeable southern entrepreneurs with a single guide through what had become an overgrown thicket of specialized shops. In the 1890s these were supplemented by the appearance of the independent southern agency, which bundled different lines of machinery along with services and supplies; the most famous of these agents, D. A. Tompkins of Charlotte, North Carolina, extended his reach into promotion as well, becoming one of the great practical publicists of the New South. Unhappy with the agents' conflicts of interest, the larger shops established their own agencies, bundling the offerings of smaller producers to fill gaps in their own lines. After 1900 both marketing consolidation and cutthroat competition led to a major shakeout and consolidation in the machinery industry.[22]

21. Navin, *Whitin Machine Works*, 209–35; Gibb, *Saco-Lowell Shops*, 272–73, 351–56, 416–19. On the importance of solving the problem of "fitting" to the emergence of American-style mass production of precision machinery, see David A. Hounshell, *From the American System to Mass Production, 1880–1932*, Studies in Industry and Society, 4 (Baltimore: Johns Hopkins University Press, 1984).

22. On the rise of the independent mill engineer, see Navin, *Whitin Machine Works*, 121–23, 209–11; Samuel B. Lincoln, *Lockwood Greene: The History of an Engineering Business, 1832–1958* (Brattleboro, Vt.: Stephen Greene Press, 1960), 73–116. Charles T. James, the antebellum New Englander who has been generally

Thus, like their British counterparts, New England machine makers and other suppliers of services responded to the conditions of an increasingly mature, slow-growth industry by aggressively encouraging the proliferation of new customers in less-developed regions of the world—only in their case a less-developed region within the boundaries of their own country. Furthermore, like other new producers around the world, southern textile industrialists persisted in their dependence on metropolitan technology. By the late nineteenth century textile technology was largely set, but into the early twentieth century important innovations continued to be generated by the core producers. New and Old England boasted a plenitude of skilled machinists. Moreover, while machine-making had spun off into an independent industry, many larger mills maintained in-house machine shops, and a number of the most important developments, such as the ring spindle, developed through collaboration between practical millmen and shopmen. Some shops, such as George Draper and Sons in New England, pioneered in research and development, as well as in the aggressive use of patent law, to build competitive "moats" around their products. Sharing a common language and constant flow of information, skilled workers, and investigators, British and New England technologies cross-fertilized each other—Americans contributing the high-speed ring spindle to Britain, the British offering the revolving flat card to their Yankee cousins. Finally, old-line producers began concentrating their attention on refining their productive processes through economies of scale, specialization, consolidation, and, in New England, adoption of "American System"–style interchangeability of parts. Although western Europe developed its own important textile technology community—with important consequences down the line—the developing-world industries of the late nineteenth century generally relied on the accumulated, and increasingly widely available, skills and experience of the "Englands."[23]

While the machine builders' relentless cultivation of the southern U.S. market mimicked the British export of the textile industry abroad,

regarded as the first of these independent consulting engineers, was an important proponent of southern industrialization; see Lozier, *Taunton and Mason,* 375–88. On the southern agency, see Navin, *Whitin Machine Works,* 217–23; Gibb, *Saco-Lowell Shops,* 269–70, 351–52, 414–15.

23. Gibb, *Saco-Lowell Shops,* 210–16, 344–46; Farnie, "Textile Machine-Making Industry," 154–57; Mass, "Technological Change and Industrial Relations," 54–77.

their general neglect of foreign sales reflected the great peculiarity of the American textile industry in a global context: its essential confinement to the home market. Despite the great size of the American textile machinery industry—second only to the British industry, and indeed surpassing it by World War I in value of product—it was historically but a minor factor in supplying the world industry. The labor market for the American textile industry was, by world standards, a high-wage market, and accordingly, its technology tended to substitute capital for labor, adding to the cost of American-made equipment relative to that of its British competitors. As a result, markets outside the United States were largely closed to American producers. Historians of the major firms find but scattered foreign orders in the nineteenth century, and even in the 1920s and 1930s, when they were at their most competitive, American producers accounted for only 5 percent of world export tonnage and 10 percent of export value.[24]

Similarly, the southern textile industry was unique among the "developing world" textile industries in that it was wedded to the American home market. Southern yarn makers arose as feeders to the specialized weavers and hosiers of Pennsylvania and Rhode Island; unlike their counterparts in India, they could make little headway in opening the vast yarn market of China.[25] The integrated bulk producers, for their part, fed their products into a marketing system designed to serve the needs and requirements of a vast, expanding nation with a sophisticated distribution system.[26] The rapid settlement and urbanization of the United States assured them a growing market; the fact that they were the lowest-cost producers in the most commodified branches of the industry allowed them increasingly to take business from their northern competitors.

This is not to say that southerners lacked all interest in developing export markets. For instance, a number of the large bulk producers in upper South Carolina and adjacent districts placed much of their output in China, thanks largely to the aggressive marketing efforts of com-

24. Farnie, "Textile Machine-Making Industry," 152, 166–67; Gibb, *Saco-Lowell Shops,* 271, 480–81.
25. Ralph M. Odell, *Cotton Goods in China,* U.S. Department of Commerce and Labor, Bureau of Foreign and Domestic Commerce, Special Agents Series, No. 107 (Washington: Government Printing Office, 1916), 43–47.
26. Carlton, "Revolution from Above."

mission houses such as Deering, Milliken and Company, and Wood-ward, Baldwin and Company. At times, indeed, Woodward, Baldwin was marketing as much as 75 percent of the production of its Piedmont mills through its office in Shanghai, managed by a member of the Baldwin family; thanks largely to its efforts, South Carolina manufacturers accounted for nearly half of American textile exports in 1900. American—primarily southern American—producers dominated the market in North China and especially Manchuria, where a cool climate and masses of impoverished people generated strong demand for simply constructed unfinished plain goods. By the turn of the century such giant factories as the legendary Loray Mill of Gastonia, North Carolina, were being created exclusively for the China trade.[27]

Despite these developments, southern producers remained minor factors in the international markets. In 1900, the Census of Manufactures asked cotton goods manufacturers whether the goods they produced were intended for export. While southern mills reported somewhat greater export dependence than northern mills did, they still expected less than 10 percent of their product (by value) to go abroad. Export dependence was most pronounced in South Carolina, which accounted for three-quarters of southern exports; even the Palmetto State, however, only devoted a quarter of its production to the export trade. To be sure, the manufacturer-reported totals accounted for only two-thirds of actual exports; thanks to the complex marketing channels of the American textile industry, large quantities of American cotton goods entered international trade without the manufacturers' knowledge. But if the extra amount is allocated by region (a reasonable assumption), southern mills still only exported around 15 percent of their products.[28]

Why so little? For one thing, the export trade required special attention

27. *U.S. Census, 1900,* vol. 9, *Manufactures, Part 3, Reports on Selected Industries,* 25, 65–68, and table 24; Mary Baldwin Baer and John Wilbur Baer, *A History of Woodward, Baldwin and Co.* (n.p., 1977), 36–37; W. A. Graham Clark et. al., *Foreign Markets for the Sale of American Cotton Products,* U.S. Department of Commerce and Labor, Bureau of Manufactures, Special Agents Series, No. 11 (Washington: Government Printing Office, 1907), 11–13, 20–23, 36–37. On the early history of the Loray Mill, later the site of the most notorious strike in southern textile history, see James L. Love, *R. C. G. Love, a Builder of the New South: A Story of Reconstruction Days* (Chapel Hill: University of North Carolina Press, 1949), 41.

28. *U.S. Census, 1900,* vol. 9, *Manufactures, Part 3, Reports on Selected Industries,* 25, 65–68, and table 24.

to the varying requirements of foreign countries with respect to taste and distribution channels, concerns to which southern producers, and perhaps more important, their commission houses, comfortable with their established, familiar markets, tended to be oblivious. The fit between the Manchurian market and the low-cost bulk production of southern producers was uncommon; indeed, Americans were unable to compete with the British in South China, where marketing requirements were more complex. Moreover, foreign markets could be fraught with political hazard—as Woodward, Baldwin and the promoters of Loray discovered to their grief at the time of the Boxer Rebellion and the Russo-Japanese War. While one sees sporadic interest in exporting during slack periods in the industry, for most mills such interest went little beyond the desire to dump surplus production, and it tended to fade when prosperity returned.[29]

More important, when it ventured out into the world the southern textile industry lost its primary advantage, that of being the lowest-cost producer. Here again, while its development resonated with larger world developments, the American South, for all the parallels of its experience with that of the underdeveloped world, was above all *American*. Its real wage levels, while lower than those in the North, were among the highest in the world, well above those of Great Britain. Southern producers compensated for their high wage rates with a high productivity rate per worker, thanks in part to their substitution of relatively expensive capital equipment for labor (the automatic loom was virtually unknown outside the United States); economic historian Gregory Clark has estimated that, correcting for the greater utilization of labor in Britain, southern workers cost the same as British. However, the higher cost of capital in the South—unexpected in a capital-short region, but necessary in a skill-short one—left the region, by Clark's rough estimates, still at a competitive disadvantage to the British in world trade, even without considering Lancashire's superior experience and marketing savvy.[30]

29. Copeland, *Cotton Manufacturing Industry of the United States,* 220–31. The various country-level reports on the cotton-textile trade prepared by agents of the U.S. Department of Commerce and Labor between 1907 and 1916 describe the deficiencies of American textile marketing abroad in detail. See, in particular, U.S. Department of Commerce and Labor, Bureau of Manufactures (later Bureau of Foreign and Domestic Commerce), Special Agents Series, Nos. 11, 31, 36, 86, and 107 (Washington: Government Printing Office, 1907–1916).

30. Clark, "Why Isn't the Whole World Developed?" 146, 148, 150, 152, 164.

Thus, for the most part, the outlets of southern cotton textile manufacturers were confined to the American home market. Up until World War I, however, their failure to expand much abroad did not represent a big problem for them. The American market for bulk goods was enormous and expanding, and southern producers, as the lowest-cost producers in the industry, were assured places at the table.

That all changed dramatically in the 1920s. After a war-induced boom in production, and a dramatic inflation of prices, the American industry lurched into a long-term depression. The immediate causes of this depression were multiple: overexpansion during the war, sharply higher costs for raw materials and labor, and an increasing role for fashion in clothing, making the bulk production of staple goods less viable. But the longer-term problems were rooted in longer-term developments and were worldwide in character. With much of its production consisting of relatively undifferentiated commodity lines, and with a highly standardized technology that could be substituted for poorly developed human capital, textiles had become a mature industry in which too many producers were fighting for shares of a stagnating market and could only gain advantage through cutting costs. In these circumstances the old "core" industries of Britain and the American Northeast, which had maintained surprising vigor in the early years of the twentieth century, spiraled into sickening decline, their market shares snatched by emerging low-wage industries in India, Japan, and, of course, the American South.[31]

But at this point the paradoxical position of southern textiles in a world context became even clearer. By 1930, as old-line New England firms went bankrupt or began transferring assets to the South, the southern Piedmont became the new center of the American textile industry, for southerners a shining symbol of the "New South" and for northerners an unsettling threat to the "American" (read "northern") standard of living irremediable by traditional protectionism. But the "victory" of the South was in part pyrrhic, for by consequence it lost much of its major competitive advantage. No longer the low-cost upstart, the southern industry was now setting the cost standard. By the

31. Jack Blicksilver, *Cotton Manufacturing in the Southeast: An Historical Analysis* (Atlanta: Bureau of Business and Economic Research, School of Business Administration, Georgia State College of Business Administration, 1959), 89–118; Claudius T. Murchison, *King Cotton Is Sick* (Chapel Hill: University of North Carolina Press, 1930); Rose, *Firms, Networks, and Business Values,* 206–19.

1930s, in fact, many old-line southern manufacturers in the northern Piedmont were beginning to discover that their major competitors were now farther south, in states such as Alabama, where a surfeit of farm labor was driving wages yet further down. By 1932 the head of one of the largest firms in North Carolina was complaining, in good New England fashion, that wages in South Carolina, Georgia, and Alabama were "so ridiculously low that we would be ashamed to run a business based on them."[32] Southern managers responded with massive cost-cutting measures; while they were aided by the advent of an important new labor-saving technology, long-draft spinning, they primarily sought to intensify the work pace—only to usher in an era of unprecedented labor conflict that sent hundreds of thousands of previously "docile" southern workers into sometimes violent battles with management and state authority.[33]

Thus the South, having long exploited the advantages of its "peripheral" position in the American economy, began to discover that, with respect to textiles, it had become part of the "core." More important for the long term, it began to have to reckon with the fact that, in a larger world context, it had always been simply a less-developed part of a "core" economy all along. In East Asia, especially in its prized Manchurian market, it had faced mounting difficulties even earlier, as Japanese and British competitors began running the "chops" (or brands) of southern mills out of the market. In the aftermath of World War I, the southern industry's position in international trade deteriorated further. Because the United States emerged from the world war as, for the first time in its history, a creditor nation, the relative cost of American cotton sharply rose, damaging world markets both for the raw material itself and for the products made from it. The rising relative costs of southern goods, along with the consequences of revolution and Japanese imperial expansion, led Woodward, Baldwin and Company, the leading conduit of southern cotton goods to China, to close its Shanghai office in 1916 and withdraw from the market entirely in 1931.[34]

32. Kemp P. Lewis to Dave S. Joseph, New York City, Aug. 19, 1932, Folder 417, Kemp P. Lewis Papers, Southern Historical Collection, University of North Carolina, Chapel Hill.

33. Jacquelyn Dowd Hall et al., *Like a Family: The Making of a Southern Cotton Mill World* (Chapel Hill: University of North Carolina Press, 1987), 183–236.

34. Clark, *Cotton Goods in Japan;* Baer and Baer, *History of Woodward, Baldwin,* 37–38.

Especially did the South find itself in an increasing disadvantage to the emergent industry of Japan. Arising at roughly the same time as the southern industry and as part of the same "breakout," in the late nineteenth century, Japanese producers had been far less efficient than American, although they had the competitive advantage of close proximity to China and aggressive government aid in opening markets. But Japan was unique among "developing world" textile industries in that from early on it began to shed its dependence on outside technology and began to develop its own stock of skills and, especially, its own capital-goods industry. Domestic demand in Japan was shaped by the empire's strong and deeply rooted handloom industry, which produced goods to which British looms were poorly adapted. The failure of the British to dominate the Japanese loom market opened the gate for an indigenous inventor such as Sakichi Toyoda to develop a specifically Japanese power-loom. By 1924 Toyoda's company (the ancestor of the modern Toyota Motor Company) had progressed to the introduction of its own automatic loom, adapted to the specific needs of Japanese manufacturers. Partly because of such technical developments, partly because of its easily controlled labor force of young, transient females, Japanese managers were able to dramatically increase their firms' productivity, and by the 1930s were dominating East Asian markets formerly controlled by the "core" producers, Britain and the American South.[35]

Thus, by the 1930s, the southern textile belt was displaying many of the characteristics of an established industrial region, while at the same time clinging to the strategies—bulk production of staple constructions at low cost—that it had used to establish its position, and that now made it vulnerable to outside competitors who could beat it at its own game. Fortunately, southern manufacturers still had the home market, and enough of the old-line New England bulk producers remained to allow southerners to continue to seize market share. They continued to cut costs by adopting such innovations as long-draft spinning and used their extraordinary power over their workers to successfully fend off labor unions in an era of heightened union power. World War II brought booming demand, and the postwar world offered pent-up domestic demand, a

35. Otsuka, Ranis, and Saxonhouse, *Comparative Technology Choice in Development;* Susan Walcott, "The Perils of Lifetime Employment Systems: Productivity Advance in the Indian and Japanese Textile Industries, 1920–1938" *Journal of Economic History* 54 (June 1994): 307–24.

world full of ragged customers desperate for resupply, and devastated Japanese competitors.[36]

The postwar world, though, also saw the effective completion of the textile industry's transfer from the North to the South. Moreover, it brought the United States fundamentally new responsibilities in the world, both military and economic. The New Deal represented, among other things, the displacement of the traditionally protectionist Republicans by the traditionally low-tariff Democrats, many of whom were rural-oriented southerners such as Secretary of State Cordell Hull. Convinced that such policies as the 1930 Smoot-Hawley Tariff had seriously worsened the depression, they enacted a policy of liberalizing trade through reciprocal agreements negotiated on a country-by-country basis. As the world lurched from depression to world war, the catastrophe came to be blamed in part on "beggar-thy-neighbor" protectionist policies, of which imperialism was seen as the ultimate expression. Accordingly, among the outgrowths of the famous Bretton Woods Conference of 1944 was a process for liberalizing trade across the globe, formalized in 1947 as the General Agreement on Tariffs and Trade (GATT). The push to open America's gates to foreign goods was yet further impelled by the national security imperatives of the Cold War, as the United States used access to its enormous market to shore up its allies and battle the Communist bloc for the "hearts and minds" of the less-developed world.[37]

As it happened, the best strategy available for developing and recovering countries in their effort to "crack" the American market was precisely the strategy that the South had used in the late nineteenth century—bulk production of low-end staples at the lowest cost. Here the Japanese, again, led the way. In the mid-1950s, after a decade of postwar recovery and the negotiation of an advantageous trade agreement with the United States, Japanese manufacturers inaugurated a systematic plan to selectively invade and dominate specific low-end, high-volume markets within the United States. By the late 1950s southern producers were beginning to feel the heat; mills were going on short time, and laid-off millhands began to appear in gathering spots for casual labor

36. Blicksilver, *Cotton Manufacturing in the Southeast,* 119–56.
37. A good, if jaundiced, overview of this transformation in U.S. trade policy can be found in Alfred E. Eckes Jr., *Opening America's Market: U.S. Foreign Trade Policy since 1776* (Chapel Hill: University of North Carolina Press, 1995), esp. ch. 5.

hiring in small towns around the region. By the 1960s some mills, especially older ones, were shutting down for good—even as the South was in the full flush of its postwar industrial expansion.[38]

The response of the southern industry to the Japanese invasion, and that of other developing countries in later years, was multipronged. Mills continued to cut costs, in large part by abandoning obsolete multilevel plants for single-storied, air-conditioned bunkers where materials could flow through the plant more easily. By the 1970s a wave of revolutionary new machines—air-jet and water-jet looms, open-end spinning, and the like—transformed factory floors throughout the region, a change that, among other things, dramatically reduced employment in the industry. Some firms, such as South Carolina's Milliken and Company, began to invest massively in research on new technology and innovative products—a task that few firms had undertaken in the past, being content to piggyback on research undertaken by government and by private suppliers such as machinery firms and (from the 1920s forward) synthetic fiber producers.[39] A few firms began to redirect their business strategy toward niche lines, such as home furnishings and industrial fabrics, that benefited from relative insulation from foreign bulk producers. The most sophisticated of these were "boutique" mills that offered sophisticated fabrics, quick response, and design services to high-end customers. Certain subindustries, such as North Carolina hosiery makers, developed cooperative strategies for sharing technology and exploring new markets.[40]

38. Blicksilver, *Cotton Manufacturing in the Southeast,* 156–62; Eckes, *Opening America's Market,* 169–77.

39. Julia C. Bonham, "Robotics, Electronics, and the American Textile Industry," in *Hanging by a Thread: Social Change in Southern Textiles,* ed. Jeffrey Leiter, Michael D. Schulman, and Rhonda Zingraff (Ithaca, N.Y.: ILR Press, 1991), 163–80; Brian Toyne et al., *The U.S. Textile Mill Products Industry: Strategies for the 1980's and Beyond* (Columbia: University of South Carolina Press, 1983), pp. 3–28; David L. Carlton, "Textile Town Settles In: 1950 to 1974," in *Textile Town: Spartanburg County, South Carolina,* ed. Betsy Wakefield Teter (Spartanburg, S.C.: Hub City Writer's Project, 2002), 209–31. On the role played by fiber producers in one important textile specialty, tufted carpeting, see Randall L. Patton with David B. Parker, *Carpet Capital: The Rise of a New South Industry* (Athens: University of Georgia Press, 1999), 118–20, 186–87, 267–73; for another example, see Annette C. Wright, "Strategy and Structure in the Textile Industry: Spencer Love and Burlington Mills, 1923–1962" *Business History Review* 69 (Spring 1995): 42–79.

40. A good description of a state-of-the-art "boutique mill" in North Carolina is Jim Phillips, "Valdese Weaves ERP Success Story" *Textile Industries* (May 2001), via

But the most visible response of the industry was defensive. By the late 1950s the leaders of the textile industry, and politicians representing textile-dependent southern states, had become vocal, indeed downright xenophobic, protectionists. The political scientist Alfred Hero, surveying the attitudes of southern textile executives in the early 1960s, found them (in his eyes) dishearteningly parochial toward trade liberalization and toward the outside world in general. They tended to blame imports (which at the time he was writing accounted for only 7 percent of U.S. consumption) for a number of plant closings, regardless of whether competition from imports was the decisive factor or simply (as was often the case) a contributing factor to the demise of a firm plagued by poor management, obsolete plant and equipment, or a behind-the-times commitment to bulk staple production.[41]

And, in truth, many firms found it difficult to adapt. The many independent firms in the industry lacked the profit margins needed to attract the capital required to remake themselves. But even technology had its limits as a savior. Like most "developing-world" textile industries, the South had based its growth on technology furnished from the outside; unlike Japan, it had never developed a significant industry of its own. While some elements of the American textile machinery industry relocated southward in the twentieth century, the center of production remained in New England well after World War II. In the meantime, the machine makers had grown technologically stodgy with age. Historically, New England manufacturers, the Drapers excepted, had never invested heavily in research and development; innovation came incrementally, generated by the larger community of talented mechanics and practical millmen in which the machine makers were embedded. As that pool of textile talent began to dry up in the interwar period, the machine firms were unable to make the transition to internal development of innovation. Content with their existing markets, buoyed by postwar growth, they increasingly fell victim to 1960s-era conglomerates who coveted them as "cash cows." By the 1970s the old-line machine makers were los-

http://www.textileworld.com/News.htm?CD=107&ID=483, accessed Aug. 18, 2004; the work of Hickory, North Carolina's Hosiery Technology Center is featured in Ayelish McGarvey, "When the High Road Isn't Enough," *American Prospect* (Jan 1, 2004): 53–56.

41. Alfred O. Hero Jr., *The Southerner and World Affairs* (Baton Rouge: Louisiana State University Press, 1965), 153–62.

ing ground, and they hang on today chiefly as suppliers of spare parts for aging, obsolete equipment.[42]

Accordingly, when the technological revolution of the later twentieth century made its appearance, its bearers were foreign, mainly European, builders. To be sure, the German, Swiss, and other firms eagerly cultivated the business of Americans, who just as eagerly snapped up the new technology. From the 1960s on, German and Swiss firms established sales and assembly operations in such southern textile centers as Spartanburg, South Carolina, anchoring what subsequently became an explosive growth in foreign investment along the I-85 "autobahn."[43] But continued reliance on outside technology scarcely provided the southern textile industry with a leg up on its competition, for these new air- and water-jet looms and open-end spinning frames were made widely available to producers around the world. The lack of a distinctive technological community left southern bulk producers with little to distinguish themselves from their counterparts in, say, Pakistan.

But, most important, the problem with southern textiles was that it clung to a business strategy that, however important to its growth, could not sustain it during the very different circumstances of its maturity. As one of the "developing world" industries arising in the late nineteenth century, it had sought to make use of what the economist Gary R. Saxonhouse has referred to as "shelf technology"—generic and highly portable—developed elsewhere to create firms whose chief competitive advantage was their ability to outdo firms of the "core" at massive production of staple goods at low cost. For these upstart industries, developing new markets was of less interest than seizing market share from older producers in already established markets.

As long as the "established market" in question was the U.S. domestic market—enormous to begin with, and fed by massive immigration, the shift from farm to city, and sharply rising incomes—the strategy was

42. Toyne et al., *U.S. Textile Mill Products Industry,* ch. 3; Glenn Bridges, "The Draper Story: Rise and Fall of a Loom-Making Giant," in *Textile Town,* ed. Teter, 257–59.

43. On this development, see Carlton, "Textile Town Settles In," 229; Laura Hendrix Corbin, "An International Influx: Following Textiles to Spartanburg," in *Textile Town,* ed. Teter, 254–55; Rosabeth Kanter, *World Class: Thriving Locally in the Global Economy* (New York: Simon & Schuster, 1995), 242–83; Marko Maunula, "Guten Tag, Y'All: The Arrival of Foreign Corporations in Spartanburg County, 1960–1992" (Ph.D. diss., University of North Carolina, Chapel Hill, 2004).

unproblematic. But, as the twentieth century increasingly revealed, the American South was unique among "less-developed" regions in that it was *American*. However poor they seemed by northern standards, southern workers commanded high wages by world standards, while the inflexibility of the bulk-production model made it difficult for them to compete in many world markets with the more agile British. The British dominated most world textile markets up to World War I because they, in effect, played General Motors to the American South's Ford; their broad range of goods and sophisticated marketing largely trumped the Model-T–like mass-production model of southern producers. But above all, the bulk-production-with-shelf-technology model was broadly available to countries with far lower labor costs than southern firms enjoyed. As the globe has shrunk, the contradictions of a "Third World" development strategy in the heart of a "First World" country have become unendurable.

All of which is not to say that the story of southern textiles is ending. One recent study, at least, has suggested that the industry is in fact "reinventing" itself, as new firms continue to enter the field even as older ones vanish.[44] The experience of American automakers, who, despite their own mass-production heritage, have expanded exports to the developing world as average incomes have risen, suggests that southern textile producers may be able to exploit niches even in the global marketplace. But the surviving industry will inevitably be an industry transformed— a high-technology, human-capital-intensive industry reliant on flexibility and creativity to make its way in the world. And such an industry—for better or worse—will represent a very different South than the one it played such a central role in shaping over the past century and a quarter.

44. Jim Levinsohn and Wendy Petropoulos, "Creative Destruction or Just Plain Destruction? The U.S. Textile and Apparel Industries since 1972." National Bureau of Economic Research, Working Paper 8348 (June 2001), via http://www.nber.org/papers/w8348, accessed Aug. 18, 2004.

Beginnings of the Global Economy

Capital Mobility and the
1890s U.S. Textile Industry

Deth English

Beginning in the 1890s, the center of cotton textile manufacturing in the United States underwent a regional transition from New England to the South. This relocation was an early step in the process of globalization within the industry, starting in the United States from one region to another at the turn of the last century, and continuing today from nation to nation. Late-nineteenth- and early-twentieth-century New England textile mill owners recognized that the highest profits could be made in the underdeveloped, overwhelmingly rural South, where labor was abundant, cheap, and unorganized, and opportunities for gainful employment were few. As seen through the lens of the Dwight Manufacturing Company, a Massachusetts-based producer of cotton textiles that eventually relocated to Alabama, these general globalizing tendencies characterized the industrialization of the post–Civil War South and led to the eventual deindustrialization of New England's textile manufacturing sector. Late-nineteenth-century southern industrial boosters and many state legislators linked the South's economic development inexorably to the maintenance of the region's low-wage, pro-business status quo. While successful in attracting the mobile capital of New England textile companies seeking to decrease their production costs by opening mills below the Mason-Dixon Line, this strategy for southern industrialization ultimately circumscribed the possibility for diversified economic growth and stifled the widespread establishment of high-wage industries that employed skilled workers. Indeed, the South's economy continued to rely on staple-crop cultivation and the transformation of raw materials into simple manufactured goods well into the twentieth century. Because many of the dynamics that shaped the Dwight Company's movement of capital from Massachusetts to Alabama during the 1890s are still at work within the worldwide economy, understanding the origins of the relocation of the cotton textile industry from New England to the South, particularly the parts played by labor, management, and state governments in this process, provides a historic reference point for and helps inform ongoing discussions about capital mobility, corporate decision-making, and the globalization of labor.

In 1880, Massachusetts cotton manufacturers looked forward, optimistically, to a long and lucrative future for their New England mills. But, as southern competition in the industry became a force with which to reckon during the depression years of the 1890s, these mill owners watched their profits shrink, and some began looking southward for relief from their economic woes. Thus, the process of transferring mill money, machinery, and jobs from one region to another in the U.S. textile industry began. "For some days the newspapers have been filled with accounts of the investments of large sums of money in the far South by the great cotton mill corporations of New England," wrote Carter Glass, owner and editor of the *Lynchburg News* in 1895. "They said their object in coming South is to get away from the meddlesome and restrictive laws enacted at the instigation of 'walking delegates' and lazy agitators. Their hope is to get among conservative people who want work and so [do] not hamper and hinder great enterprises."[1] Glass's short editorial boiled down two of the motives behind this turn-of-the-century capital flight: organized labor in the mills and "restrictive laws," often passed at the behest of unionized workers.

Massachusetts was one of the nation's first industrialized states, and as such, it was also a leader during the nineteenth century in enacting state regulations for manufacturing businesses. Massachusetts labor laws did not apply to all wage earners in the state equally, and compliance with the statutes varied from place to place and industry to industry. Never-

1. *Lynchburg (Va.) News*, Jan. 18, 1895.

theless, at the turn of the century, Massachusetts arguably had the most rigorous and detailed system of industrial legislation and enforcement of any state in the nation. After passing the Commonwealth's first labor law in 1836, the general assembly added new statutes, strengthened existing workplace regulations throughout the following decades. Massachusetts legislators passed the nation's first general factory safety act in 1877, and by 1898, they had sanctioned stringent education regulations for minors employed in manufacturing establishments, outlawed night work in factories by minors and women, and effectively limited the operation of textile mills in the state to fifty-eight hours per week.[2]

Despite the Commonwealth's labor laws and the contention of Bay State textile manufacturers that age and hours regulations would make them incapable of competing successfully with producers outside

2. The 1836 labor law regulated the employment of children under the age of fifteen in manufacturing establishments. Passed in 1874, the first law also covering adult factory workers limited the hours of work to sixty per week for all women and persons under the age of eighteen employed in manufactories. Although this law only applied to women and minors, the preponderance of women and minors working in the textile industry meant that no mill could function without them and had the practical result of making the sixty-hour week standard for all textile operatives. In 1892, legislators changed the provisions of this law to lower the maximum hours that women and minors could legally work from sixty to fifty-eight. On the development of Massachusetts labor legislation through the nineteenth century and the role of labor unions in the process, see Sarah Whittelsey, *Massachusetts Labor Legislation: An Historical and Critical Study* (1901; reprint, New York: Kraus Reprint, 1970), 9–13, 80–83, 107–43; Charles Persons, "The Early History of Factory Legislation in Massachusetts, from 1825 to the Passage of the Ten-Hour Law in 1874," in *Labor Laws and Their Enforcement with Special Reference to Massachusetts,* ed. Susan Kingsbury (New York: Longman, Green, 1911), 4–125; Henry Farnham, *Chapters in the History of Social Legislation in the United States to 1860* (Washington, D.C.: Carnegie Institution of Washington, 1938), 225–30, 253–65; Thomas Dublin, *Women at Work: The Transformation of Work and Community in Lowell, Massachusetts, 1826–1860,* 2nd ed. (New York: Columbia University Press, 1979), 108–31; David Montgomery, *Beyond Equality: Labor and the Radical Republicans: 1862–1872* (1967; reprint, Chicago: University of Illinois Press, 1981), 117, 230–47, 262–67; Robert R. R. Brooks, "The United Textile Workers of America" (Ph.D. diss., Yale University, 1935), 1–15; Mary Blewett, *Constant Turmoil: The Politics of Industrial Life in Nineteenth-Century New England* (Amherst: University of Massachusetts Press, 2000), 102–40; Tom Juravich, William Hartford, and James Green, *Commonwealth of Toil: Chapters in the History of Massachusetts Workers and Their Unions* (Amherst: University of Massachusetts Press, 1996), 51–52; Leon Fink, *Workingmen's Democracy: The Knights of Labor and American Politics* (1983; reprint, Chicago: University of Illinois Press, 1985), xii-xvi, 3–37, 219–33; Massachusetts State Federation of Labor, *History of the Massachusetts State Federation of Labor* (Boston: Federation, 1935), 14–23.

Massachusetts, where such restrictions did not exist, the late 1880s were profitable years for the state's textile industry. Dividends of the late 1880s, however, often turned into losses during the 1890s as the U.S. economy fell into a general depression. Between 1893 and 1897, numerous New England companies significantly curtailed operations or closed completely. Mill building and textile production in the Piedmont South, meanwhile, continued unabated, only adding to the difficulties Massachusetts manufacturers faced in selling their textiles domestically and abroad during the severe economic downturn. Within the context of the fifty-eight–hour week imposed by the state legislature in 1892 and growing labor unrest in mills throughout the state, expanding textile production in the South engendered a sense of impending disaster among many Massachusetts mill owners. During the depression years of the 1890s, therefore, the New England textile industry press and manufacturers' organizations increasingly focused their attention on devising solutions to the problem of southern competition.[3]

Three arguments dominated the discussion among Massachusetts manufacturers about how best to counteract the growing threat posed by southern mills. Many proposed avoiding competition with Piedmont mills entirely by switching their production from coarse to fine goods. Others advocated the complete replacement of old machinery in their mills with new equipment, citing the fact that the majority of southern mills were decades younger than New England mills, and their owners had installed the most technologically advanced automatic looms and ring-spinning machines when the mills were built. Retraining a workforce to make fine goods, breaking into the fine-goods market, which was dominated by British and European producers, and completely retooling mills with thousands of looms and hundreds of thousands of spindles necessitated a substantial outlay of money and the investment of a significant amount of time. The issues of time, money, and markets determined that these strategies, even if implemented immediately, would do little to alleviate the distress felt by Massachusetts textile companies during the depression years.[4]

3. Patrick Hearden, *Independence and Empire: The New South's Cotton Mill Campaign, 1865–1901* (DeKalb: Northern Illinois University Press, 1982), 97–98; Melvin Copeland, *The Cotton Manufacturing Industry of the United States* (1912; reprint, New York: Augustus M. Kelly Publishers, 1966), 221–24.

4. *Transactions of the New England Cotton Manufacturers' Association,* Annual Meeting, 1896, 61–62; Semi-Annual Meeting, 1886, 129–53, hereinafter cited as

A third proposed strategy for dealing with southern competition garnered the most attention and support from Massachusetts mill owners:
securing a moratorium on the passage of new regulatory labor laws and
working for the repeal of those already enacted. According to the leading millmen of Massachusetts, the state-mandated regulations with
which they were forced to comply, when coupled with the lower wages
paid to southern operatives, made it impossible for their goods to compete successfully with those manufactured in southern cotton mills. These
factors, mill owners contended, would ultimately lead to the "stagna-
tion" of the industry in the Bay State. Indeed, while state legislation
made the workweek in Massachusetts textile mills fifty-eight hours, other
New England mills ran sixty hours a week, and mills in the Piedmont
South typically operated sixty-six to seventy-two hours per week.[5]
Individual mill owners as well as lobbyists representing the Arkwright
Club and New England Cotton Manufacturers' Association brought before the general assembly their claims of being unfairly disadvantaged
by the regulatory legislation. Staunch opposition from lobbyists representing textile unionists and from state legislators friendly to labor, however, doomed the repeal agenda of the textile manufacturers. Arguments
began surfacing from among manufacturers' groups that the solution to
the problem of southern competition was not to be found in lowering
standards for Massachusetts mills, but in raising those prevalent in
southern mills. Yet, agitation and support for federal labor legislation
meant to equalize conditions in northern and southern mills remained
limited, and movements through the late 1890s to secure national regulations failed.[6]

NECMA Transactions. David Doane, "Regional Cost Differentials and Textile Loca-
tion: A Statistical Analysis," Explorations in Economic History 9 (Fall 1971): 22; Jac-
quelyn Dowd Hall et al., Like a Family: The Making of a Southern Cotton Mill World
(Chapel Hill: University of North Carolina Press, 1987), 46, 51; Alice Galenson, The
Migration of the Cotton Textile Industry from New England to the South, 1880–1930
(New York: Garland Publishing, 1985), 39–42; Mary Oates, The Role of the Cotton
Textile Industry in the Economic Development of the American Southeast: 1900–1940
(New York: Arno Press, 1975), 6–8; Chen-Han Chen, "Regional Differences in Costs
and Productivity in the American Cotton Manufacturing Industry, 1880–1900,"
Quarterly Journal of Economics 55 (Aug. 1941): 566.
    5. Arkwright Club, Report of the Committee on Southern Competition, 1897, 3;
Hall et al., Like a Family, 77.
    6. Arkwright Club, Report of the Committee on Southern Competition, 6–8; Amer-
ican Federation of Labor, Massachusetts State Branch, Proceedings of the Thirteenth

As Bay State textile manufacturers continued to discuss among themselves how best to neutralize the effects of southern competition, the city of Chicopee, Massachusetts, felt the full brunt of the 1893 economic depression. The city's two largest employers, the Dwight Manufacturing Company and the Chicopee Manufacturing Company, were cotton textile concerns. Throughout the 1890s the Dwight Manufacturing Company was the largest manufactory in the city with at least 1,600 operatives on its payroll.[7] As profits contracted and the fifty-eight–hour law curtailed working hours during 1893, labor-management conflict flared at the Dwight Manufacturing Company when a wage cut precipitated a strike by unionized weavers in the Dwight mills. The owners of the Dwight Company believed their control over the production process was undermined by the progression of labor laws passed by the state legislature as well as by this walkout of an estimated 600 unionized weavers. This local labor crisis, therefore, ultimately intersected with state labor legislation and an interregional fight for control of the coarse-goods textile market to create the conditions that marked a turning point in the history of the Dwight Manufacturing Company.[8]

The Dwight Company's intensified focus on labor costs in the face of southern competition dictated that it would not let unionized workers prescribe wage rates that could put the company at an even greater dis-

---

Annual Convention, 1898, 13–14. The American Federation of Labor had long advocated federally mandated labor standards for industry. During the depression, some New England manufacturers also began calling for national legislation similar to that endorsed by the AFL. *NECMA Transactions,* Annual Meeting, 1897, 93–94; American Federation of Labor, *Report of the Nineteenth Annual Convention,* 1899, 107; Hearden, *Independence and Empire,* 88, 101–4.

7. Vera Shlakman, "Economic History of a Factory Town: A Study of Chicopee, Massachusetts," in *Smith College Studies in History,* vol. 20 (Northampton, Mass.: Department of History of Smith College, 1935), 160, 168, 175; *Springfield (Mass.) Republican* 22 (Aug. 1893); *"The Blue Book" Textile Directory of the United States and Canada, 1891* (New York: Davidson Publishing, 1891), 78; see also directories from 1892 through 1899. The series is hereinafter cited as *Blue Book.* Shlakman estimated that the Dwight Company employed 2,000 and the cited *Springfield Republican* article noted that "Dwight employed over 2,000 hands," 400 workers more than the 1,600 employees listed as working for the Dwight Company in the *Blue Book* series throughout the decade.

8. *Springfield Republican,* Sept. 5, 1893. For a day-by-day account of the 1893 strike and events leading up to it, see also Aug. 22 and 23, and Sept. 6, 8, and 18, 1893; Shlakman, "Economic History of a Factory Town," 213–14.

advantage in the coarse-goods market. Given the surplus of goods in its warehouses, the limited demand for cotton textiles overall, and the fact the strike only affected three of Dwight's seven mills, the company felt no obligation to negotiate with the unionized weavers. In fact, Dwight management believed that any bargaining with the strikers would only encourage workers to use collective action as a negotiating tactic in the future. As had been their practice during previous periods of labor strife, management refused to deal with the weavers. Through the creation of a blacklist and evictions from company-owned boardinghouses, moreover, management also used the strike to purge its mills, albeit temporarily, of militant operatives.[9] Less than two weeks after the weavers' walkout, the near-impossibility of finding work elsewhere in a depression-plagued industry and the intransigence of the company forced the majority of the strikers back to work at the reduced scale of wages.[10]

In the wake of the weavers' strike, and while Chicopee remained mired in economic depression, the owners of the Dwight Manufacturing Company settled on a new strategy meant to ensure the company's long-term stability and profitability. They decided to build a branch plant in the South. The Dwight Company wanted to bolster its share of the coarse-goods market without having to abandon the millions of dollars invested in mills, manpower, and machinery in Chicopee, and company directors believed this could be achieved by expanding its productive capacity to a location where the company could pay its workers

9. Unions continued to exist at the Dwight Manufacturing Company into the twentieth century. It was after a major strike in the spring of 1925, however, that Dwight's owners decided to permanently close the Chicopee mill and move all production to Alabama. On strikes at the Dwight Manufacturing Company and attempts by Dwight management to prevent organized labor from becoming firmly entrenched in its mills before 1893, see *Springfield Republican*, Apr. 6, 7, 13, 15, 16, 18, 23, and 30, and May 4 and 9, 1874; Signed Petition for Old Rate of Wages to George Bedlow, Chicopee Agent, Apr. 1874, Dwight Manufacturing Company Collection, MO-2, Folder 13, Baker Library, Harvard Business School, Boston, Mass.; Signed Contracts, Dec. 1, 1881, and May 11, 1883, Dwight Manufacturing Company Collection, MO-2, Folder 13; George Hills, Lymann Mills agent to James Cumnock, Dwight Manufacturing Company Chicopee agent, Sept. 10, 1885, Dwight Manufacturing Company Collection, ML-A, Folder 11; Shlakman, "Economic History of a Factory Town," 188.

10. *Springfield Republican*, Sept. 9 and 18, 1893. In light of the depression, unorganized operatives and unionized mulespinners and loomfixers in the company's employ did not think that conditions were favorable for winning concessions from the company and did not support the weavers' actions with walkouts of their own.

less and could operate without the restrictions imposed upon it in Massa-chusetts by striking workers and state regulations. Dwight's corporate officers banked the future of the company on its ability to compete suc-cessfully in the coarse-goods market by supplementing the production of its Chicopee factory with goods manufactured in the Piedmont South at a lower price.

The Dwight Company was one of a handful of Massachusetts mills in the 1890s that chose not to try to find ways around competing with southern mills but, instead, to capitalize on the "advantages" that textile production in the Piedmont South offered. After more than fifty years in business, the Dwight name as well as its "White Star" and "Anchor" trademarks were known worldwide. Operating a southern mill was a way for the company to couple its name recognition with the lower costs of operation that southern mills had by virtue of their regional location.[11] The Dwight move to build below the Mason-Dixon line il-lustrated, according to the *Commercial Bulletin,* the "disposition of manu-facturers . . . to make no important additions or extensions of their enterprises in Massachusetts, but to go outside her borders . . . where the labor agitator is not such a power, and where the manufacturers are not constantly harassed by new and nagging restrictions."[12]

By the winter of 1894, the directors of the Dwight Company had de-cided that their new mill would be located in Alabama. The first fully integrated cotton textile mill in the state of Alabama began operations in 1832, and during the 1840s, two more mills were constructed in the state.[13] When the Civil War began, Alabama had fourteen cotton mills, over half of which were spinning mills with few or no looms. Only six of Alabama's mills were cotton factories that carried on the entire process

11. Marvin Fischbaum commented on the importance of a recognizable trade-mark for New England-made coarse goods to remain competitive with those pro-duced in the South. Fischbaum argued that by World War I northern textile mills that did not have southern branch plants "largely gave up the manufacture of goods in direct competition with the South, producing goods only when a trade-mark or superior finish" added a small amount to the value of the cloth on the mar-ket. See Marvin Fischbaum, "An Economic Analysis of the Southern Capture of the Cotton Textile Industry Progressing to 1910" (Ph.D. diss., Columbia University, 1965), 107–8.

12. *Commercial Bulletin,* Sept. 28, 1894.

13. Phillip Taft, *Organizing Dixie: Alabama Workers in the Industrial Era* (West-port, Conn.: Greenwood Press, 1981), 5.

of textile production from raw cotton to unfinished cloth.[14] As was the case in all southern states, Alabama's textile industry did not reach a size or levels of managerial and technical maturity achieved in New England and the Mid-Atlantic states during the antebellum period. In 1860, when the Dwight Manufacturing Company alone was capitalized at $1.2 million and employed 1,600 workers, cotton mills in the entire state of Alabama represented $1.3 million in invested capital and had a textile workforce numbering just slightly over 1,300.[15] Through the 1870s and into the first decades of the early twentieth century, however, Alabama experienced what historian Philip Taft dubbed a "mini-industrial revolution," within which the Dwight Manufacturing Company's mobile capital played an important part.[16]

In published materials and in the halls of the state legislature, during the 1880s and 1890s industrial boosters in Alabama embarked on increasingly aggressive campaigns intended to facilitate industrialization within the state's borders. Eager to attract investments in textiles, mining, and metals manufacturing which could jump start a statewide economic reconstruction, state legislators and local civic groups worked in tandem to create an image of Alabama as a place where natural resources abounded, invested money would bear fruitful returns, labor was cheap and "docile," and entrepreneurs would not be harassed by state regulations.

During the 1886–1887 session, Alabama state representatives passed legislation intended to advertise the state to would-be investors. Although an attempt to establish a state Industrial and Immigration Bureau failed in 1884, state-sanctioned action "to encourage immigration and investment of capital in the State of Alabama" became law in February of 1887. The statute appropriated two thousand dollars to purchase the copyright of Benjamin Franklin Riley's text, *Alabama as It Is; or the Immigrant's and Capitalist's Guide Book to Alabama*, as well as an additional

14. Robert Eugene Perry, "Middle-Class Townsmen and Northern Capital: The Rise of the Alabama Cotton Textile Industry, 1865–1900" (Ph.D. diss., Vanderbilt University, 1986), 27, 60; Taft, *Organizing Dixie*, 5.

15. Shlakman, "Economic History of a Factory Town," 157; Wayne Flynt, *Poor but Proud: Alabama's Poor Whites* (Tuscaloosa: University of Alabama Press, 1989), 19; Jonathan Wiener, *Social Origins of the New South: Alabama, 1860–1885* (Baton Rouge: Louisiana State University Press, 1978), 139; Taft, *Organizing Dixie*, 5; Perry, "Middle-Class Townsmen and Northern Capital," 27.

16. Taft, *Organizing Dixie*, 3.

fifteen hundred dollars to publish and distribute five thousand copies of the book. *Alabama as It Is* became the state-endorsed instrument meant not only to exhibit the diversity of and potentialities for Alabama's natural resources, but also to demonstrate why these resources placed Alabama "in advance of any other State of the American Union." The goal was to show why one should invest in Alabama but, more important, why one should choose it over other southern states.[17]

In *Alabama as It Is,* Riley divided Alabama into four sections and systematically analyzed county-by-county data on each. Speaking directly to possible northern investors, he also made the point of mentioning that "Northern people will meet with no jealousies or indignities. The animosities of the war are all buried and forgotten . . . man is esteemed according to his moral, intellectual and industrial worth—not for his political sentiments." *Alabama as It Is,* however, was much more than an assurance for skittish Yankee capitalists or a simple compendium of facts and figures. Riley forwarded the argument that diversified farming in conjunction with industrialization was an absolute necessity and the best way to stimulate development within Alabama's economy. His study illustrated how establishing industries that used the state's cotton crop and its timber and mineral resources could lead to economic prosperity, and stressed the fact that the growth of industrial and urban populations would create a need for foodstuffs and generate local markets for those who raised livestock and farmers who grew fruits, vegetables, and grains. As such, *Alabama as It Is* was a blueprint of the overall objectives of Alabama's post–Civil War economic boosters.[18]

Promotional campaigns conducted at the local level supplied information and reflected goals similar to those found in *Alabama as It Is.* In towns and cities throughout Alabama, leading community members produced a body of booster literature targeting outside investors, especially northern manufacturers. Civic boosters used editorials and advertisements in regional and national newspapers to inform readers of the "advantages to capital" found within a particular locale. In 1887, full-

17. Alabama, Secretary of State, Administrative Division, *House and Senate Journals of the General Assembly of Alabama, 1884–1885;* Alabama, Secretary of State, Administrative Division, *Acts of the Fifty-Fourth General Assembly of Alabama, 1886–1887;* Benjamin Franklin Riley, *Alabama as It Is; or the Immigrant's and Capitalist's Guide Book to Alabama,* 2nd ed. (Atlanta: Constitution Publishing, 1888), 218.
18. Riley, *Alabama as It Is,* 11–215, quotation on 19.

page advertisements placed by "young progressive towns of Alabama" began appearing regularly in the pages of the *Manufacturers' Record,* each listing the reasons why astute entrepreneurs should invest and build manufacturing establishments there. Community boosters also prepared and published detailed brochures meant to generate interest in their towns.[19] The "Citizens of Gadsden," for example, distributed a pamphlet intended to make their city and the surrounding area stand out as having the greatest potential for industrial and agricultural development of any place in Alabama. The publication called attention to the three railroad lines running through Gadsden, its location on the Coosa River, and the town's location fifty-four miles northeast of Birmingham and ninety-two miles south of Chattanooga, a boon for investors wanting easy access to markets. The pamphlet touted the iron, clay, stone, and coal deposits along the Coosa, the stands of timber on nearby Lookout Mountain, the fertile farmland in the countryside, where farmers grew "some of the best grades of cotton," a healthful location, mild climate, good schools, and numerous churches. Howard Gardner Nichols of the Dwight Manufacturing Company would later note that the transportation infrastructure, the city's proximity to major urban areas, the cotton available from farms in the valley, and the coal located in the Gadsden area helped persuade the company to choose adjacent Alabama City as the location for its textile mill.[20]

Through the 1870s and 1880s, much of the industrial growth in Alabama occurred in mining and the iron industry. In 1880, Alabama's textile

19. *Manufacturers' Record,* vol. 12, no. 2. Alabama towns placing advertisements included Gadsden, Bessemer, Tuscaloosa, Anniston, Decatur, and Florence. These advertisements continued intermittently in the paper through the early 1890s. On the importance of publicity generated by civic boosters, see Gavin Wright, *Old South, New South: Revolutions in the Southern Economy since the Civil War* (Baton Rouge: Louisiana State University Press, 1986), 43; Perry, "Middle-Class Townsmen and Northern Capital," 4; Paul Gaston, *The New South Creed: A Study in Southern Mythmaking* (New York: Knopf, 1970), 73.

20. Citizens of Gadsden, *Gadsden, Alabama: Its Climate, Its Agricultural and Mineral Resources; A Handbook of Useful Information for the Settler and Investor* (New York: South Publishing, 1887), 1–6, quotation on 4; *Gadsden (Ala.) Times-News,* May 3, 1895. David Carlton argued that economic considerations, including access to transportation lines, were the primary reasons why southern textile mills often located in and around towns. See David Carlton, *Mill and Town in South Carolina, 1880–1920* (Baton Rouge: Louisiana State University Press, 1982), 46; Wright, *Old South, New South,* 44.

industry was virtually the same size as it had been in 1860.[21] "The iron industries and kindred interests have attracted so much attention in Alabama for several years that the business men of that State have failed to appreciate the importance of cotton manufacturing," wrote Richard Edmonds in 1887. Mills established in Georgia and North and South Carolina, he added, "almost without exception, appear to be enjoying great prosperity . . . not only making money for their owners but . . . furnishing employment for thousands of hands . . . and also creating a home demand for diversified agricultural products." Alabama, Edmonds argued, "needs to build such mills." Many in Alabama came to agree with Edmonds, and through the 1890s state legislators and civic boosters increasingly focused their attention on attracting outside investments to aid exclusively in the expansion of the state's cotton manufacturing industry.[22]

The confluence of poor business conditions, mill curtailments and closures, labor unrest, mounting competition from southern mills, and the passage of regulatory legislation in New England taken together with aggressive campaigns to attract northern investments, improved transportation networks, the availability of cheap and abundant southern labor, and inducements offered by state governments in the South resulted in a wave of New England textile investments in Alabama during the 1890s. Between 1890 and the turn of the century, northern monies invested in Alabama's textile industry were crucial to its growth. Commission houses, machine manufacturers, and non-southern entrepreneurs and corporations, including the Dwight Manufacturing Company, provided 52 percent of the capital spent on new textile mills being built in

21. In 1860, the Alabama textile industry consisted of fourteen mills with a total capitalization of $1.3 million and 1,312 workers. By 1880, Alabama had sixteen mills, representing $1.3 million in invested capital and 1,400 workers. Perry, "Middle-Class Townsmen and Northern Capital," 27, 57–61; Taft, Organizing Dixie, 3–4.

22. Manufacturers' Record, vol. 12, no. 1. Several historians point to the importance of agrarian protest movements, especially Populism, in pushing wealthy planters as well as many members of Alabama's legislature to encourage development of the textile industry during the 1890s as a means of relieving economic distress and calm tensions in the countryside. See Sheldon Hackney, Populism to Progressivism in Alabama (Princeton: Princeton University Press, 1969), esp. 138–39; Perry, "Middle-Class Townsmen and Northern Capital," 170; Wiener, Social Origins of the New South, 226–27; Dewey Grantham, Southern Progressivism: The Reconciliation of Progress and Tradition (Knoxville: University of Tennessee Press, 1983), 46–47.

the state between 1880 and 1895, and 71 percent of the capital between 1895 and 1900.[23] New England firms had constructed three branch factories in the state by 1900, representing over 100,000 spindles and a total capitalization of more than $4 million.[24]

When put into practice, this agenda for expanding Alabama's industrial base with capital from outside the region was one part of the process of making the economy of the New South dependent on low-wage, low-skill industries. The availability of cheap, accessible labor in the Gadsden area was a key factor in drawing the owners of the Dwight Manufacturing Company there. From the beginning of the region's cotton mill boom in the 1880s until the late 1890s, labor was easily obtainable by managers of southern textile mills. In addition to low wage rates and long operating hours, this availability of labor gave southern mill owners a significant advantage over their Massachusetts counterparts. The Arkwright Club of Boston estimated that these three factors made the operating costs of southern mills about 40 percent lower than those of New England mills.[25]

The wages paid to southern textile mill operatives during the final decades of the late nineteenth century were closely linked to fluctuations in the cotton market and the effect that these changes had on farming families throughout the Piedmont South. At the end of the Civil War, demand for cotton was high, especially by the textile mills of the Northeast that had closed or drastically curtailed operations during wartime when supplies were nearly nonexistent. Through the remainder of the 1860s, southern cotton farmers received high prices for their crops. This quickly changed as the numbers of farmers engaged in cotton cultivation steadily rose through the 1870s and 1880s, increasing

23. Perry, "Middle-Class Townsmen and Northern Capital," 140–48, 182–88; Wright, *Old South, New South,* 135.

24. *Blue Book,* 1899–1901; Perry, "Middle-Class Townsmen and Northern Capital," 165–68; Fischbaum, "An Economic Analysis of the Southern Capture of the Cotton Textile Industry," 106–7. Articles discussing movements of Massachusetts textile money to Alabama appeared in *Manufacturers' Record,* vol. 35, no. 19, and vol. 37, no. 1.

25. Arkwright Club, *Report of the Committee on Southern Competition,* 1897, 3. While the hours worked and wages paid varied from mill to mill and state to state, Mary Oates described the overall differences in wages and hours between Massachusetts mills and mills in the Piedmont South as "striking." See Oates, *The Role of the Cotton Textile Industry,* 116.

the amount of the staple on the market and driving down prices. Cotton, nevertheless, remained one of the few commodities southern farmers could raise as a means of securing credit in the cash-poor, post–Civil War South, and prices fell steadily through the early 1890s. In 1894, a pound of cotton cost ten cents to grow and bring to market but sold for only five cents. It would be a decade before cotton prices returned to the levels seen in the early 1880s.[26] While many southern farmers were mired in a cycle of debt, cotton prices appeared to be on an upswing often enough during the bad years to keep many farmers engaged in cotton cultivation in the hopes that they would earn enough with the next season's crop to pay their creditors in full.

At the same time, working and earning cash wages in nearby manufactories was a strategy that poor, white farmers throughout the Piedmont South increasingly embraced as a means through which they might find an escape from their financial hardships.[27] As late as December 1897, the southern industry press reported "4 and 5 cent cotton has run the small tenants off the farms, like rats leaving a sinking ship. . . . [T]he result is that the cotton mills at North Alabama are glutted with help."[28] The Dwight Manufacturing Company chose Alabama City as the location for its branch plant and began operations there at a point when white farming families throughout Alabama's Coosa Valley were looking to waged work in local manufactories as a way to alleviate their economic burdens.

Beyond the pool of labor available to owners of cotton mills, inducements at the state and local levels worked in concert to secure the investment of textile dollars, particularly northern ones, in Alabama. Tax exemptions for new textile industry expenditures were one kind of state-sponsored incentive. In February 1893 the Alabama legislature enacted a law "for the purposes of encouraging the building and operating of factories for the spinning of thread, yarns, and the weaving of cloth and other fabrics," authorizing counties, cities, and towns to free property, buildings, and machinery used in textile manufacturing from taxation for five years. In February 1897, the Alabama General Assembly passed a

26. Hall et al., *Like a Family*, 6; Douglas Flamming, *Creating the Modern South: Millhands and Managers in Dalton, Georgia, 1884–1984* (Chapel Hill: University of North Carolina Press, 1992), 29.

27. Hall et al., *Like a Family*, 3–13.

28. *Southern and Western Textile Excelsior*, Dec. 11, 1897.

law exempting from state taxation "any person, copartnership [sic], association of individuals, or corporations incorporated under the laws of the State of Alabama" that within five years of the passage of the law "invest, expend, lay out and pay at least fifty thousand dollars in money in the erection, building and construction of cotton mills or factories" in the state.[29]

Although the Dwight Manufacturing Company was incorporated under the laws of the Commonwealth of Massachusetts and began construction on its southern mill two years prior to the passage of the 1897 tax exemption act, the 1893 statute allowing counties, towns, and cities to forego taxing textile manufactories was an important consideration in the company's decision to build its branch factory in Alabama. Acting on the prerogatives allowed them by the state, Etowah County and Alabama City officials assured the Dwight Company that there would be no taxes levied on a new mill constructed there. The Alabama City Land and Development Company also gave land to Dwight free of charge, which company representative Howard Gardner Nichols later described as "liberal and . . . of course a large consideration." The combination of free land and no taxes, according to Nichols, "had much to do" with the Dwight Manufacturing Company's choice of location for its southern mill.[30]

The issue of state labor regulation in Alabama, however, played an equal, if not more important, role in the Dwight Company's decision-making. In 1887, Alabama was the first southern state to enact a law regulating working hours and child labor in manufactories. The 1887 bill prohibiting the "compelling" of women to work for more than eight hours in mechanical and manufacturing businesses, establishing an eight-hour day for children under the age of fourteen employed "in any factory, workshop or other place used for mechanical or manufacturing

29. Acts of Alabama, 1892–1893 and 1896–1897. See also Hackney, Populism to Progressivism in Alabama, 138. For an in-depth discussion of tax exemptions granted to New England industries from the eighteenth century through the Civil War and their similarities to those passed in southern states after the war, see Fischbaum, "An Economic Analysis of the Southern Capture of the Cotton Textile Industry Progressing to 1910," 134–68.

30. Gadsden (Ala.) Times-News, May 3, 1895. The Alabama legislature issued a charter of incorporation for the Alabama City Land and Development Company in 1891 at the same time that Alabama City received its charter. See Acts of Alabama, 1891.

purposes," and making illegal the employment of children under the age of fifteen in coal or iron mines passed the Alabama Senate and House with only one dissenting vote. Punishment for violation of this law was a fine of five to fifteen dollars, but legislators wrote no enforcement mechanisms into the statute.[31]

Assemblies of the Knights of Labor based in urban centers like Birmingham, Mobile, and Montgomery, with the assistance of labor-friendly state representatives they had helped to elect, led the campaign for the passage of the 1887 law. During the same session, legislators enacted the statute to encourage industrial investment through the purchase and distribution of B. F. Riley's *Alabama as It Is,* but the overwhelming majority of the state's lawmakers represented rural or nonmanufacturing districts and viewed the potential passage of the age and hours regulations with indifference. For those representatives of coal-mining areas where mine owners employed children, the lack of enforcement provisions made the act toothless. Because of the small number of textile mills operating in Alabama at that time, moreover, no organized bloc of textile industry lobbyists existed to oppose the legislation.[32] The strength of the Knights of Labor in the South, however, began to wane by 1888 and except for a small number of independent unions based mostly in urban areas, the region was virtually union-free for a decade.[33]

It was during this lull in organized labor activity in Alabama that the Dwight Manufacturing Company announced that it would build a southern subsidiary mill. Community boosters trying to secure the investment of Dwight's capital in their locales sent treasurer J. Howard Nichols letters and pamphlets "pressing the claims and setting forth the advantages of various sites." One such sales pitch came from Alabama

31. The only dissenting vote came from a senator from Elmore County, home to a textile mill since 1866. *Acts of Alabama,* 1886–1887; Elizabeth Davidson, *Child Labor Legislation in the Southern Textile States* (Chapel Hill: University of North Carolina Press, 1939), 18–20.

32. Melton Alonza McLaurin, *The Knights of Labor in the South* (Westport, Conn.: Greenwood Press, 1978), 39–50, 80–112; and *Paternalism and Protest: Southern Cotton Mill Workers and Organized Labor, 1875–1905* (Westport, Conn.: Greenwood Publishing Company, 1971), 80–82; Davidson, *Child Labor Legislation in the Southern Textile States,* 18; George Sinclair Mitchell, *Textile Unionism and the South* (Chapel Hill: University of North Carolina Press, 1931), 23–25.

33. McLaurin, *Paternalism and Protest,* 120; Mitchell, *Textile Unionism and the South,* 22; I. A. Newby, *Plain Folk in the New South: Social Change and Cultural Persistence, 1880–1915* (Baton Rouge: Louisiana State University Press, 1989), 547.

City businessmen Robert Kyle and James Elliot and Gadsden's mayor, R. A. Mitchell. In addition to the advantages of railroad lines, quality cotton, and readily available labor, which the three men brought to the attention of Nichols, the promises of tax breaks and free land in Alabama City piqued the interest of the Dwight Company's owners.[34]

What the owners of the Dwight Manufacturing Company wanted, however, even more than free land, tax incentives, and cheap labor was the guarantee that their new mill would be located in a state where, unlike in Massachusetts, there would be no "interference" with its management's ability to determine who would work and for how long. "Labor agitation was directly the cause which induced us to come south," noted Howard Gardner Nichols, ". . . labor agitators . . . have been weaving a web of oppressive laws around cotton manufacturing industries in Massachusetts till they are almost strangled in its meshes."[35] The Dwight Company's corporate officials perceived Alabama's law regulating working hours and the employment of children, regardless of the laxity in its enforcement, as a major deterrent to their investing there.

Why, then, did the Dwight Company build its branch factory in Alabama, the only southern state with recently passed labor legislation, rather than the leading southern textile states of North Carolina, South Carolina, or Georgia? Dwight officials dismissed North Carolina as an option because they believed there were too many mills already located there and not enough cotton grown locally to supply them all. They rejected South Carolina because of "oppressive taxation." The choice was between Alabama and Georgia, and a Dwight official admitted, "the difference in their advantages was not great."[36]

What swayed the Dwight Company to choose Alabama over Georgia were actions taken by the Alabama legislature in 1894. In November 1894, the house representative from the legislative district covering Gadsden and Alabama City, introduced a bill "on request" from Governor William

34. *In Memoriam, Howard Gardner Nichols* (Cambridge, Mass.: Riverside Press, 1897), quotation on 17; unidentified newspaper clipping in Gadsden Industries (Textiles) Vertical File, Gadsden Public Library, Gadsden, Ala.; Steven Howard, "Alabama City's Industrial Roots Run Deep," *Gadsden Times,* June 20, 1988, in Gadsden-Alabama City Vertical File, Gadsden Public Library. Announcements that the Dwight Company would build its mill somewhere in the South appeared in the *Manufacturers' Record* in July 1894 and in the *Commercial Bulletin* in Sept. 1894.
35. *Gadsden Times-News,* May 3, 1895.
36. Ibid.

Oates that would repeal the 1887 age and hours law "so far as the same related to Etowah county." With approval from the governor, the legislature went one step further and on December 5, 1894, it passed a law repealing the 1887 statute entirely.[37] "Alabama had been the first state to regulate child labor in 1887," child labor reformer Irene Ashby would later remark, ". . . and the first to repeal restrictions . . . at the urging of Dwight mill officials from Chicopee, Massachusetts."[38]

Governor Oates was an ardent advocate of Alabama's industrial development.[39] He supported the 1894 reversal of the 1887 law, seeing it as a guarantee that the Dwight Company would immediately begin construction on its mill in Alabama City. He accepted statewide nullification, believing that for other New England corporations it would stand as evidence of Alabama's willingness to act in the interests of invested capital. Indeed, as events showed, Alabama was not only willing to pass legislation that favored the owners of textile manufactories, but it was also willing to revoke old laws and prevent the passage of new ones that did not. After the repeal of the 1887 law, Howard Gardner Nichols was confident that he and the Dwight Company had the ear of the governor and the support of a pro-business legislature, acknowledging that the actions of the governor and state representatives proved to the Dwight Company "that Alabama was governed in a common sense and economical way, and that we had less to fear here from hostile legislation . . . than in any other southern state."[40]

Work on the Dwight Manufacturing Company's Alabama City mill

37. *Journals of Alabama,* 1894–1895; *Acts of Alabama,* 1894–1895. See also Davidson, *Child Labor Legislation in the Southern Textile States,* 20; Hackney, *Populism to Progressivism in Alabama,* 74–75; Perry, "Middle-Class Townsmen and Northern Capital," 171–73.

38. Ashby quoted in Flynt, *Poor but Proud,* 270. R. A. Mitchell, the mayor of Gadsden in 1894, later referred to a trip he and Howard Gardner Nichols took to Montgomery in 1894 where Mitchell introduced Nichols to "my friends, Governor Jones and Governor Oates." Although the author has not been able to locate a source explicitly stating it, it is presumed that a topic of conversation between Nichols, Mitchell, and Oates during this 1894 trip was the repeal of the age and hours restriction law. For the reference to the Montgomery trip, see *In Memoriam, Howard Gardner Nichols,* 66.

39. For an example of Oates's pro-industrialization attitude, see William Oates, "Industrial Development of the South," *North American Review* 161 (Nov. 1895): 566–74.

40. *Gadsden Times-News,* May 3, 1895.

began in the spring of 1895. The citizens of Alabama City and Gadsden looked upon the construction of the Dwight mill as evidence of a "great progressive movement for this region of Alabama," and a "conspicuous signal of the faith of capital that is keen and cautious to the last degree to the advantages of the cotton belt for the manufacture of cotton."[41] The initial capitalization for Dwight's southern subsidiary mill was $1.2 million. The main mill building measured 130 feet wide, 500 feet long, and was 3 stories high. This building housed 27,000 spindles and 800 looms, making it one of the largest textile mills in Alabama at that time. The Alabama City mill complex included a cotton warehouse, water reservoir holding 5 million gallons of water and covering 2 acres, a boiler house and engine rooms, and a brick smokestack 200 feet in height. The Dwight Company also constructed a mill village of 150 homes to house its initial workforce of 500 employees. But, the size of the Alabama City mill paled in comparison to the Dwight facility in Massachusetts. When construction began on the southern branch, the Chicopee complex included 7 mills, housed 130,000 spindles and 3,400 looms, and the Chicopee mill workforce numbered 1,600.[42]

The Dwight Company, however, planned to expand the Alabama City mill if it proved profitable. "We anticipate the surplus earnings of the Dwight Manufacturing Co. will very likely be expended here," declared Howard Gardner Nichols, agent of the new mill, "and not in Massachusetts."[43] The Alabama City mill showed a profit for the Dwight Manufacturing Company slightly over a year and a half after the start of production in February 1896, and it continued to do so in the following years.[44] In December 1897, L. A. Aumann, agent for the Dwight mills in Chicopee, told treasurer J. Howard Nichols that he was "pleased to see the showing" of the Alabama City mill, adding that he was "very glad to

41. Ibid., Jan. 7, 1896.

42. *Blue Book,* 1895–1896, 47, 69; *Gadsden Times-News,* Apr. 16, 1895. Updates about the progress of the construction of Dwight's Alabama City mill appeared in the *Manufacturers' Record,* vol. 26, no. 24; vol. 26, no. 26; vol. 28, no. 23.

43. *Gadsden Times-News,* May 3, 1895.

44. Profits for the six months ending Nov. 1897 were $32,123.15 for the Alabama City mill and $38,839.09 for the Chicopee mill; profits for the six months ending May 1898 for the Alabama City mill were $54,072.29 and $47,297.95 for the Chicopee mill; profits for the six months ending Nov. 1898 for the Alabama City mill were $58,181.90 and $48,202.95 for the Chicopee mill. Journals, Dec. 1891–Nov. 1899, Dwight Manufacturing Company Collection, DB-9.

see that we are not as badly off as some of the other [Massachusetts] Co[mpanie]s."[45] In his testimony the following year before the Massachusetts Legislative Labor Committee, William Lovering, treasurer of the Whittenton Mills of Taunton, Massachusetts, argued that the Dwight Company's ability to make profits during the slack years of the 1890s was due to the fact that it had a branch plant in Alabama. "Southern mills opened by Northern capital, in several cases as 'dependencies' of Massachusetts corporations," he pointed out, "earned dividends upon their capital stock during 1897, while the Northern ones failed to do so."[46]

True to Howard Gardner Nichols's prediction in 1895, the Dwight Company did not expand its operations in Chicopee for over a decade but more than doubled the productive capacity of its Alabama City mill. By 1905, Dwight's southern mill housed 1,800 looms and 60,000 spindles and employed 1,000 workers.[47] The Dwight Manufacturing Company made cotton textiles in both Massachusetts and Alabama until 1927, when the company suspended its Chicopee operations and began the complete removal of its production to the Alabama City facility.

The closure of the Dwight Manufacturing Company's Chicopee mill and relocation of its production lines to Alabama City was one of a growing number of textile mill closures that occurred throughout Massachusetts during a depression that beset the U.S. textile industry after World War I, lasted through the 1930s, and exacerbated the effects of persisting regional disparities in working hours, wages, and numbers of unionized workers. By the 1920s, New England mill owners and unionists alike had been grappling with southern competition for over thirty years. Yet, the development of a strong interregional textile union, the passage of adequate state legislation in the South, and the enactment of enforceable federal regulatory statutes that might have mitigated the North-South divide had not come to pass. As bankruptcies and closures ravaged the New England industry, textile mills of the Piedmont South continued to expand, increasing their share of total textile workers in the nation from 46 to 68 percent between 1923 and 1933. Within the same time period, 40 percent of all New England textile manufactories closed, resulting in the unemployment of over half the

45. L. A. Aumann, Chicopee agent to J. Howard Nichols, treasurer, Dec. 28, 1897, Dwight Manufacturing Company Collection, MK-3.
46. Testimony quoted in Whittelsey, *Massachusetts Labor Legislation,* 41.
47. *Blue Book,* 1904–1905, 59, 93; and 1906–1907, 53, 89–91.

region's textile industry workforce.[48] By the 1930s, the southern textile states had supplanted New England as the leading textile manufacturing region in the United States, topping the number of wage earners and value of products manufactured in 1923, the number of active spindles in 1925, and the number of looms by 1931.[49] Over twenty-two thousand Massachusetts textile employees lost their jobs between 1920 and 1933, as ninety-three Massachusetts mills permanently closed their doors. Eleven of the mills, including that of the Dwight Manufacturing Company, were owned by textile corporations with southern branches.[50]

What happened in Chicopee, Massachusetts, with the shut-down of the Dwight Manufacturing Company in 1927 became the norm in mill towns throughout New England over the next forty years. The capital flight and mill closures that defined the state of the industry there by the end of the 1920s accelerated through the 1930s, 1940s, 1950s, and 1960s. In the decades after World War II, however, southern mill owners began to face competition from lower-wage, nonunion areas as their New England counterparts had before them. The American South, as noted by historian James Cobb, had become a high-wage region in comparison with many labor markets around the globe, and cotton goods made internationally sold for cheaper prices than those produced in southern mills.[51]

48. Hall et al., *Like a Family*, 197.

49. George Brown Tindall, *The Emergence of the New South, 1913–1945* (1967; reprint, Baton Rouge: Louisiana State University Press, 1999), 75; James Hodges, *New Deal Labor Policy and the Southern Cotton Textile Industry, 1933–1941* (Knoxville: University of Tennessee Press, 1986), 12.

50. Massachusetts Department of Labor and Industries, Division of Statistics, *Record of Cotton Mills in Massachusetts Which Went Out of Existence during 1921–1934 Exclusive* (n.p., 1935), 1. For averages of idle spindles by state, 1921–1935, see Oates, *The Role of the Cotton Textile Industry*, 200.

51. James Cobb, *Selling the South: The Southern Crusade for Industrial Development, 1936–1980*, 2nd ed. (Baton Rouge: Louisiana State University Press, 1993), 268; John Gaventa and Barbara Ellen Smith, "The Deindustrialization of the Textile South: A Case Study," in *Hanging by a Thread: Social Change in Southern Textiles*, ed. Jeffrey Leiter, Michael Schulman, and Rhonda Zingraff (Ithaca: Cornell University Press, 1991), 181, 183–85; Nancy Francis Kane, *Textiles in Transition: Technology, Wages, and Industry Relocation in the U.S. Textile Industry, 1880–1930* (Westport, Conn.: Greenwood Press, 1988), 139–44; Flamming, *Creating the Modern South*, 308–11. For global comparisons of hourly wages paid in the textile manufacturing industry between 1975 and 1993, see International Labor Organization, *Globalization of the Footwear, Textiles, and Clothing Industries: Report for Discussion at the Tripartite Meeting on the Globalization of the Footwear, Textiles, and Clothing Industries* (Geneva: International Labor Office, 1996), table 2.1.

As worldwide competition increased through the 1970s, 1980s, and 1990s, so too did its negative impact on the profits of textile mills located in the southern United States. During these decades, mill owners throughout the region began embracing strategies to maintain company profitability and viability similar to those that the Dwight Manufacturing Company had used as early as the 1890s. Southern textile manufacturers attempted a variety of solutions, including extracting concessions from the small number of textile unions in the region on matters of wages and workload standards, lobbying for industry-friendly legislation, and ultimately, establishing branch factories abroad and closing their production facilities in the United States. The Dwight Manufacturing Company, purchased by Cone Mills of Greensboro, North Carolina, in 1951, closed in 1959, when management, looking to cut costs in the face of increasingly tight foreign competition, refused to bargain with the Dwight local of the Textile Workers Union of America that struck the mill during contract negotiations in March of that year. Cone Mills would later close other factories located throughout the southern United States and open production facilities in Mexico.[52] The Cone Mills closures and the relocation of part of its manufacturing operations outside of the country were part of a widespread trend in both the U.S. textile industry and the nation's manufacturing sector as a whole, resulting in significant job losses. Between 1973 and 1996, almost one million workers in the U.S. textile and apparel industries lost their jobs, a nearly 40 percent decrease, and employment in these industries is projected to decline another 200,000 in the near future.[53]

It is nearly impossible to halt the constant search for business-friendly, low-wage, union-free areas by owners of industries seeking to maximize profits. Neither is it likely that local, state, and national governments seeking to build and expand their manufacturing sectors will change policies on offering investment incentives to corporations. In fact, some analysts estimate that business owners seeking lower operating costs will move up to 5 million U.S. jobs overseas by 2015.[54]

52. *Gadsden Times*, Mar. 3, 6, 17, and 31, and Apr. 10, 1959; *New York Times*, Dec. 14, 2000.

53. Mark Mittelhauser, "Employment Trends in Textiles and Apparel, 1973–2005," *Monthly Labor Review* 120 (Aug. 1997): 24, 25, 34 n. 1; Steven Greenhouse, "As Factory Jobs Disappear, Workers Have Few Options," *New York Times*, Sept. 13, 2003.

54. *New York Times*, Sept. 5, 2003.

Arguments abound that the restructuring of the U.S. economy result-ing from such relocations will ultimately produce positive effects, in-cluding the creation of a more efficient, specialized, and advanced economy that employs a highly skilled and better paid workforce. Yet, as this tran-sition occurs, many displaced workers struggle to obtain employment that affords them a standard of living similar to that they previously maintained. Short-term fixes such as extended unemployment benefits and job-retraining programs only go so far and only help so many when manufacturing businesses that are the foundation of local and regional economies relocate. The key to finding long-term solutions to problems caused by capital flight, therefore, might best be found by looking to the past and gaining a better understanding of the factors that historically have facilitated industrial relocations. The lessons to be learned from examples like those provided by the story of the Dwight Manufacturing Company are particularly important for today's workers and communi-ties, so that they might anticipate change and be proactive in meeting the challenges presented by mobile capital in the global economy.

Throughout the 1880s and early 1890s when southern competition first became an issue for the northern portion of the U.S. textile indus-try, New England textile unionists focused their organization and leg-islative lobbying efforts locally and intraregionally, ignoring the conditions that made the South a potential haven for runaway companies. The lim-ited solidarity and cooperation between northern and southern opera-tives during these early years of the South's "cotton mill boom" meant that southern state legislators and local boosters went unchecked as they catered to New England capitalists. New England operatives' commit-ment to organizing their southern counterparts and working for the de-velopment of better labor legislation and workplace standards in the southern textile states over the next several decades remained limited at best, with the result that the disparity between northern and southern wage and working conditions as well as the South's pro-business, anti-union, laissez-faire status quo would only become more firmly entrenched. Such a myopic outlook continued through the "Buy American" cam-paigns of the 1970s and 1980s, and extends to current efforts made by U.S. manufacturers and unions alike to fight foreign competition by se-curing tariff policies meant to establish barriers to the marketplace suc-cess of products made more cheaply outside of the United States.

The elements shaping the process of the Dwight Manufacturing Com-pany's relocation from Massachusetts to Alabama in the 1920s, and the failure decades later of protectionist agendas to stop the flow of jobs from the United States to nations abroad, make clear the necessity for workers and communities to recognize that job security and the best workplace standards are inexorably tied to the worst that exist in any industry. Labor organizations in industrialized nations, therefore, must embrace an international outlook and, as was necessary for New England textile unionists to do with southern millhands during the late nineteenth and early twentieth centuries, to see foreign workers in their industry not as competitors per se, but instead, as coworkers with whom they have a shared cause. As such, cooperation must occur across regional and national lines, and a concerted effort must be made to bring about an equalization of conditions so that when change does happen it is toward the highest, not the lowest, common denominator. As the labor markets available to corporations have shifted over time from local to regional, and from regional to national and international, so have the difficulties that workers within the global labor force face in finding a middle ground between job loss and deindustrialization in highly developed nations and job creation and economic growth in less-developed nations that is responsible, just, and beneficial to workers, communities, and corporations alike. For sure, the improvement of global labor standards will be a long, difficult, and ongoing movement, and how this raising of the bar can most effectively be achieved remains an open question. But, the movement of capital that has occurred in the past highlights the importance of a concerted, collaborative effort among workers to ensure that corporate profit-seeking does not come at the expense of the world's labor force.

Black Workers, White Immigrants, and the Postemancipation Problem of Labor

The New South in Transnational Perspective

Erin Elizabeth Clune

In the first decade of the twentieth century, a multitude of southern commentators expressed concern about a labor shortage in cotton production. As James Sprunt wrote to a business associate in New York in October 1906, a "very serious feature just now is the lack of labour: we are retarded greatly in our work here for the first time since twenty years, and the mills around about here are equally troubled." Such reports reached Sprunt from area planters, as well as from contacts out of state. On his way to synod in Laurens, South Carolina, Rev. Alexander Sprunt wrote to his brother that he was "much interested in the cotton fields as we passed them by the way. It seemed to me the cotton was 'suffering' for lack of pickers," Alexander wrote. "The fields seemed full and so few pickers." Having toured through Clarendon, Sumter, and other points in South Carolina, Alexander found that "everywhere the same conditions seemed to prevail."[1]

The head of a transatlantic cotton-shipping firm in Wilmington, North Carolina, James Sprunt was a fairly typical ideologue of the New South.

1. James Sprunt to A. B. Gwathmey, Oct. 8, 1906, Correspondence, Box 2; Alexander Sprunt to James Sprunt, Oct. 30, 1906, Correspondence, Box 2, Alexander Sprunt and Son, Inc., Papers, Rare Book, Manuscript, and Special Collections Library, Duke University.

He was an elite white businessman who embraced the rise of free labor, industrialization, and a more modern economic liberalism. New South leaders like Sprunt were not the only southerners to raise the alarm about labor shortages. They were, however, one of the most vocal and active groups to address shortages whenever they seemed to occur, waging widespread public campaigns to bring more laborers, either from the North or abroad, to work in the southern states. As Paul Gaston wrote of New South boosters, they were agreed "that their program of agricultural renascence and industrial development required large-scale immigration."[2] C. Vann Woodward noted that "state bureaus, land companies, and numerous immigration societies of businessmen" took up the cause of labor recruitment, and that every "state had an immigration bureau of some sort by 1900."[3]

While foundational studies established the prominence of immigration campaigns, they handled the topic summarily. Concerned implicitly with the question of why the South had failed to modernize on a par with the industrial North, earlier studies focused on the inefficacy of immigration efforts. C. Vann Woodward merely pointed to the redundancy of the campaigns, noting that the South had sought immigrants since "the time it was a colony of England," to "fill up its sparsely settled territories, develop its resources, and supplement its labor supply."[4] Rowland T. Berthoff charged that fewer than half a million people of foreign birth resided in twelve southern states by 1910, while there were more than thirteen million foreign-born in the rest of the United States. Largely due to widespread nativism and xenophobia, the "appeal to foreign laborers and settlers was but a minor and futile phase of the New South."[5]

Methodologically, of course, the questions we ask of history help to determine the conclusions we reach. Earlier scholars evaluated the immigration campaigns according to the foremost stated goals of the New South movement, asking whether immigration helped the southern econ-

2. Paul Gaston, *The New South Creed: A Study in Southern Mythmaking* (New York: Knopf, 1970), 75.

3. C. Vann Woodward, *Origins of the New South: 1877–1913* (Baton Rouge: Louisiana State University Press, 1951), 297.

4. Ibid.

5. Rowland T. Berthoff, "Southern Attitudes toward Immigration, 1865–1914," *Journal of Southern History* 17 (Aug. 1951): 342, 360.

omy to develop along the lines of the industrial Northeast.[6] But we begin to see the New South movement in a different light when we try to uncover other motives and ideologies behind the immigration efforts. As Demetrius L. Eudell observes in his comparative study of emancipation in Jamaica and South Carolina, the categorical evaluation of political strategies in terms of success or failure "responds to only one side of the historical question."[7] When we consider that immigration efforts took place within a larger public discourse about a labor problem in the late nineteenth and early twentieth centuries—and within the racialized political climate of segregation and disfranchisement—it is clear that the campaigns' ideological foundations are vital to understanding the New South. The fact that many of the targeted immigrants were "white" was not incidental to the movement and cannot be explained simply in terms of southern development in the northern image. Rather, the immigration campaign arose from a profound, historically specific concern to control the labor of people of African descent.

Indeed, the writings and political activities of white ideologues demonstrate that the immigration efforts were part of a broader campaign to construct new racial and labor systems in the New South, so many decades after the end of slavery. Far beyond simply trying to increase the labor supply for southern industrial growth or agricultural development, white businessmen were waging an ongoing emancipation struggle. Moreover, it was a struggle that put them in line with ruling classes throughout the modern postemancipation world. Like their contemporaries in the Atlantic world, white ideologues were centrally concerned with constructing a new society in the wake of emancipation. They attempted to use immigration not simply to increase production, but for the larger social purpose of controlling the transition from slavery to freedom, and thus establishing new hierarchies of race and labor. Focusing on immigration efforts in the first decade of the twentieth century, this chapter uncovers some of the more complex, and often contradictory, motivations of a New South elite as they

6. Woodward, *Origins*, 147–48, 157–58, 291; Gaston, *New South Creed*, 189–91, 205–6.

7. Demetrius L. Eudell, *The Political Languages of Emancipation in the British Caribbean and the U.S. South* (Chapel Hill: University of North Carolina Press, 2002), 64.

sought to mobilize black workers for the new southern economy but maintain white supremacy and labor control.

This reexamination of southern immigration campaigns builds on postemancipation world scholarship as it identifies the New South as a critical field of comparison. But it also moves beyond comparative history to recast southern immigration movements through transnational methodology. For as they grappled with their own postemancipation problem of labor, they borrowed from and negotiated with politicians, intellectuals, and business figures from various European, Latin American, Caribbean, and African societies. The historical importance of these campaigns resides in the fact that white ideologues brought the landscape of the Atlantic world, characterized by the end of slavery, and the onset of new forms of colonialism, to bear on the politics and public discourse of the New South.

Though the New South has not generally been considered part of the postemancipation and colonial world, its landscape in the late nineteenth and early twentieth centuries was one and the same. The British Empire abolished slavery as early as 1833; French emancipation took place in 1848; and Peru abolished slavery in 1854. But Dutch emancipation in Surinam occurred as late as 1863, and total abolition was not achieved in Cuba until 1886. While European powers partitioned Africa from the early 1880s, and imperialism became part of the Western political vocabulary, slavery did not end in many African societies until the early twentieth century.[8] As this chapter demonstrates, a more in-depth focus on the ideological workings of the immigration campaigns demonstrates that the New South movement and the political and economic color lines it helped to construct cannot be understood without reference to the rise of imperialism and the end of slavery worldwide.

As leading New South ideologues debated the perceived labor shortage in diverse local environments at the turn of the twentieth century, their efforts cohered around one notion in particular. Southern progress

8. E. J. Hobsbawm, *The Age of Empire, 1875–1914* (New York: Vintage Books, 1987), 58–60; John Iliffe, *Africans: The History of a Continent* (Cambridge: Cambridge University Press, 1995), 176, 189–90, 206–7; David Northrup, *Indentured Labor in the Age of Imperialism, 1834–1922* (New York: Cambridge University Press, 1995), 26–35; Frederick Cooper, Thomas C. Holt, and Rebecca J. Scott, *Beyond Slavery: Explorations of Race, Labor, and Citizenship in Postemancipation Societies* (Chapel Hill: University of North Carolina Press, 2000), 85–86, 120–21.

depended upon the recruitment of a larger and whiter labor force. In South Carolina in 1904, the state installed a new commissioner of immigration to "meet the cry of scarcity of labor," particularly in farms.[9] While New South boosters embraced the new bureau generally, they tended to disagree with area farmers about which immigrant groups should be targeted. James Calvin Hemphill, managing editor of the pro-New South newspaper the *Charleston News and Courier*, reported with consternation that the commissioner was limited by legislation, empowered to recruit only "white citizens of the United States, citizens of Ireland, Scotland, Switzerland, France, and all other foreigners of Saxon origin."[10] The reported controversy was not over whether immigrant workers should be "white," for participants all agreed on that point. But as scholars have noted, the definition of "whiteness" was still in flux in this period and was constructed in U.S. society through and by other identities, such as class, skill level, gender, and political ideology.[11]

Clashing with various interest groups—some opposed to immigration outright, and others opposed to only certain immigrants—New South advocates in South Carolina and elsewhere often touted the suitability of Italian laborers. As the *News and Courier* reported, Italian workers had immigrated to various southern regions, and in Louisiana, were making good "farmers, laborers, and citizens."[12] James Hemphill wrote in part to convince other white South Carolinians, who harbored both class- and race-based fears that an influx of "foreign pauper labor" would undermine white laborers and disrupt the cultural homogeneity of white communities.[13] Richard H. Edmonds, the editor of the New South journal the *Manufacturers' Record*, sustained Hemphill's position in an address to the State Farmer's Institute at Clemson College. "The Italians are already proving what they can do as independent farmers, truck-raisers, and farm laborers in Louisiana and Mississippi," Edmonds

9. "A Lesson in Immigration," *News and Courier*, Aug. 23, 1904, 5.

10. "Shutting out the Italians," *News and Courier*, June 18, 1904, 4.

11. On the fluidity of whiteness, see, for example, Matthew Frye Jacobson, *Special Sorrows: The Diasporic Imagination of Irish, Polish, and Jewish Immigrants in the United States* (Cambridge: Harvard University Press, 1995); Grace Elizabeth Hale, *Making Whiteness: The Culture of Segregation in the South, 1890–1940* (New York: Vintage Books, 1998); and Lee D. Baker, *From Savage to Negro: Anthropology and the Construction of Race, 1896–1954* (Berkeley: University of California Press, 1998).

12. "Italian Immigrants in Louisiana," *News and Courier*, July 4, 1904, 4.

13. "Opposition to Immigration," *News and Courier*, Aug. 17, 1904, 6.

asserted, espousing the racial idea that it "is the attrition of mind against mind, the intermixture of the blood of the virile white races which really produces the strongest people."[14]

While New South ideologues could conceive of Italians as white for the purposes of political discourse, actual Italian immigrants were almost exclusively embraced as farm laborers, not autonomous landowners. Even northern Italians, whose lighter complexions more commonly recommended them to southerners as reliable workers, were considered only as laborers. As the *News and Courier* reported in its section "The World's Trade," a Mississippi planter who had begun employing Italian laborers on his own plantation had traveled to Europe to "study" Italian farmers. The South should contract with "none but agriculturalists who come to this country direct from the farms of their native land," Charles Scott affirmed. "If they are from Central or Northern Italy, all the better."[15] By contrast, South Carolina's Commissioner Watson talked of bringing "Finns, Norwegians and Swedes, all of the purchasing class." But even if Italian immigrants were imagined as white citizens by New South ideologues, their whiteness was no assurance of civil treatment. As Bertram Wyatt-Brown and others have demonstrated of the Sunnyside plantation of Arkansas, for example, Italian laborers were intimidated, defrauded, and virtually forced into peonage.[16]

If the whiteness of Italian immigrants did not buy them categorical acceptance or protection in southern society, it did nevertheless fulfill one primary goal of New South immigration efforts—control of the labor and autonomy of people of African descent. As Hemphill's newspaper enjoined, South Carolina would be wise to lift immigration restrictions in order to bring "good settlers whatever their native land, always excepting of course the natives of Africa."[17] In keeping with con-

14. "South's Need of Immigrants," *News and Courier,* Aug. 15, 1904, 5. Edmonds's advocacy of racial mixing was a version of the ideology espoused by President Theodore Roosevelt, as demonstrated by Gail Bederman, *Manliness and Civilization: A Cultural History of Gender and Race in the United States, 1880–1917* (Chicago: University of Chicago Press, 1995), 179.

15. "Italians for the South," *News and Courier,* Nov. 11, 1905, 5.

16. "New Colony for Horry," *News and Courier,* July 23, 1904, 1; Bertram Wyatt-Brown, "Leroy Percy and Sunnyside: Planter Mentality and Italian Peonage in the Mississippi Delta," in *Shadows over Sunnyside: An Arkansas Plantation in Transition, 1830–1945,* ed. Jeannie M. Whayne (Fayetteville: University of Arkansas Press, 1993), 77–94.

17. "Shutting out the Italians," 4.

temporary notions of social Darwinism, New South ideologues corre-
lated whiteness with modernity and believed that as white workers were
more adept at modern industry, so white citizens were more adept at
leading modern "civilization." Translated into economic terms, white
ideologues desired to construct a society that was ruled by white citizens
but that kept black labor available for southern economic development.

Indeed, despite its modernization and free-labor tenets, New South
ideology generally reflected and reinforced the South's discriminatory
social and political relations. The development of mines, iron furnaces,
and tobacco factories offered people of African descent limited opportunities for competitive earning in new urban areas, but debt-ridden
cycles of sharecropping and tenantry still dominated black economic
life.[18] In 1900, people of African descent owned a smaller percentage of
land in the cotton South than they had at the end of Reconstruction,
even though by 1910, cotton farming still employed more black southerners than any other single activity.[19]

Textile mills, the flagship industry of the New South, virtually banned
black workers from their midst. In Leon Litwack's words, white working
families "were compensated for their low pay and terrible conditions by
a company policy of not hiring blacks to work alongside them." New
South ideologues most often explained the exclusion in essentialist terms.
As textile industrialist Daniel Tompkins said in 1895, black workers
seemed to lack the "Anglo-Saxon patience" and "tenacity of purpose"
necessary to stay alert in the mills, for their weak spot seemed to be a
"want of steadiness of purpose."[20] Yet other evidence clearly suggests
that textile owners also excluded black workers because this arrangement
served to keep white workers in line. Though stymied by the South's relatively low wages and a range of federal and legal obstacles, southern businessmen attempted to fill labor shortages in mills with white immigrants,

18. Leon F. Litwack, *Trouble in Mind: Black Southerners in the Age of Jim Crow*
(New York: Knopf, 1998), 128–143.

19. Eric Foner, *Reconstruction: America's Unfinished Revolution, 1863–1877* (New
York: Harper and Row Publishers, 1988), 597; James R. Grossman, "A Chance to
Make Good: 1900–1929," in *To Make Our World Anew: A History of African Americans*, ed. Robin D. G. Kelley and Earl Lewis (New York: Oxford University Press,
2000), 355.

20. Litwack, *Trouble in Mind*, 143; D. A. Tompkins, "The Cultivation, Picking,
Bailing, and Manufacturing of Cotton, from a Southern Standpoint," Box 5, bound
volumes, Daniel Augustus Tompkins Papers, Manuscript Division, Library of Congress.

as well. While more successful recruitment in mills and farms may eventually have led to open conflict between white mill workers and owners, efforts to exclude black people seemed to result primarily from a desire to control white workers, rather than an absolute essentialist racial philosophy. As R. T. Fewell of the Arcade Cotton Mills in South Carolina wrote to Daniel Tompkins in 1906, he sought a "full meeting of all the mills to discuss the labor shortage and adopt some concerted action by which we could secure more labor." Fewell recognized that Tompkins was a business leader and immigration advocate, and he wrote with urgency. For "[i]f it gets any worse the negro will be taken up, and I for one believe he could do as well as anyone else, but would not like to be the first one to adopt it, unless I was forced into it."[21]

New South ideologues, like other white southerners, revealed the contradictions in their own racial beliefs, particularly when they responded to black mobility and success with fear and concern. Indeed, the efforts of white businessmen to construct new racial and economic relationships indicated that far from doubting black progress, they feared the potential economic and social power of black southerners. In 1912, for instance, white residents of Edgefield County, South Carolina, threatened violence against black citizens who owned land. Daniel Tompkins wrote to a friend back in his home state and argued for the institution of legal measures to combat black progress. "[I]n driving out the negroes by volence [sic], you are cutting off your nose to spite your face. With the salubrious climate and fertile soil, Edgefield needs the negroes for labor. Instead of driving them out, you ought to execute the vagrancy law and put them to work building new roads."[22] Despite the legalized oppression of the Jim Crow era, a black middle class of landowners did emerge in the Upper South, and to some extent, in the Lower South, as well. Yet as Leon Litwack has noted, even after black southerners were no longer a "political threat," black success in the early twentieth century was still commonly met with violence and harassment.[23] For white

21. R. T. Fewell to Tompkins, Mar. 27, 1906, Correspondence, Daniel Tompkins Papers, Southern Historical Collection, Manuscript Department, Wilson Library, University of North Carolina, Chapel Hill.

22. Daniel Tompkins to John Sheppard, Jan. 2, 1912, Correspondence, Daniel Tompkins Papers, Southern Historical Collection.

23. Litwack, *Trouble in Mind*, 122, 153. Numbers of African Americans owning land varied significantly by region, though New South ideologues tended to speak

ideologues, free labor may have been important to the development of the new southern economy, but too much black freedom threatened to undermine New South civilization.

Because the resistance and mobility of working people of African descent had been constant since Emancipation, white businessmen called upon strategies like immigration to effectively curb black autonomy and economic strength. Arguably, the immigrant campaign had particularly urgent appeal in the first decade of the twentieth century because rising cotton demand appeared to contribute to a more competitive labor market. Rowland Berthoff hinted at the role of people of African descent in the southern immigration efforts when he observed: "Cheap foreign labor seemed likely not only to replace emigrating Negroes but also to break down Negro monopoly of unskilled labor and so keep wages low."[24] The dependency of white landowners on black labor had become an issue immediately after Emancipation, when people of African descent enacted their right to negotiate their labor "by moving, if only a few miles to the next plantation."[25] According to J. William Harris, white landowners in Georgia and Mississippi at the turn of the century were still struggling to control black workers through vagrancy laws, contracts, and debt strategies, struggles that help to explain "the continuing high level of mobility by tenants and laborers" in these years.[26]

It was in the economic climate of a competitive labor market, then, that the intensely racialized nature of the South's labor problem became most evident. The papers of New South ideologues tell a story of ongoing black struggle and resistance, and of white concerns to limit and control it. In November 1904, for instance, the Hemphill family received

---

for the whole South. Litwack reports that in 1900, 14 percent of black Georgian farmers owned their farms, and in 1910, only 13 percent. In 1900, an estimated 75.3 percent of black farmers were tenants or sharecroppers. Edward Ayers basically concurs, writing that in 1900, "the first year for which region-wide numbers were collected, about a quarter of all Southern black farmers owned the land they worked," and this number continued to rise until 1910. The proportions of black farmers who owned land, Ayers notes, were greatest in the Upper South, along the coasts, and in the trans-Mississippi states. See Edward Ayers, *The Promise of the New South: Life after Reconstruction* (New York: Oxford University Press, 1992), 208.

24. Berthoff, "Southern Attitudes," 331.

25. Grossman, "Chance to Make Good," 383.

26. J. William Harris, *Deep Souths: Delta, Piedmont, and Sea Island Society in the Age of Segregation* (Baltimore: Johns Hopkins University Press, 2001), 66.

word from farming relatives in Mississippi. Following an oblique reference to recent racial violence in their region, the first letter recounted that "the negrows [sic] are getting to be so bad." A few days later, however, another letter expounded on the issue in clear economic terms. Asserting that the "crop on the entire place is exceptionally good," the letter also stressed that "of course the negro labur [sic] is all that we have here. But you can't hire one to work for us at no price." Linking the high demand for cotton to the resistance of black workers, the letter concluded that the "high price of cotton has almost ruined the country. I mean as far as the negro is concerned."[27] Vocalizing a different view on the matter, Booker T. Washington nonetheless confirmed the changing labor dynamic in a 1905 letter to the white planter and ideologue Alfred Holt Stone. Washington pointed plainly to the economic climate. The improving economy "makes the laborers, in my opinion, feel an independence that results very often in their not sticking to a job in the way they would if they felt that if they gave up their present job they would have to seek many months before finding another."[28]

Seen in terms of a broader Atlantic world of postemancipation societies, New South ideologues were far from unique in their response to the resistance and mobility of people of African descent. The industrial North may have been the closest model of economic modernization, and even European immigration, but white ideologues found models elsewhere to apply to their broader social and economic agenda. Writing to the News and Courier in July 1904, a local man was one of many advocates who referenced more distant locales in support of Italian immigration. The "recent rapid industrial progress of the South," he wrote, as well as the "failure of the negro to reach any general efficiency in skilled labor," was forcing southerners to treat immigration more seriously. In both Brazil and Argentina, he noted, colonies of Italian workers had been established.[29]

When a prominent railway company brought a Brazilian consul to Texas to speak about the benefits of Italian laborers a few months later, James Hemphill's newspaper applied the example of postemancipation

27. [illegible] Taylor to Uncle Robert, Nov. 16 and 18, 1904, Correspondence, Box 11, Hemphill Family Papers, William R. Perkins Library, Manuscript Collection, Duke University.
28. Booker T. Washington to Alfred Holt Stone, Apr. 6, 1905, in The Booker T. Washington Papers (Urbana: University of Illinois Press, 1979), 8:249, on-line text.
29. "The Immigration Problem," News and Courier, July 23, 1904, 5.

Brazil more palpably to the New South. Along with Scandinavians, French Canadians, Scotch-Irish, and Germans, the column contended that Italians "would bring about a settlement of our race problem in the most satisfactory way."[30] The goal of controlling the labor and autonomy of people of African descent was plain.

"When slavery was abolished in Brazil sixteen years ago the people reached out for farmers and induced the settlement of large colonies of Italians in their country," the column recalled. While newly freed African farmers produced only four million bags of coffee per year, the contribution of Italians raised the production level up to ten million. The column directly quoted the Brazilian consul to the effect that "[f]or us, the Italian has solved the negro question and that of the slave."[31]

Two Atlantic world societies grappling with distinct postemancipation labor problems, Brazil and the American South, had long been linked in the minds of southerners. South Carolinian planters had looked to Brazil as a place of refuge immediately following the Civil War, when they were disturbed by the prospect of a changing economic relationship with freedpeople. The continuation of slavery in Brazil at that time enticed some planters to emigrate from Chester and Edgefield counties as early as 1866.[32] Ultimately, no massive planter emigration occurred, because most believed that the social revolution of Emancipation in the South would not ultimately prove unbearable. As the *Charleston Mercury* also argued at that time, however, southern planters knew that Brazil would eventually undergo emancipation, as well.[33]

In the nineteenth and twentieth centuries, many colonial societies attempted to use mass immigration campaigns to control or mitigate black freedom and autonomy after slavery. Thomas Holt has stated of postemancipation Jamaica that the struggle of people of African descent to work as free and independent laborers led to a massive effort to recruit immigrants from England, Africa, and the United States.[34] As Walter Rodney likewise perceived about British Guyana, the postemancipation

30. "The Italian and the Negro Question," *News and Courier,* Sept. 1, 1904, 4.
31. Ibid.
32. Francis Bulter Simkins and Robert Hilliard Woody, *South Carolina during Reconstruction* (Chapel Hill: University of North Carolina Press, 1932), 240.
33. Ibid.
34. Thomas C. Holt, *The Problem of Freedom: Race, Labor, and Politics in Jamaica and Britain, 1832–1938* (Baltimore: Johns Hopkins University Press, 1992), 70–79, 197–202.

decades there involved the importation of thousands of indentured immigrants.[35] Although East Indian laborers immigrated in the greatest numbers, white planters also relied on Portuguese, African, Chinese, and West Indian islanders to continue laboring for sugar, and to move the society ever so gradually toward the practice of free labor. In British Guyana, planters discussed labor shortages categorically in terms of labor control, inflected by strains of racial essentialism. "The supply of labor has no bearing on the sugar industry," one overseer plainly told the West India Royal Commission of 1897. The "whole origin of immigration hinges on this point. You may have work and plenty of it for a black man and a coloured man, and they will not do it. . . . Therefore it is absolutely necessary that you should have bound labor that you can command."[36]

With its own social "whitening" designs and relatively late date of emancipation in the Americas, the New South found its most influential model in Brazil. After slavery ended in Brazil in 1888, Brazilian planters strove to limit the extent to which they had to bargain freely with former slaves.[37] As George Reid Andrews has observed, white planters in São Paulo were interested in maximizing profit under free labor, but they also acted upon a specific racial ideology concerning the "innate laziness and irresponsibility of the black and racially mixed Brazilian masses."[38] Rather than dispense with racial distinctions after slavery, the ruling class embarked on a state-subsidized program to "Europeanize" Brazil. In the planters' refusal to negotiate freely with former slaves, they drew significant ideological power from "the currents of scientific racism sweeping the Atlantic world" at that time.[39]

Brazilian ideologues of all kinds viewed themselves as modernizing their economy not simply through the acquisition of a new labor force, but through the actual whitening of their population. While planter efforts clearly aimed at keeping labor costs low by flooding the labor market and marginalizing workers of African descent, Brazilian politicians

35. Walter Rodney, *A History of the Guyanese Working People, 1881–1905* (Baltimore: Johns Hopkins University Press, 1981), 32–34.
36. Ibid., 47.
37. George Reid Andrews, *Blacks and Whites in Sao Paulo, Brazil, 1888–1988* (Madison: University of Wisconsin Press, 1991), 47–53, see also introduction.
38. Ibid., 48.
39. Ibid.

effectuated the racial program by banning African and Asian immigrants.[40] In the forty years after emancipation, over two million European workers went to Brazil, almost half of whom "had their trans-Atlantic passages paid for by the state government."[41] Much like the Italian laborers' experience in the American South, some immigrants found working conditions so intolerable that by 1902, the "Italian government forbade its citizens to accept subsidized passages to Brazil."[42]

As they looked out to this Atlantic world landscape, New South businessmen were just as contradictory in their correlation of whiteness with progress and autonomy as were their Brazilian counterparts. The Sunnyside plantation example underscores that the experiences and treatment of white immigrants seldom matched the New South imagination. But this was not entirely surprising, since New South racial discourse also betrayed a recognition that black working people were competing for greater autonomy and economic security all the time. In August 1904, when South Carolina's immigration commissioner outlined his mandate to merchants and farmers, he cited black migration to cities as a main cause of the labor shortage, but he offered other statistics to "awaken the people to their condition" as well. Black farmers operated the majority of farms in South Carolina, Watson pronounced, and a substantial number of these operators owned their land. Watson theorized that those numbers might account "in some measure for the lack of productiveness of many of the farms" in the state. But he also conferred that despite the "loose method of agriculture employed by the small negro farmers in South Carolina," they were "raising two-fifths of the farm products in this State, measured in value." Looking at the bulletin of the United States Census Bureau, Watson concluded, shows the "great need for an increase of our industrious white agricultural population."[43]

Ultimately, it was the underlying goal of restricting black autonomy and undercutting black competition that made the New South so representative of the postemancipation, colonial world. On the ground, immigration efforts did not focus exclusively on Italian laborers, or even laborers at all. Like other organizations of its time, for instance, the

40. Ibid., 52–55, 83, see also appendix B, 249–54.
41. Ibid., 54.
42. Ibid., 84.
43. "A Lesson in Immigration," *News and Courier,* Aug. 23, 1904, 5.

South Carolina immigration bureau advertised its business in foreign countries.[44] Of the hundreds of letters that the department reportedly received from England and Scotland each week, Watson shared with his audience a letter from an English man of the "better and educated class" in Liverpool. Seeking information on how to establish himself in the state, Alexander Smethurst questioned, "Can one buy land by easy installments [sic] ? What does the negro work for per day? What is the actual cost of producing cotton per acre?" As a prospective white landowner in the South, the English immigrant added a curious detail to confirm his qualifications: "I have experience of tropical agriculture in India, besides gardening here."[45] Though not connected in any way, this letter presages a note written by Daniel Tompkins about the Edgefield racial conflict eight years later. In that letter, Tompkins declared that ever since the abolition of slavery, the "rights and privileges" of the black population had been too much at issue. Tompkins criticized the excesses of the "anti-slavery movement" in light of the British Empire. "We all here in the South know that they have over done the thing. We also [know] that England has the same problem in India, and that the southern view of the race problem is identically the same as the English view of it in India."[46]

In fact, while black labor control remained central to all immigration efforts, a campaign to recruit white English immigrants in this decade provides even more expansive insight into the racial ideology—and the transnational context—of the New South movement. In contrast to the Brazilian example, New South ideologues did not draw on specific campaigns waged by the British Empire around the world. Rather, British and southern businessmen together explored prospects for the immigration of British farmers and landowners to the American South. Insofar as New South businessmen sought immigrants to buy and work land, and British manufacturers sought ways to increase the global cotton supply, their immediate economic interests concurred. As the campaign suggested, however, the two groups held sufficiently similar ideologies about race and labor in their global economies to explore common immigration goals. The British struggle to grow cotton, sugar, and other

44. One example is "Mr. Watson at Anderson," *News and Courier,* Oct. 6, 1904, 1.
45. "A Lesson in Immigration," 5.
46. Daniel Tompkins to George Brunson, Jan. 15, 1912, Correspondence, Tompkins Papers, Southern Historical Collection.

goods with profitable, manageable, and nominally free workforces in Africa and the Caribbean was, to be sure, one of the social agendas that brought British and southern manufacturers onto common ground.

The immigration campaign was catalyzed by vast publicity in the first decade of the twentieth century about a cotton shortage in Great Britain. As the *News and Courier* reported in "Cotton Rivals of the South" in April 1904, the British board of trade issued a report on the extension of cotton cultivation in Egypt and the intent to develop cotton agriculture in the British Sudan, Nigeria, Rhodesia, and other African "protectorates." The director of the Imperial Institute denounced the almost complete British dependence on American cotton, which had come about because of the deterioration of cotton in India, the replacement of cotton by sugarcane in the West Indies, and the continually improving quality of cotton from the American South. While the South still monopolized the cotton trade, the expansion of southern textiles appeared to be increasing domestic consumption of raw cotton, thereby also diminishing the export supply.[47]

In response to the southern cotton monopoly, the British House of Commons moved that it was "incumbent upon the Government to encourage the growing of cotton in Africa and elsewhere in the British possessions" and to cooperate with commercial associations toward that end. As reported, the British Colonial Office and the Cotton Growers' Association also arranged to work together to finance the development of the cotton industry in southern Nigeria and Sierra Leone. Contributing to the debate was the representative from the textile region of Lancashire, who emphasized "the danger of Great Britain being dependent on one source of supply." Alfred Lyttleton, secretary for the colonies, noted that extensive experiments were being made in various British colonial possessions "with every prospect of success."[48]

While many southerners had long believed that the region would benefit from the limitation of cotton production, New South leaders called immediately for increased production.[49] As Daniel Tompkins told the National Cotton Convention in Shreveport, Louisiana, in December 1904, cotton production in Africa represented a serious threat to the

47. "Cotton Rivals of the South," *News and Courier,* Apr. 24, 1904, 1.
48. "Cotton in West Africa," *News and Courier,* Apr. 28, 1904, 1.
49. On farmers' efforts at limiting cotton production, for example, see Woodward, *Origins,* 412.

South's "practical monopoly" over cotton. "It is idle for us to rest in the present situation and to feel that the Europeans can accomplish nothing," Tompkins told his audience. At this meeting, as at the annual meeting of the American Economic Association one year before, Tompkins suggested that southern labor shortages were the crux of the problem, which only technological advance and immigration could solve. New manufacturing interests in the South, Tompkins argued, "are drawing so much labor from the farms that our production of cotton must of necessity be checked."[50] "If we can get a successful cotton picker and could turn one-quarter of the European emigration now coming into the United States to the cotton states," Tompkins proposed at Shreveport, "we will have supplied all the deficiency of labor" that exists.[51]

Like many of his fellow business leaders, Daniel Tompkins took an early, individual role in promoting the idea of mass immigration. In May 1905, Samuel Dale of the *Textile World Record* of Boston was preparing to attend the International Congress of Cotton Spinners and Manufacturers Association in England. Tompkins sent along some printed material on immigration issued by southern cotton mills. As Tompkins told him, he did not oppose "the movement to raise cotton in other parts of the world" but felt sure that "the quickest way to insure the production of sufficient cotton for the world's consumption is to get immigration here in the South." Tompkins attempted to address the fact that English immigrants might be loathe to encounter social discord in the South. "We have no apprehensions about the present race problem, nor about any with the Italian," he contended. The South would "forget there ever had been such a thing as a 'race problem' if we did not hear more or less of it from the North from time to time."[52]

Even if Tompkins represented the South disingenuously, it was also true that English immigration was intended to solve the "race problem" by bolstering the racial hierarchy and thereby diminishing black resis-

50. D. A. Tompkins, "The Cotton Industry," in *Papers and Proceedings of the Sixteenth Annual Meeting, Part 1, New Orleans, December 29–31, 1903,* by the American Economic Association (New York: Macmillan, 1904), 151.

51. D. A. Tompkins, "Address before National Cotton Convention held at Shreveport, La., Dec. 12–15, 1904," in Box 2, Tompkins Papers, Manuscript Division, Library of Congress.

52. Tompkins to Samuel Dale, May 5, 1905, Letterbook S-8, Tompkins Papers, Southern Historical Collection.

tance. At least one successful settlement in North Carolina demonstrates what he more than likely had in mind. In March 1906, Daniel Tompkins received a letter from a business associate, Captain Alexander Thompson. The two men were working to generate interest among their English colleagues. "I have a cotton growing scheme, on hand, and was pleased to find that every body in any way connected with the cotton trade, seemed to know you and know you well," Thompson wrote from the state of Washington. Though he provided no more detail, Thompson specified the notion that white English immigrants would come to the South, first as landowners, and then possibly as workers. "The plan I have outlined to the English Cotton men, is the one you spoke of, that of the manufacturers combining, and buying up land, importing labour and growing their own cotton."[53]

A short time later, Alex Thompson wrote to Tompkins as the European representative for the Carolina Trucking Development Company of Wilmington, an immigration business centered around truck farming that James Sprunt later called a "pronounced success."[54] Sprunt praised his friend and Carolina Trucking Development company founder, Hugh MacRae, for his success in modernizing the economy of Wilmington. "Of how much greater service to mankind is he who plants a colony of small farmers in a wilderness of waste land," Sprunt wrote, "and by the application of modern scientific methods makes that wilderness blossom and bear fruit and food products a hundredfold!"[55] As James Hemphill worked to generate support for immigration through Charleston, he expressed a similar sentiment about the company. "The Wilmington plan might be adopted in Charleston and in other parts of this State and in the South Atlantic States," Hemphill opined, "with equally good results." Specifying the issue at stake, he continued that what "we need and must have is more white people in the South, unless we have concluded that the negro shall continue to be our main dependence in the development of our soil."[56]

53. Capt. Alex Thompson to Tompkins, Mar. 24, 1906, Correspondence, Tompkins Papers, Southern Historical Collection.

54. See Alexander Thompson to Tompkins, May 9, 1906, Correspondence, Tompkins Papers, Southern Historical Collection; James Sprunt, *Chronicles of the Cape Fear River, 1660–1916* (Raleigh: Edwards & Broughton Printing, 1916), 676.

55. Sprunt, *Chronicles,* 675.

56. "Immigrants in North Carolina," *News and Courier,* Sept. 9, 1907, in Scrapbook F-4278, Hemphill Family Papers, Duke University.

A privately funded enterprise, the Wilmington company exemplified the kind of economic and racial relationships that New South ideologues hoped to perpetuate through their transatlantic efforts. The second vice president of the Carolina Trucking Development Company, C. Van Leuven, provided insight into the class, racial, and gender designs of the business. Having acquired options on thousands of square miles of land around Wilmington, he explained, the company aimed to "secure men, of families, possessing some means, if possible, to start the colonization." Providing agricultural supplies to immigrant families they recruited, the company laid out a small town, built roads and drainage systems, and sold the land in a kind of share system in multiples of ten acres. Ultimately, the company settled five distinct groups, a blend of white ethnics: "North Italian, Polish, Greek, Hungarian, German and English" settlers populated the land. Given that eastern European immigrants were not necessarily considered "white" in the North, where they lived in greatest numbers, their presence again suggests some flexibility in the New South conception of ideal white replacement labor.[57]

If the company's efforts resonated ideologically with the broader campaign in the New South, the racial contradictions of the company's strategies, particularly its equation of whiteness with industry and modernity, were as evident as its racial goals. "Our English colony has been so far the least successful," Van Leuven ultimately admitted to Hemphill at the *News and Courier*. "They come to this country expecting success to come to them without hard work . . . and they nearly all feel that the real work should not be done by them, but by others whom they employ for wages."[58] Because of the perceived labor shortage, Van Leuven explained, the company had hoped to enable "a man with a family of reasonable size to work his own land entirely independent of labor outside of his own household."[59]

Evidently, the New South message about the economic role of white immigrants was mixed, for one company pamphlet seemed to promote quite a different arrangement, aimed at the construction of a labor hierarchy with black labor at the bottom. It "has only been during the last few years that ambition has reasserted itself in the South and invited

57. "The Way to Handle Immigrants," *News and Courier,* Sept. 9, 1907, 8; on Polish immigrants, for instance, see Jacobson, *Special Sorrows,* 182–200.
58. "The Way to Handle Immigrants," 8.
59. Ibid.

Capital and Labor to come and assist in the development of their vast resources," the pamphlet announced. Despite the stated goal of fostering independent small farmers, the pamphlet seemed to imply that black labor was available, noting that strawberry cultivation would be highly profitable in part because the "Negroes of the locality pick them for 32 cents a crate."[60] Another contemporary account, though, simply points to the larger racial agenda of diminishing black autonomy. As Robert Vincent wrote in the *World's Work* in November 1908, "every deed issued" to the immigrants "contains a clause restricting the land from passing to a Negro."[61]

Whether black workers were competing in the farm labor market or withdrawing from it, white ideologues cast black economic activity as incompatible with modern civilization, and therefore, necessitating white control. As editor Richard Edmonds had articulated during his Clemson College address, a "great incoming of immigration would mean an increase in value of every acre of land in the South," not to mention great business opportunities, more wealth, and better infrastructure. Moreover, with an increase in the white population, the black worker will "learn that with active competition in every field of employment, in the household and on the farm alike, his only hope will be in sobriety, honesty, and work."[62] In February 1906, Edmonds was still locating the problem of labor in the proclivities and behaviors of working people of African descent. The "movement of negroes from the agricultural regions to the towns steadily progresses in spite of increased farm wages," Edmonds wrote. Though it was not possible to dispense with black labor in many places, the positive outcome of white immigration had already been demonstrated. "Their coming has had an influence for good upon the remaining negroes, who seem to have been impressed with the fact that unless they endeavor to keep pace with the whites the time will not be far distant when they will be debarred from opportunity to work at all."[63]

60. "Wealth in Carolina Truck Farms," Carolina Trucking Development Company, Wilmington, North Carolina, undated, Warshaw Collection of Business Americana, North Carolina Geographic File, Box 1, Folder 4, Development, Archive Center, National Museum of American History, Smithsonian Institution.

61. Robert W. Vincent, "Successful Immigrants in the South," *World's Work* (Nov. 1908): 109–10.

62. "South's Need of Immigrants," 5.

63. "South's Need of Workers," *Manufacturers' Record,* Feb. 8, 1906, 83.

Many New South ideologues responded to the perceived labor problem as they did precisely because they viewed the situation through a global lens. In December 1905, the *News and Courier* reported on a paper given at the American Economic Association by Alfred Holt Stone, the writer and planter who had conducted his own "experiments" with black plantation labor in Mississippi. Speaking along with R. C. Bruce of the Tuskegee Institute and W. E. B. Du Bois of Atlanta University, among others, Stone discussed the South's labor shortage. Typically, Stone cast the problem in terms of black economic behavior, rather than wages, labor conditions, or hardship. He noted that vagrants and idlers were everywhere, and steady labor was scarce even with high wages. Suggesting that the economic and social turmoil of other post-emancipation societies was the fault of the freedpeople, Stone mused: "I sometimes wonder if the story of Jamaica and the West Indies is to be repeated in the South." Indeed, he made explicit his own global framework. "It seems difficult to escape the conclusion that back of all this lie the characteristics that apparently have always been a curse to the race—whether in Africa, the Southern states, or the West Indies—shiftlessness and improvidence."[64]

Violent conflicts punctuated the southern racial scene and helped to catalyze the immigration campaign. This racial violence also reveals the extent to which black progress threatened to destabilize the class and racial hierarchies of the white New South. In the Atlanta race riot of September 1906, furious white mobs assaulted and killed black people and destroyed black businesses. As Edward Ayers has noted, the riots were marked by the horrible irony that although Atlanta was touted as the embodiment of progress for all southerners, this was clearly "New South violence" directed at black southerners alone.[65] According to the *New York Times,* a white mob armed with clubs, cans, guns, and stones "rushed upon a negro barber shop, just across from the Federal building." The white rioters killed the two barbers, mutilated their faces, and tore off their clothing "as souvenirs or waving them above their heads to incite

64. "A Warning for the Negro," *News and Courier,* Dec. 30, 1905, 1; Alfred Holt Stone, *Studies in the American Race Problem* (1908; reprint, New York: Negro Universities Press, 1969), 192, 199, 196. On his "experiments," see 114–24, 128–34.

65. Ayers, *Promise of the New South,* 435–36. Also see Tera W. Hunter, *To 'Joy My Freedom: Southern Black Women's Lives and Labors after the Civil War* (Cambridge: Harvard University Press, 1997), 124–28.

further riot." The mob then dragged the barbers' bodies across the street to a statue of the New South prophet Henry Grady, killed another black man there, and left all of the bodies together.[66]

Fueled by white workers' resentment over their own financial hardship, the riots betrayed the fact that the New South gospel was as classbound as it was racist. Immediately after the riots, the *New York Times* reprinted an editorial from the *Atlanta Constitution,* formerly Henry Grady's newspaper, commenting that the outbreak of violence "came as a logical culmination of a series of crimes and attempted crimes which had wrought Anglo-Saxon patience and endurance to a preternatural tension."[67] In fact, while alleged assaults by black men on white women had contributed to the white hysteria, so had incendiary disfranchisement rhetoric in the governor's race.[68] As David Levering Lewis has noted, black men and women in Atlanta were only guilty of "setting terrible examples for their country cousins by throwing off three hundred years of servility" and representing a "labor reserve against white workers."[69] Contemporary observers offered their own economic explanations. Atlanta was "essentially an industrial town," the *New York Times* reported, "it has grown rapidly, and a large part of its population, white and black," was new to the city. Somewhat consonant with northern elite fears of urban growth and deviancy, but reflective of southern concern over black autonomy, the paper endorsed an *Atlanta Constitution* proposal, that the city enforce its law against vagrancy and send "every one found loafing to the chain gang." The chain-gang solution "tends to meet, moreover, the one controlling fact in the situation, that the South has, needs, and cannot possibly spare negro labor. If the non-workers among the negroes, and the whites as well, can be reduced to the lowest practicable number, the indispensable services of the rest can be retained."[70]

Though it noted the culpability of white residents in the riot, the following day's editorial page linked the riot to extant immigration proposals. "Though its progress since the close of the civil war has been the

66. *New York Times,* Sept. 24, 1906, 2.
67. Ibid.
68. Ayers, *Promise of the New South,* 436.
69. David Levering Lewis, *W. E. B. Du Bois: Biography of a Race, 1868–1919* (New York: Henry Holt, 1993), 334.
70. "The Atlanta Riots," *New York Times,* Sept. 25, 1906, 8.

wonder of the modern world," the column submitted, "its labor system is backward in many regards, and is deeply complicated and seriously retarded by the conditions growing out of negro slavery." Indeed, the paper seemed to succumb entirely to the postemancipation labor perspective that guided the immigration campaign. "It is not to be denied that disturbances such as those now going on in Georgia must tend to discourage immigration of the right sort," the paper posited. But once started, it will "tend both to raise the standard of industry and lead to a higher and more efficient type of social and political organization. To some extent it will drive out the negroes, especially of the lower class, but it will also influence public sentiment in favor of more regular and enlightened modes of social life."[71]

Ultimately, however, the movement to recruit English immigrants advanced not only in response to the social agenda on the ground, but also with encouragement from across the Atlantic. Apart from owning a shipping firm, James Sprunt had served as British vice consul in North Carolina since 1884.[72] Because his post required him to promote British interests, Sprunt contributed to official investigations into southern economic conditions. As Foreign Office records indicate, one such investigation took place in 1906. In April 1906, the Foreign Office requested a report on the productivity of North Carolina truck farms. Shortly thereafter, a cable from the Foreign Office was logged as "Emigration Report, Truck Farms, N. C.," explicitly linking the issue of farming with that of immigration. On May 4, 1906, the Savannah consulate received the farming report from Wilmington, a document for which James Sprunt most certainly gathered facts, if he did not write it, with respect to an investigation into prospects for British immigration.[73]

Though it is difficult to connect the Foreign Office investigation with specific actions on the part of southern businessmen, transatlantic cooperation increased with time. That same year, James Sprunt drafted an

71. "Immigration to the South," *New York Times*, Sept. 26, 1906, 8.
72. Sprunt's tenure is documented in Robert J. Cain, "Cotton for the Kaiser: James Sprunt, Contraband, and the Wilmington Vice-Consulate," *North Carolina Historical Review* 74 (Apr. 1997): 163.
73. See specific log entries relating to Wilmington on Apr. 12, 1906; May 2, 1906; May 4, 1906; and May 5, 1906. For the full span of Foreign Office interest in the issue, also see log dates of June 13 through Dec. 26, 1908. Foreign Office Register of Savannah, 1905–1914, F.O. 550, piece #3, Foreign Office Records, National Archives, Kew Gardens, England.

essay on the status of southern cotton production. Following an embittered reflection on class politics and farmers' movements, Sprunt noted the arrival of a new era.[74] This new era was characterized by an unprecedented demand for cotton in the modern world and the recognition that the South had a global responsibility to meet this challenge. Sprunt wrote sympathetically of the British demand for more cotton, warning that a "failure of the cotton crop in the South would be a stupendous disaster to the cotton industries of the world, especially to that large population of England dependent upon the cotton mills for its daily bread." As a result, British statesmen had understandably centered their cotton concerns upon "the wide and almost limitless" British territory in Africa and the rest of the world.

As Sprunt viewed it, however, there was another important English movement "more interesting to us in the South"—the recent visit to the United States of a commission of British textile owners to investigate the cotton and textile industries. Upon its return to Liverpool, Sprunt wrote, the commission reported "that the possibilities of Cotton growing in the Southern states" were "practically unlimited, millions of acres being available." Because of this hopeful activity, the reign of King Cotton "will long continue in the South." In a closing comment noteworthy for its location of the New South in a global framework, Sprunt lauded a future that would preserve the "beloved South which has risen from the ashes of humiliation and sorrow to a place of exaltation among the nations of the Earth."[75]

In the years 1906 and 1907, groups of British businessmen did visit the South, sustaining the development of the immigration campaign. Though they would ultimately fail to spur mass immigration, New South ideologues viewed their transatlantic campaign as support for their broader social struggle, and this struggle in turn infused public debate in the South and throughout the United States. Immigration schemes like these sustained the dominant class outlook in the South, and as the *New York Times* editorial about the Atlanta riots demonstrates, garnered

74. Undated article, in Correspondence, Box 9, Alexander Sprunt & Son, Inc., Papers, Duke University. I would date this article late spring or summer of 1906. A reference to the newspaper at the opening suggests that this article was written for the *Wilmington Star,* the newspaper that Sprunt later partially owned. Publication status is unknown.

75. Ibid.

support in the North, as well. As Demetrius Eudell has recently observed, even if they failed to settle substantial numbers of laborers, the enduring implication of such campaigns was that the "general well-being of the social order depended on such a solution."[76] While some scholars have observed that sectional tensions between North and South lessened with the rallying cry of the Spanish-American War around the turn of the century, the transatlantic political campaigns of the New South ideologues may well have had a similar effect, at least among the cosmopolitan business elite.[77]

The New South newspaper editor Richard Edmonds played an early role in inducing the Lancashire Private Cotton Investigation Commission to visit the South in 1906. In August 1904, Edmonds reportedly urged American manufacturers to engage European businessmen in the project of fostering greater mutual understanding of their international economy. Echoing his New South colleagues and their interests in the project, Edmonds wrote that "it would be far more profitable for the cotton consumers of Europe to fully understand this situation and lend their co-operation to the expansion of cotton-growing in the South than undertake the losing venture of seeking to develop cotton-growing in other lands."[78] However they were ultimately convinced, six members of the Lancashire Private Cotton Investigation Commission traveled to the United States the following spring to meet with cotton producers. After touring the cotton-growing areas of the South, the Lancashire commission also attended a large meeting with American cotton growers and manufacturers. In fact, the general purpose of both the visit and the conference was to generate discussion on topics of cotton trade, regulation, and handling between planters and textile owners.[79]

But the prospect of British immigration and investment was at the forefront of the New South agenda. From the day they alighted from the *Saxonia,* the British group became the object of Edmonds's newspaper crusade. "While there have been frequent newspaper declarations that the commission has been looking for a large tract of land in the South

76. Eudell, *Political Languages,* 61.
77. One such observation about the Spanish-American War is in Ayers, *Promise of the New South,* 329–31.
78. "An Epoch-Making Gathering for the Cotton Trade," *Manufacturers' Record,* Sept. 5, 1907, 187.
79. "English Spinners' Visit," *Manufacturers' Record,* Mar. 29, 1906, 271; "Our English Textile Guests," *Manufacturers' Record,* Apr. 12, 1906, 341.

on which an experimental cotton farm might be established by British spinners," one article conceded, no conclusive or public report had yet been made. But the columm insisted upon positive thinking. The visit might "with propriety be denominated a voyage of discovery," he suggested, "and that in making their investigations everything connected with cotton culture has been considered, even to the point of raising cotton on Southern plantations by English and other foreign spinners." It would "thus appear," it concluded, "that agitation of a momentous character is on and is engaging the attention of cotton spinners on both sides of the Atlantic."[80]

While the Lancashire visit that year did not yield any concrete immigration plans, southern businessmen were clearly hopeful, evidenced by the fact that they did not merely advertise it in public arenas. Its ideological importance to them was also manifest in their private writings. Daniel Tompkins, who had pursued the idea of British land investment with Alex Thompson only a month earlier, was disappointed for a time, because the English group skipped his home base of Charlotte on their tour through the South.[81] Tompkins nonetheless viewed the visit as a potential boon for the South. At the end of May, Tompkins instructed his brother to delay the sale of their land. Labor migration from farms to factories in North and South Carolina was one reason Tompkins offered, and in "the new situation cotton production is a very attractive occupation," he wrote. "There has already set in a moderate tide of immigration from the bleak northwest and also from Europe to take advantage of the new profitable agricultural conditions. In this situation land is bound to go up in price."[82] Only a few months later, Tompkins wrote to his brother again and warned him not to sell their farmland at current prices. "I believe we are on the eve of quite a movement of immigration," he wrote. "The newcomers will have to have land. At the present price of cotton, good cotton land will be much sought after in the next five years."[83]

80. Albert Phenis, "New England Cotton Manufacturers in Session," *Manufacturers' Record*, Apr. 26, 1906, 403; also see "International Cotton Conference," reprinted in *Manufacturers' Record* from *Textile World Record*, Apr. 26, 1906, 403; "International Cotton Conference," *Manufacturers' Record*, Feb. 1, 1906, 58.

81. Tompkins to W. A. Hildebrand, Apr. 3, 1906, Letterbook S-9, Correspondence, Tompkins Papers, Southern Historical Collection.

82. Tompkins to Mr. A. S. Tompkins, May 31, 1906, Letterbook S-9, Correspondence, Tompkins Papers, Southern Historical Collection.

83. Tompkins to Mr. A. S. Tompkins, Oct. 11, 1906, Letterbook S-9, Correspondence, Tompkins Papers, Southern Historical Collection.

At the end of 1907, in fact, the idea of recruiting English immigrants seemed only more plausible to the New South ideologues. In October, more than one hundred representatives of the textile industry of England and the Continent planned to tour the South, on their way to the International Conference of Cotton Growers, Spinners and Manufacturers in Atlanta.[84] Publishing a precise itinerary of the trip and an informational column about southern industry, Richard Edmonds reminded his potential British readers of the racial imperatives of the immigration campaign. Black workers were "in a steadily-diminishing majority" as farmers, Edmonds wrote, and "neither the factories nor the fields will be equipped as to workers equal to the opportunities in the South for raising and manufacturing cotton." Soon enough, the "South must look elsewhere for its full equipment of workers. The South's guests from foreign lands will please make a note of that."[85]

Both larger and better organized than previous tours, the 1907 tour satisfied ideologues throughout the New South.[86] As president of the Manufacturers' Club in Charlotte, Daniel Tompkins appointed a committee of businessmen to entertain the visitors, and accompanied the group on part of their tour.[87] Thomas Parker of Monaghan Mills served on the committee to receive the foreign guests in Greenville, Mississippi.[88] As the *Manufacturers' Record* recounted, the European visitors also inspected the cotton plantations of the Lower South. They investigated the cotton plantation of J. A. Crawford at Heathman, Mississippi and "at Dunleith, in the same State, several of the party left the train for the afternoon and rode over the plantation, rejoining the others at Greenville the next day."[89]

The Dunleith plantation visit highlights the extent to which New South

84. "An Epoch-Making Gathering for the Cotton Trade," 187; "Foreign Cotton Manufacturers Welcomed by Southern Authorities," *Manufacturers' Record*, Sept. 26, 1907, 57. Also see "To Greet Foreign Spinners," *Manufacturers' Record*, July 25, 1907, 29.

85. "Vest-Pocket Facts for Foreign Visitors," Sept. 26, 1907, *Manufacturers' Record*, 60.

86. "Cotton Growers and Spinners Confer at Atlanta," Oct. 10, 1907, *Manufacturers' Record*, 45.

87. C. B. Bryant to unnamed, Oct. 4, 1907, Correspondence, Tompkins Papers, Southern Historical Collection.

88. Parker to Tompkins, Oct. 4, 1907, Correspondence, Tompkins Papers, Southern Historical Collection.

89. "The Foreign Spinners," Oct. 17, 1907, *Manufacturers' Record*, 49.

ideologues viewed this immigration campaign as a solution to a post-emancipation labor problem, rather than simply a labor shortage, or a question of increasing production. Until roughly 1905, Dunleith had been host to the racialized labor "experiment" of Alfred Holt Stone, the well-known immigration proponent and planter. Despite the fact that Stone had acknowledged in 1901 the growing number of black farmers who were independent cultivators in the Mississippi Delta, over the years he came to fixate on the "restless, migratory tendency" of black workers as a major cause of the South's labor problems.[90] Most important, Stone commonly employed a kind of postemancipation, colonial lens through which to cast working people of African descent in essential racial terms. Black labor demonstrated similar patterns, Stone suggested, whether facts were drawn "from the fields of the Southern states, from the diamond mines of Kimberley, or from the gold workings of the Rand." Indeed, Stone maintained, black racial traits presented "the greatest obstacle to the real, general, permanent advancement of the race, whether in this country, Africa, or the West Indies."[91] Whether or not the Dunleith visitors participated in discussions about race and labor control is unknown. Yet it is difficult to imagine that Stone did not take the opportunity to discuss with his guests examples from around the Atlantic world, commonly recognized tales of white elites who replaced free laborers of African descent with immigrant farmers, workers, and landowners.

In the end, it turned out that New South ideologues had predicted the outcome of their immigration campaign as incorrectly as they assessed the capacities of black southerners. The departure of the 1907 visitors led to much speculation again, but Richard Edmonds only seemed more desperate when he advertised that "we are assured there will in the not distant future be some very large investments of European capital in the South."[92] M. V. Richards of the Southern Railway revealed later in the same journal only that "[s]ome of the visitors made inquiries about the country as a field for Europeans, and expressed the idea that they saw many opportunities for people of their own countries

90. In his discussion of Stone, Edward Ayers also notes the historical prosperity of black farmers in the Delta, as early as the 1880s and 1890s. See Ayers, *Promise of the New South*, 195; Stone, *Studies in Race Problem*, 84, 145, 114–24, 128–34.

91. Stone, *Studies in Race Problem*, 145.

92. "Leaders in Europe for the South," Oct. 24, 1907, *Manufacturers' Record*, 43.

to settle."[93] What the southern businessmen did achieve was a measurable degree of influence on public debate in the New South and even in the North, where the general public seemed eager enough to leave the South to its own devices in these years. Writing to a British associate three years after the peak of the southern immigration movement, for instance, Samuel Dale of Boston was only more convinced of the New South cause. Regardless of who ultimately immigrated, Dale wrote, it was "essential in promoting emigration to the South that the will of the Southern people be respected. They have willed that their country shall be a white man's land, that is, that the white man shall be dominant, and that is the sentiment of the American people."[94]

At its peak in the first decade of the twentieth century, the immigration campaign failed for many legal and political reasons that have not been examined here, as well as for the contradictions that clearly adhered within New South ideology itself.[95] In the course of their efforts, white ideologues contributed to a climate of racial hostility and coercion, while in their own mills and farms they served to deprive black working people of basic economic freedoms. If white ideologues hoped to create a modern, industrial society like that of the North, they were also intent on solving their postemancipation labor problem along with other societies of the broader Atlantic world.

For racial ideologues like Tompkins, Sprunt, Hemphill, Edmonds, and Stone, there was no great challenge in casting the racial and economic conflict of the New South as part of a global struggle. As Alfred Holt Stone said at the second annual meeting of the American Sociological Society in 1907, the future of racial conflict in the United States depended on both groups, but racial antipathy seemed likely to endure among Anglo-Saxons. Never in the history of "English speaking people" had they granted equality to equal numbers of people of African descent. The determination to discriminate, Holt argued, rendered the

93. "The Tour of the European Spinners in the South," Jan. 2, 1908, *Manufacturers' Record*, 90–91.

94. Samuel Dale to Thomas Crook, Mar. 7, 1910, enclosures with Samuel Dale to D. A. Tompkins, Mar. 7, 1910, Correspondence, Tompkins Papers, Southern Historical Collection.

95. These obstacles and contradictions are discussed at great length in Erin Elizabeth Clune, "Emancipation to Empire: Race, Labor, and Ideology in the New South," (Ph.D. diss., New York University, 2002).

South "practically a political unit to this day. In South Africa we see the same determination of the white man to rule, regardless of the numerical superiority of the black."[96] Only five years, later, of course, South Africa would adopt the Native Lands Act, prohibiting Africans from purchasing land outside of designated "reserves" and even from entering into sharecropping contracts in white farming areas.[97]

Through their immigration campaigns, white businessmen of the New South attempted to capitalize on their links to the postemancipation world by presenting their ideas as necessary solutions to modern global problems. Yet the modern reality was also that people of African descent continued to resist, both in the South and throughout the Atlantic world, until their own visions of freedom were realized. W. E. B. Du Bois captured this reality in the formal response that he provided to Stone's paper in 1907. "Emancipation was simply the abolition of the grosser forms of that physical force," he noted, but "we all hope for gradual emancipation in thought and custom." Du Bois warned, however, that "it is peculiarly dangerous for a people of today, who expect to keep up with modern civilization, to base their hope of peace and prosperity on the ignorance of their fellows or the lack of aspiration among working men." Moreover, Du Bois seemed to suggest directly to Stone and his colleagues, "even if a people like those in the South do hope that the Negro is not going to aspire and not going to demand equal rights and fair treatment, then they are bound to disappointment." Pointing to ongoing black resistance, Du Bois stated that there "is today in the South growing protest from the mass of negroes, protest to which whites are yielding today, and must yield. . . . without it there would be no race problem."

In a comment fit for the white immigration campaign, Du Bois contended: "Mr. Stone has often expressed the cheerful hope that the Negro would be supplanted by the white man as worker in the South." But, Du Bois continued, "the thing does not happen. On the contrary there are today more Negroes working steadily and efficiently than ever before in the world's history." Just as Stone maintained that racism was global in character, Du Bois suggested that the struggle of people of African descent

96. Stone, *Studies in Race Problem*, 227.
97. George Frederickson, *White Supremacy: A Comparative Study in American and South African History* (New York: Oxford University Press, 1981), 241.

had an important global dimension in the first decade of the twentieth century and well into the future. "If we assume the white South as planted immovably on the proposition that most human beings are to be kept in absolute and unchangeable serfdom and inferiority to the Teutonic world," Du Bois posited, and that people of color throughout the world "are determined to contest this absurd stand to the death, then the world has got some brisk days ahead, and race friction will inevitably grow not only in the United States but the world over."[98]

98. W. E. Burghardt Du Bois, response to Stone, "Is Race Friction between Blacks and Whites in the United States Growing and Inevitable?" *Papers and Proceedings, Second Annual Meeting of the American Sociological Society, 2,* by the American Sociological Society (Chicago: University of Chicago Press, 1908), 104–7.

Contributors

Shearer Davis Bowman, born and raised in Richmond, Virginia, received his B.A. from the University of Virginia and his M.A. and Ph.D. from the University of California at Berkeley. He is the author of *Masters and Lords: Mid Nineteenth-Century U.S. Planters and Prussian Junkers* (1993). He has taught at Hampden-Sydney College in Virginia and the University of Texas at Austin. Currently he lives in Lexington, Kentucky, and teaches at both Berea College and the University of Kentucky.

David L. Carlton is associate professor of history at Vanderbilt University. He is the author of *Mill and Town in South Carolina* (1982) and, with Peter Coclanis, *The South, the Nation, and the World: Perspectives on Southern Economic Development* (2003).

Erin Elizabeth Clune is currently assistant professor of history at Stonehill College in Massachusetts, where she teaches U.S., African American, and Atlantic world history courses. The essay in this volume is developed from her larger manuscript, tentatively entitled *Emancipation and Empire: Race, Labor, and Ideology in the New South*.

Peter Coclanis is Albert R. Newsome Professor of History and associate provost for international affairs at the University of North Carolina, Chapel Hill. He is the author of numerous works in southern and international economic history, and most recently, with David L. Carlton,

The South, the Nation, and the World: Perspectives on Southern Economic Development (2003).

Susanna Delfino is senior researcher and a professor of American history at the University of Genoa, Italy. Her interests focus on the society and economy of the antebellum South. Among her recent publications is *Neither Lady nor Slave: Working Women of the Old South* (2002), coedited with Michele Gillespie, in which she has an essay on female labor in the Upper South's iron and mining industries.

Stanley L. Engerman is John H. Munro Professor of Economics and professor of history at the University of Rochester. His publications include *Time on the Cross: The Economics of American Negro Slavery* (1974), coauthored with Robert W. Fogel, and *A Historical Guide to World Slavery* (1998), coedited with Seymour Drescher. He is currently coeditor with David Eltis of the four-volume *Cambridge World History of Slavery.*

Beth English received her Ph.D. in American history from the College of William and Mary. She is the author of *A Common Thread: Labor, Politics, and Capital Mobility in the American Textile Industry, 1800–1959,* forthcoming from the University of Georgia Press as part of its Society and Economy in the Modern South series.

Michele Gillespie is Kahle Associate Professor of History at Wake Forest University. Her publications include *Free Labor in an Unfree World: White Artisans in Slaveholding Georgia* (2000). This volume marks her second collaboration with Susanna Delfino, with whom she coedited *Neither Lady nor Slave: Working Women of the Old South* (2002).

Emma Hart is lecturer in modern history at the University of St. Andrews, Scotland. Her main interests lie in the field of colonial American history, and she is currently completing a book on eighteenth-century Charleston and the British Atlantic world.

John Majewski is associate professor of history at the University of California, Santa Barbara. His book *A House Dividing: Economic Development in Pennsylvania and Virginia before the Civil War* was published by Cambridge University Press in 2000.

Brian Schoen is assistant professor of history at California State University, Sacramento. A graduate of the University of Virginia, he taught there and lectured at Georgetown University before recently moving west. He was a resident postdoctoral fellow of the Program of Early American Economy and Society at the Library Company of Philadelphia in the spring of 2004. He is revising his dissertation, "The Fragile Fabric of Union: The Cotton South, Federal Politics, and the Atlantic World, 1783–1861," into a book manuscript.

Viken Tchakerian received his doctorate in economics from the University of California, Los Angeles, and is currently an associate professor of economics at California State University, Northridge. His research interests include early manufacturing and economic development in the antebellum South and Midwest and the California wine industry before Prohibition.

Index

agrarian bourgeoisie, formation of, 113–14

agrarian periodicals, 116

Alabama: foreign investment in, 71; labor legislation in, 189–90, 191–92; northern investment in, 186–87, 188–89; promotion of, 183–85; protective tariffs and duties in, 72; state-sponsored industrial development in, 62; textile industry in, 175–76, 182–98

Alabama City Land and Development Company, 189

Albion, Robert, 56

Alexander Brown and Company (Baltimore and Liverpool), 66

American Farmer, 116

American Midwest: cash crops of, 133, 135; land-use patterns in, 134, 143–44; manufacturing in, 133; per capita income in, 88, 133; post–Civil War economic development of, 10–11, 18; railroad development in, 136, 139, 146

American North: economic comparisons to South, 2–3, 10, 17, 18–19, 22, 24–25, 86; industrialization of, 86, 112, 132; migration of ex-slaves to, 24; railroad development in, 146; southern dependence on, 6, 51, 55, 60, 61, 70, 73, 74, 107, 111

American South: backwardness of, 76–77, 88, 105–7, 116, 117, 123, 127–28; cash crops of, 5, 18, 20, 28, 66, 75, 82, 90–91, 109, 117, 133, 176; class formation in, 2, 114–15; economic diversification (rejuvenation) of, 61, 63–66, 107–8; exceptionalist bias toward, 4, 10, 104, 106; exploited by northern elite, 10; growth of markets in, 10, 131–32; industrialization of, 1–2, 6, 7, 8, 9, 11, 15–25, 61–63, 66, 69, 86–87, 90, 119–20, 130; inefficiencies in, 17, 133–34, 137–43, 150; land-use patterns in, 134, 143–49; manufacturing distribution in, 134–37; manufacturing in, 1–2, 63–65, 69, 111, 119–20, 132–33; marginalization (isolation) of, 5, 9, 12; modernization of, 10, 118, 123, 129, 200; natural resources of, 69, 90; per capita income in, 24, 25, 83–84, 87–88, 89, 133; political economy of, 6; post–Civil War economic performance of, 88–91; pre–Civil War economic performance of, 2, 7–8, 17, 22–23, 118; railroad development in, 9, 58, 61–63, 73, 77, 79, 80–81, 139–42, 145–46; regional economy of, 5–6, 75; revisionist history of, 1–5, 6, 17; subregions of, 79

American West: economic comparisons

233